Dau

D1118711

p. 172 written comp——
of A and Tsvetaeva

ANNA AKHMATOVA

Anna Akhmatova in 1922

ANNA AKHMATOVA

A Poetic Pilgrimage

AMANDA HAIGHT

A poet is someone from whom nothing must be
taken and to whom nothing must be given.
ANNA AKHMATOVA

NEW YORK *and* LONDON
OXFORD UNIVERSITY PRESS
1976

Oxford University Press

NEW YORK LONDON OXFORD
GLASGOW TORONTO MELBOURNE WELLINGTON
CAPE TOWN IBADAN NAIROBI DAR ES SALAAM LUSAKA ADDIS ABABA
KUALA LUMPUR SINGAPORE JAKARTA HONG KONG TOKYO
DELHI BOMBAY CALCUTTA MADRAS KARACHI

ISBN 19 211731 9

© *Oxford University Press 1976*
Library of Congress Catalogue Card Number: 76-22841

Set in Great Britain by
Gloucester Typesetting Co. Ltd., Gloucester
Printed in the United States of America

For
CLARE

CONTENTS

ILLUSTRATIONS

PREFACE

I first met Anna Akhmatova early in 1964. I had vague plans for a thesis and had just started an attempt at making a full and accurate collection of her work. I was living in Moscow and assumed her to be in Leningrad. I thought I would go there some day and sit at her feet and try to ask some not too unintelligent questions. Instead I discovered she was in Moscow and I became, in time, a friend.

There is no doubt that I turned up at the right moment. Banned from publication for years, Akhmatova was at this time being asked constantly for poems to print. Her position as a translator of poetry had helped to make this possible, as well as the general change in the literary and political climate in the Soviet Union. There was still, however, confusion as to her exact position in the literary world. At the same time increasing interest was being shown abroad in her work and in that of her contemporaries. Various publications were reaching her and she was extremely irate at the number of mistakes they contained. When I first met her she was in high dudgeon over S. Makovsky's memoir of Gumilyov, her first husband, which she had just read in a French translation. 'Go and talk to some people who really knew me then,' she said —and I went willingly to whomever she sent me to: friends and contemporaries who had known her at different periods of her life, for whose kindness and patience in the face of my ignorance I have unending gratitude.

In 1965 Akhmatova came to England to receive the honorary B.Litt. conferred upon her by the University of Oxford. She returned to Russia via Paris and in both England and France received people who had come from all over the world to see her: old friends, scholars, and admirers of her work, even a nephew she had never met. I was fortunate enough to be with her all through this time, and the following summer I visited her again at her *dacha* at Komarovo, near Leningrad. She died early the following spring. I arrived in Leningrad in time to go with her close friends and family to lay flowers on her grave on the fortieth day after the funeral.

While I was writing the doctoral thesis upon which this book is based, I was fortunate to have work which took me regularly to the Soviet Union. I was thus able to check the development of my ideas and the accuracy of my interpretations with Akhmatova's friends there and with scholars who knew her work. With their help I was also able to correct the frequently inaccurate versions of her work being published abroad. At the same time I retained contact with several of the poet's close friends whom I had met in 1965 in England and in France.

Mistakes of any kind were anathema to Akhmatova. The poetic word was too precious a thing to be misused. I would like to have known what she thought of my work, but when it was finished I could no longer ask her questions. I could only ask them of her poetry.

ACKNOWLEDGEMENTS

I should like to acknowledge my very great debt to Dr. Georgette Donchin for her unfailing help and encouragement during the writing of my doctoral thesis, *Anna Akhmatova: Life and Work. An Interpretation in the Light of Biographical Material* (University of London, 1971). I wish also to acknowledge my gratitude to Peter Norman for allowing me to use our joint translations of the cycle 'Requiem' and for checking my translations of the other poems quoted here. Many of Anna Akhmatova's friends, some of whom are now dead, helped me in my research into the poet's life and patiently assisted me with many textual and bibliographical queries. I am most grateful to Boris Anrep, Boris Ardov, Mikhail Ardov, Viktor Ardov, Sir Isaiah Berlin, Lyubov' Bol'shintsova, Iosif Brodsky, Lidiya Chukovskaya, Emma Gershteyn, Salomea Halpern, Anna Kaminskaya, Nikolay Khardzhiev, Nadezhda Mandel'shtam, Dmitri Maksimov, Mikhail Meylakh, Anatoly Nayman, Nina Ol'shevskaya, Irina Tomashevskaya, Mikhail Zenkevich, and Vladimir Zykov. I also wish to acknowledge my indebtedness to the Worshipful Company of Goldsmiths and the University of London Central Research Fund for assistance enabling me to visit the Soviet Union in connection with my research.

A.H.

London, June 1975

'INSTEAD OF A FOREWORD'

Upon you is the mark of God . . .
O. MANDEL'SHTAM, 1910

Anna Akhmatova, a Russian woman poet who had already found fame before the beginning of the First World War, seems to have been chosen by fate to test all the intuitive and inherited values of her contemporaries, first, against the enthusiastic creeds spread by a revolution dreaming of a future paradise and then, by its repressive and paranoiac aftermath: the Stalinist totalitarian state.

Together with certain other poets of her generation, Akhmatova found herself pushed into a position where her very existence was threatened by the fact that she wrote poetry. Questions, which in other circumstances might simply have been subjects for intellectual speculation, became matters of life and death. To write or not to write—either could at times have meant imprisonment and death for her, or worse, for her son. To do either was no longer something of merely personal significance, but a political act. That the poet should discover, contrary to all logical expectation, that she had no alternative but to continue to write, even despite herself, at such times, and that this extreme test should have revealed once more the vital importance and power of the poetic word, is an answer to those who question the function of literature.

Akhmatova's personal life had helped prepare her for this task. She had to learn early to accept the fact that the sacrifice of her poetic gifts could not make her what she was not, an ordinary woman. Only late in life, when she had fully accepted what had often from childhood seemed a predestined and tragic role, was she able to enjoy the simple everyday contacts of loving relationships in which most women find themselves. What to many people is most difficult, the deep spiritual contact, came easily to her: the extraordinary was available, but the ordinary was not. Her marriages were unhappy and her day-to-day relations with her son and with her step-daughter difficult. When finally she was able to establish this more ordinary type of relationship with her step-grandchild, Anya Kaminskaya, and with her close friend, Nina Ol'shevskaya, and her children, she valued it highly. It was important for her that at last

I

she was able to be not only a woman of depth and understanding, but simply a grandmother, a friend.

But Akhmatova won this right to be also what she was not by nature, by fully accepting what she was—a poet. Her affirmation of this, after profound conflict in her personal life, meant that, when she was later subjected to attack, she had already deeply questioned her motives for writing and had discovered that it was her only true source of strength. She was thus most vulnerable, for she knew that poetry was her life-line, but at the same time strong, because she had recognized her true identity.

From the start, Akhmatova was concerned with the necessity of giving voice to the woman's point of view in a culture where women's voices, although beginning to be heard, were few and far between and where women were still suffering from the illusion that to be equal with men, they must be like them. A deeply religious and at the same time passionate woman, with close ties to nature, Akhmatova was forced to examine and reject the false doctrine that placed physical desire so often in opposition to God's purpose. She re-examined and rejected the attitude to her sex which had caused so much suffering over the past century, which had divided women into those who were 'pure' and those who were 'fallen'. When in her poetry she tried to heal this split, she was taunted for years with being 'half nun, half harlot'.

The life and work of Anna Akhmatova reflect the development of her own understanding and self-knowledge. If for a moment she had lost her ability to structure the raw material of her life into a poetic biography, she would have been overwhelmed by its confusions and tragedy. The triumphal processions she made, at the end of her life, to western Europe—to Taormina and to Oxford—were for her not so much a personal triumph as a vindication of her own and others' defence of the poet's inner truth. She went to receive honours in Sicily and England as much for those poets who had not survived to do so, for Osip Mandel'shtam and Nikolay Gumilyov, as for herself. She went as a poet, knowing what it really meant to be a Russian poet of what she called the 'True Twentieth Century'.

I

1889-1914

And I was bold and bad and gay
And did not know that this is happiness.

And the clouds were stained
With the red scum of Tsushima.

Anna Akhmatova herself drew the backdrop to her birth: 'Dostoyevsky's Russia'—with rustling skirts, plaid rugs, mirrors in walnut frames, plush chairs and the yellow light of oil lamps (I.308).*

She was born 11 June (Old Style)† 1889, on the Black Sea coast at a place called Bol'shoy Fontan (Great Fountain), not far from Odessa. Her father, Andrey Gorenko, was a naval engineer and she was the third of five children, Andrey and Iya being older than she, and Irina (Rika) and Viktor younger. When Anna was five, Rika, who was only four, died of tuberculosis. Her death was kept a secret—she had been taken away to stay with an aunt—but her sister guessed what had happened in that strange unformulated way of children and later said that because of this a shadow lay across the whole of her childhood.‡

Eleven months after Anna's birth, the family moved north: first to Pavlovsk and then to Tsarskoe Selo, the Tsar's village, now called after Pushkin, who spent his youth there and walked up and down the avenues of the great park as she was so often to do. It was a funny little 'toy town', as she recalled it later, dominated by the palaces and the park, destroyed in the war and now rebuilt, but not the same. The poet's first memories were of Tsarskoe: 'the damp green splendour of the parks, the meadow where my nanny used to take me, the racecourse where little horses of various colours galloped, the old station...' (I.43). Every summer the family returned to the Black Sea coast, to Streletskiy Bay, not far from the ancient monastery at Khersones, where the child Anna 'made friends with the sea'.

It was in many ways a strange household for a future poet to grow up in. There were virtually no books in the house except for a large volume of the works of Nekrasov which Anna was allowed to read at holidays. Her mother must have had some feeling for poetry, however, for she recited poems by Nekrasov and also Derzhavin to her children. And somehow, before she had ever written a line, everyone was convinced Anya, as she was called, would be a poet. Her father teased her, calling her a decadent poetess, and later it was he who was responsible for her becoming Anna Akhmatova not Anna Gorenko. Hearing of her poems, when she was seventeen, he told her not to bring shame upon his name. 'I don't need that name,' she answered and chose a Tatar name—that of

---

* Bracketed references in the text are to the two-volume Russian edition, *Anna Akhmatova: Sochineniya*, ed. G. P. Struve and B. A. Filippov (Munich and Washington, D.C.: Inter-Language Literary Associates, vol. I, 2nd ed., corrected, 1967; vol. II, 1968), cited by volume and page number. Other sources, to which superscript figures in the text refer, are given in the Reference Notes at p. 202.

† 23 June in the western calendar.

‡ Her sister Iya was to die of T.B. as well, at the age of twenty-seven.

the last Tatar princes of the Golden Horde. A strange choice, as she said later, for a Russian poetess, but Akhmatova was the name of her Tatar great-grandmother and the Tatars in the south had always seemed to her mysterious and fascinating.

Akhmatova described her mother in her elegy 'Prehistory' as 'a woman with transparent eyes (so blue that one could not but recall the sea as one gazed into them) with an unusual name and small white hands and a goodness which I, it seems, inherited—an unnecessary gift in my cruel life' (I.308). Inna Erazovna was apparently no ordinary woman, and not particularly domestic. She suffered, as did other female members of the Gorenko family, from tuberculosis, and her relationship with her husband was not entirely happy. Certainly Akhmatova's childhood was not to be remembered for traditional childhood things:

> And I had no rosy childhood
> With freckles, teddies and toys
> Kind aunts and frightening uncles and even
> Friends among the river pebbles.[1]

> I grew up in the patterned silence
> In the cool nursery of the young century
> And people's voices were not dear to me
> But I could understand the voice of the wind.
>
> (I.239)

In early childhood, listening to the older children's lessons, Anna began to speak French. When she was ten, she was sent to school in Tsarskoe Selo. A few months after this, she became very ill. She was delirious for a week and it was thought she would not live. When she recovered, she was deaf for a time. Apparently the doctors had no idea at all what was wrong with her. Later, a specialist suggested it might have been smallpox—leaving, however, no obvious pockmarks. It was after this she began to write her first poems and in some way she always knew that the beginning of her poetry was connected closely with this mysterious illness. A photograph of her then shows a solemn child with a shaven head.

Books or no books, by the age of thirteen the young poet loved poetry and already knew Baudelaire and Verlaine and the *poètes maudits* in French. She was hardly a book-worm, however; more at home in the water than on land, she wandered around in summer without stockings and just a dress over her bare body which she clutched to hide the rip all along the thigh, and had a tendency to jump into the sea from unexpected places. When her aunt chided her for this, saying that if she were her mother she would cry all the time, Anna replied: 'It's best for both of us that you aren't my mother.'

It was with this girl at an age hardly older than this that another young poet, Nikolay Gumilyov, fell passionately in love. To him she was a water nymph or mermaid with sorrowful eyes, the moon girl, Eve.[2] For ten years she was to dominate both his poetry and his life and later, at the very end of hers, she came to a new and deeper appreciation of this young man's prophetic vision—an image of herself as someone more tragic and more terrifying than she was at that young age prepared to come to terms with.

The two young poets met just before Christmas 1903.* Anna was on her way to buy decorations for the tree with her friend Valeriya Tul'panova (later Sreznevskaya), whose family lived in the bottom half of the same house, and who was to remain her lifelong friend. Anna, Valeriya, and her brother Seryozha ran into the Gumilyov brothers, Mitya and Kolya, near the large department store, Gostinyy Dvor, in St. Petersburg. Valeriya already knew them—they had the same music teacher. The young people walked along the street together, Valeriya with Mitya, the elder of the two, Anya with Kolya, the younger. The two Gumilyov boys saw the girls home and although the meeting seemed to have made no special impression on Anya, this was not the case with her escort. After this, Valeriya noticed Kolya hanging about when Anya was due back from school and he made efforts to get to know her elder brother, Andrey, to gain entrance to the rather closed Gorenko household.

Kolya Gumilyov was a rather wooden young man three years older than Anna, with a certain arrogance of manner covering up his shyness. He read a great deal, had started writing early, and was at this time particularly fond of the French Symbolist poets. In his own poetry he saw himself as a conquistador and in life did not like to fail in anything he attempted. Anya had grown tall and graceful, with long, thick, straight dark hair and beautiful white hands. Her grey eyes looked out of an almost unnaturally pale face. Swimming in the dark still waters of the ponds of Tsarskoe Selo, she did seem like some mermaid or water nymph and Gumilyov was so entranced by this image of her that he not only called her that in his poems, but also persuaded a friend to paint the walls of his room as the sea with a mermaid swimming in it.

In a study of Akhmatova's early work, published in 1915, the critic

---

* Valeriya Sreznevskaya, whose account of this meeting I follow,[3] remembered the year as 1902. Akhmatova told me she met Gumilyov in 1903. In the posthumously published and often contradictory biographical note included in *Pamyati A. Akhmatovoy* (In Memory of A. Akhmatova) (Paris, 1974), she gives the date as 24 February 1903.

A. Gizetti traced her development from the pagan child of 'By the Sea Shore', her long poem written in 1913, to the Christian who, in July 1914, covered her face with her hands and prayed that she might be taken as a sacrifice to prevent war, and suggested that the young poet's inability to find again her early 'pagan' *joie de vivre* might be due to the fact that it was unshared.[4] And indeed, her first poems, written after her illness the year she first went to school, may well have been produced by the shock of contact with a world outside the familiar one of home.

The innocent world of Anya's childhood ended sharply and suddenly in 1905. That January she learnt of the destruction of the entire Russian fleet by the Japanese at Tsushima. It was, she said, a shock to last the whole of one's lifetime, and particularly terrible as it was the first. Coming as she did from a naval family, this senseless destruction struck her closely. Then, at Easter, Gumilyov, despairing at her refusal to take his love for her seriously, tried to kill himself. Shocked and horrified by this, she quarrelled with him and they stopped meeting.

In the summer her home broke up: her father retired and her parents separated, her father going to live in St. Petersburg, her mother going south with the children to Evpatoriya on the Black Sea. Money was now scarce. News of the abortive revolution of 1905 reached them distantly.

As she had not yet finished school, Anna spent the winter working with a tutor to prepare for the entrance examination for the final year. This had its bright side: the young tutor fell in love with his pupil. The result was twice as many lessons as were necessary. But the winter was not all spent in studying. The sixteen-year-old girl had another important occupation: writing poetry.

In that year of 1905, she had faced the meaning of death, both on a personal level, with Gumilyov's attempted suicide, and on the larger, historical level with the tragedy of Tsushima, and the 'shadow that had lain across her childhood' was brought to the forefront of her consciousness. In her memoir of Modigliani, written at seventy, Akhmatova talks of how the future, which 'casts its shadow long before it enters, knocked on the window, hid behind the street lamps, cut into dreams . . .' (II.159). It was, in fact, only in 1955, after a large portion of her life had been lived, that she could understand and write of this aspect of her childhood:

> I seemed to myself from the beginning
> Like someone's delirium or dream,
> Or a reflection in someone else's mirror
> Without name, flesh or cause.

Already then I knew the list of crimes
That I was to commit.
Stepping out like a sleepwalker,
I walked into life and life frightened me:
It lay spread before me like the meadow
Where once Proserpine had wandered.
I was like some ungainly foundling
Yet unexpected doors were opening
And people would come in and cry
'She's come. She's come herself.'
And I would look round at them confounded
And think 'They have gone mad!'
And the stronger their praise for me became,
The more delighted with me they seemed,
The more terrible it was to live in the world;
And the more powerful my urge to awake;
And I knew I would pay a hundredfold
In prison, in the grave and the madhouse,
Places suitable for such as me
To wake in—but the torture of happiness continued.[5]

'By the Sea Shore', the poem written more than forty years before, which Gumilyov loved so dearly that he asked her to dedicate it to him, is also about herself as a child. It has for its theme childhood brought to an end by contact with death, and though it has not the frightening understanding of 'And I had no rosy childhood', quoted above, it is full of the innocence that is specially potent when a writer is still not completely divorced by time from the child he once was. It is here that we may find reflected perhaps more clearly than anywhere else in Akhmatova's work the world of the child poet who 'understood the wind better than human speech'.

The heroine of the poem is a child of about thirteen to whom the green fish swims and the white seagull flies as she sits on the shore drying her salty hair. She is at one with nature, can divine water and is considered 'lucky' by the local people, but hates to go inside houses. She is innocent with the innocence of an animal and with unconscious cruelty turns down the proposal of the grey-eyed boy who loves her and wants her to marry him. She is, after all, waiting for a prince, her tsarevich.

The young pagan on the sea shore is not the only figure in the poem. There are two others, Lena her twin sister and the Muse. Lena is in a sense more than just her sister, for she seems to be the other half of herself. Lena cannot act—she watches from her couch, for she cannot walk, but she understands death and sorrow and the meaning of things in a way her pagan sister is denied. One sister is the embodiment of the forces of life and nature in all its strength, innocent cruelty, and blindness, the other is the Hamlet, lamed by too much understanding.* Only at the end of the poem, as the child of nature listens to the funeral service for her dead prince, do she and Lena seem to have drawn closer.

It is to the child of the sea, not to Lena, that the Muse comes in dreams:

> In narrow bracelets and a short dress
> With white bagpipes in her cool hands
> She would sit down quietly and look long,
> Would not ask about my sorrow,
> Would not speak about her sorrow,
> Would just stroke my shoulder gently.
>
> (I.352–3)

In another poem of 1913 about her visitation by the Muse, there is again the connection with nature, with the sea. Here it is the Muse who teaches her to swim:

> At that time I was a guest upon the earth.
> I had been given the name, Anna, at christening,
> Sweetest for human lips and hearing.
> How wondrously I knew of earthly joy,
> For me there were not twelve feast days
> But as many as days in the year.
> I, dutiful to my secret instructions,
> Having chosen a free comrade
> Loved only the sun and the trees.
> Once late in the summer I met a stranger
> In the wily hour of dawn
> And we bathed together in the warm sea.
> Her clothes seemed strange to me
> And even stranger, her lips,
> And her words fell like stars on a September night.
> This slender girl taught me to swim,
> Holding my unskilled body with one hand
> In the taut waves.
> And, often, standing in the blue water,
> She would talk to me without haste.
> It seemed as if the tree tops were gently whispering
> Or like the sound of the crunching sand,
> Or the voice of a silver pipe
> Singing afar of evenings of separation.

---

* This double image could well be an externalization of the poet's dual nature which in 1946 was to be cast in her face by Stalin's henchman Zhdanov when, quoting the critic Boris Eykhenbaum's earlier, serious study, he referred to Akhmatova as 'half nun, half harlot'.

But I could not later recall her words
And often woke at night in pain.
I visualized her half-open lips,
Her eyes and her smooth hair.
As to some heavenly messenger
I prayed to that sad girl:
'Tell me, tell me why memory has failed
And why it is that you caress the ear
So painfully, only to take
Away the blessing of repetition? . . .'
And only once, when I was
Gathering grapes into a woven basket
And she, the dusky one, sat on the grass,
Covering her eyes and loosening her braids,
Languid and exhausted from the scent
Of the heavy, blue grapes and the spicy
Breath of the wild mint,
Did she place words miraculous
In my memory's treasure house
And I, dropping the full basket, fell
To the dry, stifling earth,
As to the beloved when love sings.

(I.191–2)

2

In the spring of 1906 Anna went with her aunt to Kiev, to take the school examination. Having relatives in Kiev made it a sensible and economical place for further study. She passed the examination and returned to spend the summer in Evpatoriya. Nikolay Gumilyov, who had gone to Paris after finishing school that June, came to see her there and they made up their quarrel. On his return to Paris, Gumilyov received a letter from Akhmatova which he described in a poem as a 'strange pale rose'. In the poem she is seen as Beatrice, he as the young Dante. Later this poem became part of a larger cycle, 'To Beatrice', which includes one of the most beautiful early poems he wrote to his young love.

In my gardens are flowers, in yours, sorrow.
Come to me and with splendid sorrow
Bewitch as with a smoke-coloured veil
My gardens' painful distances.

You are the petal of a white Persian rose.
Come here into the gardens of my languor
So there should be no sudden movement
Only a musical plasticity of motion,

So that from terrace to terrace is carried
The pensive name of Beatrice,
So that a choir of girls not of maenads
Should sing the beauty of your sorrowing lips.[6]

Anna returned to Kiev at the end of the summer to complete her last year at the Fundukleevskaya Gimnaziya. She and Gumilyov corresponded throughout the winter. In Paris Gumilyov became involved in publishing a small literary magazine called *Sirius*, in which he published one of her poems, 'On his hand are many shining rings'. Although this was the first time a poem of hers had been published, Anna did not take her entrée into the literary world via *Sirius* to be of much import: the magazine was just another of her friend's wild ventures.

'Why has Gumilyov got involved with *Sirius*?' she wrote in a letter of March 1907. 'It amazes me and puts me in an unusually merry mood. How many tragedies our Mikola had lived through and all in vain! You've noticed that all those taking part are about as well known and esteemed as I am? I think that his star must be in eclipse. These things happen' (II.303).

But although she found it difficult to take seriously Gumilyov's love for her, for him it was an overwhelming obsession. He took every opportunity he could to see her, coming to Kiev from Paris at the end of April 1907 and returning to Russia again that summer, to Sebastopol where Anna and Inna Erazovna were staying and where he took a room in the house next door to be close by. This time he asked her to come away with him. But the young girl had just finished school and the thought of marriage did not appeal to her. They stood in silence looking at the shore on which dead dolphins were lying. Gumilyov wrote of this moment in the poem 'Rejection':

A princess—or maybe nothing but a sad child—
She leant out over the sleepy, sighing sea
And her figure so graceful and lithe seemed so terribly slight
As it secretly strained out to meet the silver of dawn.

Dusk closing in. Some bird cried out
And there before her dolphins gleamed in the water.
They offered their shining backs to her to swim
To the turquoise palaces of the prince who loved her.

But the crystal voice seemed to ring so clearly when
It stubbornly pronounced the fatal 'No, I cannot . . .'
A princess—or maybe just a capricious child,
A tired child with a look of helpless sorrow.[7]

In despair following this refusal, Gumilyov again attempted suicide early that autumn in France. He went to Trouville in Normandy and was arrested '*en état de vagabondage*'. In October he returned to Kiev on borrowed money without letting his parents know, but his attempts at persuading Anna to marry him were no more successful than before. That December he tried to poison himself and was found only after he had lain unconscious for twenty-four hours in the Bois de Boulogne.

In the autumn of 1907 Anna had entered the Faculty of Law at the Kiev College for Women. She found herself interested in the history of law and in Latin, but felt little excitement over the purely legal part of the course. Gumilyov tried once more to persuade her the following April, coming to Kiev on his way back from Paris. They met again in the summer of 1908 when Anna was on a visit to Tsarskoe Selo, and he stopped in Kiev for two days in the early autumn on his way to Egypt. It was there in the Ezbekia gardens that he made his last attempt at suicide, which he recalled in the poem of that name written ten years later when his passionate love had become a memory.[8] After this the idea of suicide was to disgust him.

In a poem written in Kiev in 1909, Akhmatova, referring to Gumilyov as her brother, expressed her fear that one of his attempts on his life would be successful. But although Gumilyov did not succeed in killing himself, suicide did strike close to her when her brother Andrey killed himself in Greece some years later, in despair at the death of his child.*

Anna did not hear from Gumilyov after his return from Egypt until January 1909. That May he came to Listford near Odessa, where she was staying looking after her mother who was ill, and asked her to go with him to Africa. Once more she refused. In November, however, Gumilyov's persistent proposals at last met with success. In Kiev, with a cousin, Mariya Kuz'mina-Karavaeva, he went to an occasion devoted to the arts, 'The Island of Art'; there he met Akhmatova and spent the whole evening with her. This time she agreed to marry him.

In 'By the Sea Shore', which Akhmatova said was a 'distant echo' of her relationship with Gumilyov, the tsarevich does not come, he drowns on his way to her. In the five years between the ages of sixteen and twenty-one, the child of the sea, realizing the prince would now never come, decided to marry the 'grey-eyed boy' who loved her and to go north with him. Yet Akhmatova said that her marriage to Gumilyov was not the beginning, but 'the beginning of the end' of their relationship.

* Andrey Gorenko and his wife, Mariya Smuntzyla [Zmunchilla], made a suicide pact. He died, but she survived, and was discovered to be pregnant. Their child, Andrew Gorenko, came from Switzerland where he lived to see Akhmatova in London in 1965.

The following spring they visited St. Petersburg together, where another event occurred of great importance to the young poetess. She and Gumilyov had gone to the Russian Museum. Gumilyov had with him the proofs of a book of poems by an older poet from Tsarskoe Selo, headmaster of the boys' grammar school which Gumilyov had attended. This man, Innokentiy Annensky, had published little and late in life. Akhmatova recalls being stunned by his book, *The Cypress Chest*; forgetting everything else, she read it on the spot from beginning to end. Throughout her life she referred to Annensky as her teacher and without doubt this first encounter with his work was vital in her development from a young girl who wrote poetry to a serious poet.

Akhmatova returned to Kiev. Gumilyov soon followed her. On 25 April 1910, the young couple were married in the church of Nikol'ska Slobodka by the Dnieper. Akhmatova's family regarded the marriage as doomed to failure and none of them came to the church, which deeply offended her.

After the wedding the couple left for Paris. A new world opened before Akhmatova. She recalls this and a second trip they made to Paris the following spring, in her memoir of Modigliani:

Horse-drawn cabs were still much in evidence. The drivers had their own taverns known as '*Rendezvous des cochers*' and my young contemporaries were still alive, who were soon to die on the Marne or at Verdun. All the left-wing artists except for Modigliani were recognized. Picasso was as famous then as now, only then one talked of 'Picasso and Braque'. Ida Rubinstein was playing Salome and the Diaghilev Ballets Russes were becoming an elegant tradition—Stravinsky, Nijinsky, Pavlova, Karsavina, Bakst.

We know now that Stravinsky's fate was not to remain tied to the 1910s; that his creative work became one of the highest musical expressions of the spirit of the twentieth century. Then we did not know this. On 20 June 1910 *The Firebird* opened. On 13 June 1911 Diaghilev presented Fokine's *Petrushka*.

The laying of the new boulevards on to the living body of Paris (which Zola described) was still not quite finished (Boulevard Raspail). Werner, a friend of Edison, showed me in the Taverne du Panthéon two tables and said: 'And there are your Social Democrats—Bol'sheviks at that one, Mensheviks at the other.' Women with varying success tried wearing trousers (*jupes-culottes*) and practically swaddling their legs (*jupes entravées*). There was a complete desert as far as poetry was concerned and people bought it only for the vignettes by more or less well-known artists. I understood even then that painting in Paris had swallowed up French poetry.

René Ghil was prophesying 'scientific poetry' and his so-called students visited the master with extreme lack of interest.

The Catholic Church canonized Joan of Arc.

Où est Jeanne la bonne Lorraine
Qu'Anglais brulèrent à Rouen
(Villon)

I recalled these lines from the immortal ballad looking at the little statuettes of the new saint. They were in exceedingly doubtful taste and they began to appear in shops that sold religious objects. . . .   (II.160–1).

Akhmatova describes herself and Modigliani, both as yet untouched by their futures, sitting in the rain on a bench in the Jardins de Luxembourg (Modigliani was too poor to pay for chairs) under his enormous old black umbrella, reciting Verlaine to each other, or wandering round the old parts of Paris in the moonlight. And in describing Modigliani she describes what she herself was like—with her ability to guess other people's thoughts, have other people's dreams, to hold conversations that had little or no connection with the events of the ordinary day-to-day world.

Gumilyov pictures this woman to whom he had long ago lost his heart as a witch, not a wife:

> From a serpent's nest,
> From the city of Kiev,
> I took not a wife but a witch.
> I thought her amusing
> Guessed she might be capricious,
> A gay and happy song bird.
>
> You call out and she frowns
> You hug her and she bristles
> When the moon comes out she starts pining.
> She stares and groans
> As if she were burying
> Someone and wanted to drown herself.[9]

In another poem he mentions the effect the moon had on his young wife:

> But when the sounds of day were hushed
> And the moon rose over the town
> You started suddenly to wring your hands
> Became so painfully pale.[10]

This was not poetic licence, for Akhmatova said that all during her childhood and youth the moon had a very powerful effect on her. It was not by chance she had written, in her first published poem, that her ring was a gift from the moon. As she grew older this effect lessened.

3

Towards the end of June 1910, the Gumilyovs returned to Tsarskoe Selo, where they lived first in a house in the Bulvarnaya and later in the ground floor of Gumilyov's mother's house, Malaya 63.* Gumilyov's father had died shortly before their wedding.

Despite his persistence in proposing marriage, Gumilyov began almost immediately to chafe at the bondage it entailed. On 25 September, he left once more for a long trip to Africa, this time to Abyssinia. On the way there he sent a poem to his newly wedded wife. In it a man sitting by the fireside tells of his exploits in faraway lands before he became 'weak'. It ends:

> And hiding evil triumph in her eyes
> The woman in the corner listened to him.[11]

Left to herself, Akhmatova started seriously to write poetry and almost the whole of her first collection, *Evening*, was written in the house in the Bulvarnaya.†

Gumilyov was away for six months, returning only at the end of March 1911. When Akhmatova met him at the railway station he looked at her sternly and asked, 'Have you been writing?' When she said she had, he demanded to see the work there and then on the platform. He cast his eye over it, nodded, and said, 'Good.' From this time on he showed great respect for her writing, although without doubt he felt that for a poet to be married to a poetess was rather a ridiculous situation.

The couple left again for Paris. They returned to spend the summer of 1911 at Slepnyovo, the small country estate not far from Bezhetsk, in the Guberniya of Tver, belonging to Gumilyov's mother and her sister. After Paris Akhmatova found Slepnyovo extremely dull. She described it later as 'not picturesque: even squares of ploughed field in hilly country, mills, bogs, dried swamp, gates, wheat and more wheat . . .' (I.45).

Akhmatova's poems had begun to appear in journals, and in a review of an anthology published that year, the Symbolist poet and critic Valery Bryusov, deploring the absence of many young poets from the volume, included in their number the name of Anna Akhmatova.

That autumn when they returned to Tsarskoe, Gumilyov ran into the poet Sergey Gorodetsky and they decided to bring together a group of

---

* This house burnt down in 1941 or 1942. Akhmatova said all the houses she had ever lived in had been destroyed in her lifetime.

† It was probably also at this time that she attended the Raev historical-literary courses in St. Petersburg which she mentions in the short autobiographical foreword she wrote for the 1961 edition of her poems.

young poets in a 'Poets' Guild'. This came about largely through Gumilyov's break with the Symbolist poet Vyacheslav Ivanov. Although the Symbolist poets admitted that by 1910 Symbolism had reached a point of crisis, they were all-powerful in poetic circles, and Ivanov was at the time the uncrowned king of Petersburg literary life. Earlier that year he had been extremely displeased with a critique by Gumilyov of his latest work and had also come out strongly against Gumilyov's poem 'The Prodigal Son' when the latter had read it to him. For Gumilyov, a young, virtually unknown poet, to take a stand against the Symbolists in the face of opposition and ridicule was an act of considerable courage.

The Poets' Guild consisted of fifteen young poets: Gumilyov, Gorodetsky, Akhmatova, Mandel'shtam, Narbut, Zenkevich, Bruni, G. Ivanov, Adamovich, Gippius, Moravskaya, D. Kuz'min-Karavaev and his wife Elizaveta, Chernyavsky, and Lozinsky. They met two or three times a month, taking turns between the Gorodetskys' on the Fontanka in Petersburg (where the first meeting took place), the Kuz'min-Karavaevs' in Manezh Square, the Gumilyovs' in Tsarskoe, Lozinsky's on Vassil'evsky Island, and Bruni's at the Academy of Arts. Lozinsky made a list of addresses of the members of the Guild, and Akhmatova, as secretary, was responsible for sending out notices for the meetings— each one embellished with the emblem of the Guild, a lyre.* The first meeting, at the Gorodetskys', was attended as well by Aleksandr Blok,† Vladimir Pyast, and some visiting French scholars. The poets read in clockwise order, at these meetings, with either Gumilyov or Gorodetsky acting as chairman. They recited their poems, argued about them, and then had supper. After supper they recited comic verse.[12]

At one of the early meetings, probably the third, at Tsarskoe, Gumilyov proposed that they should refute Symbolism. He found the word 'acme' in the Greek dictionary. 'Acmeism' seemed to stand for what he felt was needed: clarity in the face of Symbolist mistiness, as the young poets looked with the fresh eyes of Adam upon the world, fashioning their poems with the highest skill of craftsmen, not trying to assume the position of priests. But not all the Guild agreed to be Acmeists or Adamists. The original group began to fall apart as its members, at first in need of each other's support, found themselves able to stand on their own feet. Lozinsky and Gippius refused categorically to support

---

* The lyre could be seen later on the cover of Akhmatova's first collection of poems, *Evening*, on Zenkevich's *Wild Purple*, and on Elizaveta Kuz'mina-Karavaeva's *Scythian Fragments*.

† Blok refers to the occasion in his diary,[13] describing it as an evening spent among the 'young'. In fact he himself was only six years older than Gumilyov. To say that the Acmeists comprised a 'younger generation' was even then slightly misleading.

Acmeism. Six declared themselves for it: Gumilyov, Mandel'shtam, Gorodetsky, Narbut, Zenkevich,* and Akhmatova.

Two years later Gumilyov and Gorodetsky published, a bit belatedly, their manifestoes for the new school.[14] 'For the Acmeists,' wrote Gorodetsky, 'a rose is more beautiful for itself, its petals, fragrance, and colour, than because of its abstract resemblance to mystic love or anything else.' The problem of Acmeism versus Symbolism was to absorb the critics and to call forth a lot of irritation and criticism and little praise. Gorodetsky, after the revolution, was quick to refute it when it served him to do so. Gumilyov himself admitted that his poetry became more and more like that of the Symbolists. Akhmatova has suggested that some of Gumilyov's theories came into being backwards—that is, from reading her poems—and Pyast thought the name 'Acmeism' was an unconscious echo of 'Akhmatova', whose work he considered the clearest expression of Acmeist principles before they had been formulated by Gumilyov and Gorodetsky.[15]

In retrospect it is difficult not to attach either too much or too little importance to the Acmeists' meetings and the deep concern about poetry and its function that they expressed. Gumilyov, Mandel'shtam, and Akhmatova, however different their poetry, held certain values in common, had a certain outlook on the world which, as poetry was central to their natures, found its formulation in relation to poetry. To discover the essence of Acmeism one must look beyond the form in which their poetry was written, beyond such things as the subjects they treated or even their politics. The outlook they shared was exactly in line with what the manifestoes of Acmeism demanded—a return to earth. With this went a deep understanding of the richness of European culture and the close ties between poets of all ages. At the core of Acmeism was a refusal to escape into another world, a conviction that God can be found through the here and now on earth, that life is a blessing to be lived.

In 1911 this kind of talk might seem to be just that of a group of young people reacting against an older generation. But the Acmeists' theories were to be tested in a way few young persons' are. That Mandel'shtam years later, having endured complete isolation and incredible hardship, could still insist that this world was for him 'not an encumbrance, or an unfortunate accident, but a God-given palace'[16] shows the depth of his conviction. In their outlook on life and on poetry the Acmeists were

---

* Zenkevich recalls that when he first met Akhmatova in those days, he was struck by her independence of thought and her insistence that poetry was something organic. The idea of Valery Bryusov solemnly writing a certain number of lines each day she found comic.

facing in a direction diametrically opposed to that of the Symbolists. As a result there was to be no escape for them from the world's realities as these grew harsher. It was necessary for them to try to reach God and to understand His purposes through understanding, living, and loving life. Existence was not just something to be tolerated while waiting for Heaven. And although for them the poet was not a priest, he was a formulator. Like Adam, he was the giver of names.

4

In the spring of 1912 Akhmatova's first collection of poems, *Evening*, appeared in an edition of 300 copies with an introduction by Mikhail Kuz'min. It was received favourably by the critics, some of whom, including Bryusov, made it the exception to other publications by the Poets' Guild. Akhmatova recalled later her embarrassment when this first book came out. She said Gumilyov laughed and recited to her:

> Retrograde or another George Sand,
> What does it matter, now you can gloat!
> You have a dowry, governess,
> Spit on them all and enjoy your triumph!

Since many of the poems in *Evening* date from the period of Gumilyov's extended absence in Africa in 1910–11, it is perhaps not surprising that the greater part of the volume is concerned with a woman who is either unloved or has lost her lover. Here we see Akhmatova already producing those small classics which more than anything else won her early popularity. They are without doubt the most perfect poems in *Evening*, but mark a stage from which, at any rate for the time being, the poet could develop no further. These little poems portray the high point in the drama of a relationship by means of an extremely laconic, terse, conversational style, in which emotion is often expressed through a gesture or an object, sometimes recalling Tolstoy's prose. Often in these poems, as the critic Viktor Vinogradov noted, the poet seems to be observing in a mirror the outer signs of her inner condition.[17]

> She clasped her hands under the dark veil
> 'Why are you pale today?'
> —Because I made him drunk
> On bitter sorrow.
>
> How can I forget? He went out unsteadily,
> Twisting his mouth in pain.
> I ran down, not touching the railing,
> I ran after him to the gate,

Panting I cried: 'A joke—
That's all it was. Leave and I'll die.'
He smiled quietly, dreadfully,
And said, 'Don't stand in the wind.'
(I.64-5)

Also in this volume is perhaps the most famous of Akhmatova's early
poems, which begins:

How helplessly my breast grew cold
But my steps were light
I put on to my right hand
My left-hand glove.
(I.67)

It is as if in these short poems she had reached the end of the process of
distillation Pushkin had begun with his 'Little Tragedies'. In fact, years
later, she wrote of her fascination with what she called Pushkin's 'giddy
brevity'[18] and of how he stopped writing whenever he had said all there
was to say.

As her contemporaries discovered, attempts to imitate these poems
proved disastrous. But perfect though they may be, there is a limit to the
number one can read before they begin to seem repetitive. Their very
perfection becomes a limitation. The form dictates the content which
limits the form. And, to do justice to her critics, the content of the poems
in *Evening* is extremely limited. They describe a precise state at a precise
moment in time with no development, only the moment now containing
the past. Though Akhmatova varies the external characteristics and
'props' of her heroine, the woman clasping her hands beneath her dark
veil is as much a puppet as the village woman who complains: 'My
husband whipped me with the patterned double strap . . .' (I.69).

In Akhmatova's poems we are faced with three images of the poet:
the one arising out of the facts of her biography; the one created by
Russo-Soviet criticism of the poems; and the one she created of herself in
her work. The third image emerges initially from many different versions
of 'I'. Slowly, during the course of her life, the word and the person giving
the word utterance ceased any longer to be divided, so that the voice of
the person Akhmatova can be heard speaking to us directly through her
poetry, without intermediary and with the awesome authority of complete integrity. But in the poems of her youth we find the poet searching
for heroines who can reflect a part of her own personality and set it in a
larger context, freeing her experience from the purely private.

The figure of the village woman, with her structured culture of Orthodox beliefs and her ritualistic way of life, was to provide at least a partial

solution to this problem of how to enrich and deepen her poetry and relate it to the events shattering and recreating her country around her, while remaining true to their reflection in her own life. The use of this woman as one of her heroines was the beginning of that 'extension of personal feelings to a wider sphere' which her critics demanded—a process which culminated in her cycle 'Requiem', written during the Terror, when finally the loss of the son by the mother becomes the loss experienced by Mary at the foot of the Cross.

Looking at Akhmatova's early poetry, it is easy to fall into the confusion of seeing her as the village woman, beaten by her husband, or the pale sorrowing face, so like the Annenkov portrait in *Anno Domini*, examining itself in the mirror, or even the tall girl wearing a shawl, reciting her poetry as she was later to do in the poets' night club, the Wandering Dog. In fact she is all three of these. Those of her friends and admirers who left Russia in the twenties and who wished to crystallize her as the Akhmatova of the early love poems and those critics who took the religious village woman of *Evening* as an expression of the poet's values and her Christianity, misunderstood equally the sources from which Akhmatova's poetry springs. Forced by her very nature only to write of her own personal experience, she uses external 'props' in her attempt to reach the universal through the particular.

The circumstances of Akhmatova's life were to lead her over and over to consider why she wrote poetry and whether it was important to her. Little by little, her understanding of herself, of what she felt to be her role in the larger life of her nation, and her position as a poet among poets of the world, both past and present, made it possible for her to rise above the circumstances of her own life and of her day and age and to see the patterns behind the events, the links that, close up, seemed to be divisions. Then she was able to say that she looked down at everything 'as from a tower' (II.103). But although this process of growth and integration was reflected from the start in her poetry, in *Evening* poetry is not yet seen as anything bringing a solution to the poet's problems. It will not, for instance, stop her heart breaking—on the contrary, death will stop her poetry. She describes herself as a cuckoo clock which sings when wound up. She sees nothing enviable in this: 'You know I can only wish an enemy such a fate' (I.71).

Through *Evening* runs the theme of the lost prince, the tsarevich: in dreams he appears in a crown; he is the grey-eyed king at whose death she cries 'Hail to thee, inconsolable grief!' (I.55), who seems to be the father of her child, but not her husband; and also Hamlet, who, speaking 'like all princes', sees no alternative for her but marriage to a fool or banishment to a convent. In contrast to the tsarevich is he who 'all his life has measured long and boring paths with his steps' (I.70). Fate separates her from her tsarevich, but life without him is 'a lie' (I.54). The days of the boy who played the bagpipe and the girl who wore a wreath are over now. Instead the poet pleads to be allowed 'to warm herself at the fire' (I.64). The mermaid is dead and her suffering in the land of mortals is because she wanted too much to live.

Cut off from the innocent world of her childhood, the poet still converses with the wind and calls to it in her grief to bury her. The immortal soul, won at the price of pain sometimes so great as to make it seem not worth the cost, is sucked from her by the man to whom she is tied, the man who could be her brother or her lover. Looking at her, passers-by think that she has been widowed, but what has died is not her husband but her soul.

Love is seen mainly as a source of pain and her fate is to know only this, it is not for her to cry or complain. She and her lover are to meet in Hell ('Over the Water') or are seen actually to have sought out suffering: 'We wished for stinging torment instead of undisturbed happiness' (I.64). If a solution is hoped for in death, here too is a catch, for the girl driven mad by suffering, searching for a place for her grave, is warned by the monks 'Paradise is not for you, not for sinners' (I.72). Nor does the Muse bring relief, for she comes to the girl abandoned by her lover and takes back the golden ring, 'God's gift' (I.77).

5

On 3 April 1912 the Gumilyovs left Tsarskoe once more for western Europe, this time Switzerland and Italy. The impressions made by Italian architecture and painting remained with Akhmatova throughout her life as if seen in a dream. They visited Genoa, Pisa, Florence, Bologna, Padua, and Venice, returning via Vienna and Cracow to Kiev.

Akhmatova spent the summer of 1912 with her mother at their cousin Nanichka Zmunchilla's estate near the Austrian frontier. She was expecting a child. Gumilyov wrote affectionately from Slepnyovo describing life there:

Dear Anichka, how are you, you don't write. How are you feeling, you know this is not just an empty phrase. Mama has been sewing a lot of tiny shirts, swaddling bands, etc. She asks me to send you a big kiss. I wrote one poem despite your warning not to write about dreams, about my Italian dream in Florence,* remember? I'm sending it to you, it seems rather ungainly. Write please what you think about it. I'm living here quietly, modestly, almost without books, continuously with a grammar, sometimes English, sometimes

* Possibly a reference to his poem 'A Dream' (*Sobranie sochineniy*, Washington, D.C., 1962–4, I.159).

Italian. I am already reading Dante, although of course I only grasp the general sense and some expressions. With Byron (in English) it goes worse, but I do not despair. I've also taken to riding, particularly equestrian vaulting or something like it. Already I can jump into the saddle at a trot and jump out of it without using the stirrups. I'm trying to do it at a gallop but am unsuccessful as yet. Olya* and I are going to arrange for tennis and are going to order rackets and balls tomorrow. That way at least I'll lose some weight. Our Moka has been about to have her pups for the last few days and she has a basket with straw in my room. She is so sweet everyone falls in love with her. Even Aleksandra Alekseevna† said that she is the most lovable of our animals. Every evening I go for a walk alone along the Akinikhsky road to experience what you call God's melancholy. All the malicious gossip about Acmeism disappears before it. Then it seems to me that in the whole universe there is not a single atom that is not full of deep eternal sorrow.

I have come full circle and am back to the period of *Romantic Flowers* . . .‡ but it is interesting that when I think of my latest work it seems to me from inertia to be in the enlightened tones of *Strange Sky*.§ It seems our earthly roles are changing, you will be the Acmeist, I the gloomy Symbolist. All the same, I hope to get by without an abscess.

Anichka my dear, I love you very very much always. Give my regards to everyone.

Love,

KOLYA[19]

But despite the affectionate tone of the letter and the birth of their son, Lev, on 1 October, their marriage was not turning out to be the rosy paradise Gumilyov had forecast at the time of their wedding.* Valeriya Sreznevskaya later recalled: 'Of course they both had too much independence and stature to be a pair of cooing turtle-doves . . . their relationship was more like a secret duelling—from her side, for her own affirmation of her status as a free woman; from his, because of a desire not to submit to any bewitchment and himself to remain independent and powerful. . . . Alas without power over this eternally elusive, many-sided woman who refused to submit to anyone!'[20]

In her old age Akhmatova talked of the period spent with Gumilyov as not really a marriage at all, but a relationship of two beings, connected in some way it was impossible to understand, living on secret heights with certain unclear obligations to one another. In a poem written in 1908, Gumilyov had described the girl he hoped one day to marry:

* Ol'ga Kuz'mina-Karavaeva, later Obolenskaya, the daughter of Gumilyov's mother's younger sister.
† A. A. L'vova, the wife of Gumilyov's cousin.
‡ *Romanticheskie tsvety* (Paris, 1908).
§ *Chuzhoe nebo* (St. Petersburg, 1912).
* In the poem 'A Ballad' (*Sobranie sochineniy*, I.176), which he brought with him to Kiev in April 1910.

Eve—the wanton, babbling incoherently,
Eve—the saint, with grief in her eyes,
Sometimes a moon-girl sometimes an earth-girl
For ever a stranger, eternally strange.[21]

In marriage she was to remain 'a stranger'.

Although Gumilyov and Akhmatova shared a passionate interest in poetry, neither seemed really to understand what being married was all about. In Gumilyov's collection *Strange Sky*, published that year, poems referring to his wife reveal the conflicting nature of their relationship. 'She', dedicated to Akhmatova (one of the few poems of his she did not like), dates from this time:

I know a woman: silence,
Bitter fatigue from words,
Lives in the secret flicker
Of her dilated pupils.

Her soul is open greedily
Only to poetry's bronze song,
Before the pleasures life allots
She remains haughty and deaf.

Soundless and unhastening,
How strangely her step flows along,
One cannot call her beautiful,
Yet in her lies my happiness.

When I am thirsty for self-will
And brave and proud—I go to her
To learn about pain wise and sweet
In her lassitude and delirium.

In hours of languor she is bright,
Holding lightning in her hand
And her dreams are clear like shadows
On the burning sands of Paradise.[22]

In another poem, 'That other one',[23] however, although quite clearly talking of his wife (he uses the word in the first verse), he actually refers to her as 'he'. He wants, he says, not a gay wife for inspired conversations about the old days, or a lover, as he's bored with that, but a companion from God in return for his suffering. He complains, however, of 'his' harshness, impudently taking the dreams that link them together for chains. Elsewhere Gumilyov looks back with nostalgia to the early days when they walked down the avenue: 'A schoolboy and a schoolgirl,

strangely tenderly, like Daphnis and Chloe.'[24] Akhmatova too recalls
this period:

> Books and pencil box strapped up
> Coming home from school
> These lime trees probably still recall
> Our meetings, my happy boy.
> But when he became a haughty swan
> The grey cygnet changed.
> Grief laid on my life its undying ray
> And my voice lost its ring.
>
> (I.93)

Early in the spring of 1913, having published his manifesto for
Acmeism earlier that year, Gumilyov left for what was to be his last trip
to Africa, this time as director of an expedition to Abyssinia and
Somaliland commissioned by the Academy of Sciences. He took his
seventeen-year-old nephew, Nikolay Sverchkov, with him. From Odessa
he wrote to his wife:

Dear Anichka, I'm already in Odessa and in a café almost abroad. I'll write
to you and then try to write some poetry. I'm completely better, even my
throat, but still a bit tired no doubt from the journey. But then I've stopped
having nightmares as before; once I dreamt of Vyacheslav Ivanov wanting to
do some horrible thing to me, but in the dream it all came out all right. In a
bookshop I had a look at *The Harvest*.* Your poems look very well and it's
funny how Boris Sadovskoy had toned down his comment.

Here I saw a poster that Vera Inber is to give on Friday a lecture about the
new women's dress or something like that; as well that Bakst and Duncan†
and all the heavy artillery are here.

All day I've been remembering your lines about the 'girl by the sea'.‡ It's
not just that I like them, they intoxicate me. So much is said so simply. And I
am completely convinced that out of all post-Symbolist poetry, you and of
course Narbut (in his own way) will prove to be the most significant poets.

Dear Anya, I know that you do not like it and do not want to understand it,
but it is not only pleasant for me but absolutely necessary that, as you deepen
for me as a woman, I strengthen and foster the man in myself; I never would
have been able to guess that hearts can decay hopelessly from joy and
fame,§ but then you would never have been able to concern yourself with
research into the country of Gaul or understand seeing the moon that it is the
diamond shield of the goddess of the warriors of Pallas.

---

* Probably referring to *Zhatva* (Moscow), IV, 1913.
† Isadora Duncan toured Russia from January to April 1913.
‡ 'By the Sea Shore'.
§ He is quoting here from a poem by Akhmatova (I.107).

.Curious, that I am now again the same as I was when I wrote *Pearls** and it
is closer to me than *Strange Sky*.
Young [Nikolay] has been a fine companion up to now and will, I believe,
continue to be.
Kiss Lyova for me (strange, I'm writing his name for the first time) and
teach him to say Papa. Write to me till 1 June to Diredawa, Abyssinia, Africa,
then till 15 June to Djibouti and 15 July to Port Said, then to Odessa.[25]

From Djibouti, he wrote again, asking her to send him new poems:
'. . . I want to know what you've become', and to tell Lyova he would get
his golliwog.[26] But Gumilyov knew that he had already 'lost' his wife.
It was on this last trip to Africa that he wrote the lines dedicated to her
in the poem 'Iambic Pentametre'.

> I know that life has not worked out . . . and you,
>
> You for whom I searched through the Levant
> For royal mantles of unfading purple,
> I've gambled you away as crazy Nalla
> Did Damayanti that time long ago.
> The dice fell with a ring like steel,
> The dice fell—and there sorrow lay.
>
> You said in a thoughtful and strict tone:
> 'I have believed and loved too much, I go
> No longer holding any trust or love
> And maybe before God's all-seeing face
> I am wrecking my life as I cut off
> Myself from you for ever.'
>
> I was not brave enough to kiss your hair
> Or even press your cold, thin hands in mine,
> Was hateful like a spider to myself
> And every sound frightened and tortured me
> And in a plain dark dress you walked away
> Like an ancient crucifix.[27]

In 1913, the year recalled so vividly much later by Akhmatova in her
'Poem without a Hero', the young poet Vsevolod Knyazev, with whom
Akhmatova herself may have been in love, committed suicide in Riga out
of unrequited love for her close friend, the beautiful actress and dancer
Ol'ga Glebova-Sudeykina. That his name should have been Knyazev—
derived from the word for prince, *knyaz'*—suggests that this 'prince'
who died and the tsarevich who drowned in 'By the Sea Shore', written

---

* *Zhemchuga* (Moscow, 1910).

that same year, may have been connected. But in the first dedication to
the 'Poem without a Hero' Akhmatova was clearly, purposely to confuse
Knyazev and Mandel'shtam. Thus, although the tsarevich may to some
extent have been suggested by Knyazev, it is unlikely that he is Knyazev
alone.

It is possible to read 'By the Sea Shore' as merely about the death of
childhood dreams and to see this as the significance of the tsarevich's
death. But Akhmatova said, describing her marriage to Gumilyov, that
they were linked on some secret spiritual heights, and it must have been
the loss of something like this that Akhmatova referred to as 'the end'
at which other people begin in marriage: something powerful enough to
dominate Gumilyov's poems for nearly ten years, but not the thing that
marriages are made of. And so the tsarevich and the grey-eyed boy who
wants the child of the sea to go north and live with him because he loves
her, might also be taken as two sides of the character of the man who
dominated Akhmatova's adolescence and finally married her: the
tsarevich who came from the sea—the poet; and the grey-eyed boy—the
husband. The two could be said to stand for two different kinds of love,
the one spiritual, the other the ordinary day-to-day relationship. The
tsarevich probably first 'drowned' on the day of Gumilyov's first suicide
attempt in 1905; he died again at the time of Knyazev's death, and may
have died many other times in between, for it seems likely that there
were other loves in Akhmatova's adolescence. Most important of all,
however, is the fact that the tsarevich is killed by marriage, and if he is
dead, then his sea princess's life is threatened. For it is to Lena, to the
disconnected other half of herself, that she turns to understand the
meaning of death. And Lena cannot walk, nor is it she who is visited and
strengthened by the Muse.

In a poem in Akhmatova's first collection, *Evening*, we hear the tones
of a defiant mermaid who, like Hans Christian Andersen's, refuses to go
in search of a human soul on earth where every step causes pain.
Akhmatova did not reprint this poem with others from the same book in
her second collection. She could not return to the lost innocence of
childhood. The way back to the Garden of Eden was barred and she
would only be allowed to wake up there when she had gone through the
list of 'crimes' she knew she had to commit.

Her marriage to Gumilyov was no cure for loneliness. Akhmatova
seemed, until much later in life, incapable of the simple acts of love which
make it possible to live with another person. She and Gumilyov, who was
in many ways like her, did not know why they were living in the same
house, or what to do with their child. Recognizing this inadequacy,
Akhmatova left her child to be brought up by her husband's mother,

who had little affection for her daughter-in-law; thus in effect she 'lost' her son.*

6

The year 1913 was the heyday of the poets' night club the 'Wandering Dog', the haunt of all bohemian Petersburg: a cellar with the windows blocked up and the walls painted in vivid colours by the artist Sergey Sudeykin, which Akhmatova recalls not only in the 'Poem without a Hero', but also in her poems 'We are all revellers here' and 'Yes, I loved them, those gatherings at night'. Benedikt Livshits describes Akhmatova and Gumilyov entering the Dog:

. . . swathed in black silk, with a large oval cameo at her waist, Akhmatova would glide in, stopping at the entrance, where, at the request of Pronin† who rushed to meet her, she would write her latest poems in the 'pigskin book' about which the simple 'clerks' would start guessing, seeing them only as something to tickle their curiosity.

In a long frock coat . . . without failing to notice one beautiful woman in the process, Gumilyov would back his way through the tables, whether by doing this he was observing court etiquette or whether it was because he feared a dagger-like glance at his back.[28]

Although the average reader of Akhmatova's poems considered every one of them to be tantamount to an intimate confession, and she became a familiar figure in the Wandering Dog and elsewhere, she still succeeded in keeping her private life very much to herself. She was certainly no longer in need of support in her career as a poet. She remained, however, according to Pyast,[29] as modest as before and rehearsed with great care for her recitals. The artist Yury Annenkov also describes her at this time as '. . . beautiful in an unusual way with her "uncurled fringe" covering her forehead and with a rare grace of movement and gesture. I do not recall anyone else among the other poets who could read their poems so musically. Her manner of recital, the way she read her poems, was in itself already poetry.'[30]

Among Akhmatova's close friends was the poet and critic Nikolay Nedobrovo, who wrote of her at this time to his friend, the artist and mosaicist, Boris Anrep: 'One can't exactly call her beautiful, but she is so interesting to look at that it would be worth while making a Leonardo drawing of her; a Gainsborough portrait in oil; an icon in tempera; or best of all, to place her in the most important position in a mosaic illustrating the world of poetry. . . .'[31]

* The only family photograph of the Gumilyovs is interesting in this respect, for it seems to be not of a family but of three isolated people. (It may in fact be an amalgam of three separate photographs.)
† The proprietor.

Nedobrovo was not alone in feeling that Akhmatova should be painted, and more than one poet had already added to the collection of poems describing her and dedicated to her, begun by Gumilyov. To Mandel'shtam she was a 'black angel' with the strange mark of God upon her;[32] while Aleksandr Blok saw her as possessing beauty that was strangely terrifying.[33] In 1922 Marina Tsvetaeva was to publish a whole cycle of poems dedicated to her.[34] Around Akhmatova was beginning to grow up the iconography of poems, paintings, and sculpture, which by the end of her life probably exceeded that of any other poet.*

The publication in March 1914 of her second collection, *Rosary*, made Akhmatova one of the most popular poets in Russia. Despite the war, it had gone into four impressions by 1916. Between 1918 and 1923 it was reissued five times by different publishers in Petrograd, Odessa, and Berlin. A game became popular: "Telling *Rosary*', with one person starting a poem, the other finishing it.

If *Evening* is mainly about women abandoned who can only wait for death with no promise of Paradise, in *Rosary* the poet is beginning to understand how to survive. In this collection and in those few poems from her third book, *White Flock*, which were written before the war, there is a strong note of hope intermingling with that of despair. To start with she is now prepared to fight back. 'Read my letter to the end,' she demands of her lover (I.92), and in another poem cries: 'Cast aside!. . . am I a flower or a letter?' (I.102). 'You aren't going to hurt me again like last time, are you?' she asks (I.109).

One response to the loss of love, of the beloved, is an understanding of the illusory nature of partings, of the way love can transcend time and space. Of Leningrad, in the 'Epilogue' to the 'Poem without a Hero', Akhmatova wrote from her exile in Tashkent during the Second World War:

> Our separation is illusion:
> You and I cannot be parted,
> My shadow is on your walls,
> My reflection, in your canals,
> The sound of my steps in the Hermitage halls
> Where I wandered with my love . . .
>
> (II.131)

And intentionally to refer back to her realization of this in 1913, Akhmatova chose as one of the epigraphs to the third section of '1913',

---

* Some of these poems appeared in a little book, *Obraz Akhmatovoy* (The Image of Akhmatova), edited by E. Gollerbakh (Leningrad, 1925). These were only a few, however, of the many dedicated to her by more than a hundred poets during the course of her long life and which she kept by her up to the time of her death in a folder which she called her 'striped notebook', some in the original and some copies.

Part I of the 'Poem without a Hero', a line from a poem she wrote that year: 'And under the arch of the Galernaya'—to which anyone adept at the guessing game of *Rosary* would have responded with the following line: 'Our shadows are for ever'. The lovers cannot be separated because their love has transcended the normal bounds and touched on the eternal:

> Because we stood together
> That blessed miraculous moment
> When over the Summer Gardens
> The rose-coloured moon appeared—
>
> I do not have to stand waiting
> By the hateful window,
> Suffer wearisome meetings,
> For love's thirst is slaked.
>
> You are free and I am free,
> Tomorrow more so than yesterday—
> On the shores of the dark-waved Neva
> Beneath the cold smile.
> Of Peter, the Emperor.
>
> (I.112)

The other response to the loss of the beloved is the poet's discovery of the strength to survive abandonment, or even to be the one with the strength to leave: 'My voice is weak but my will does not weaken, it is even better to be without love' (I.119). The past is losing its hold on her and soon she will be free. When her lover leaves her or she leaves him, life becomes empty but also bright. Poetry now has a positive role to play in this freedom from bondage, for what she writes at this time is 'happy' and if her lover knocks on the door she may not even hear. Having left the house of the husband or lover, the poet purveys his 'love and tenderness' in her poetry, for as a poet she can do what she could not do as a woman—make him famous. But still, threatening her freedom, her poetry, and her individuality, is the Don Juan-like figure who wants, as the shepherd boy did in *Evening*, to be with her in Hell:

> And he kept his eyes' dull gaze
> On my ring
> Not one muscle moved
> On his enlightened evil face.
>
> Oh I know: it is his pleasure
> To know intensely, passionately,

That he needs nothing,
That I can deny him nothing.
(I.113–14)

From him she cannot yet go, it is he who must leave, for she is powerless:

Oh how handsome you are, cursed one
And I cannot fly up and away
Although from childhood I've had wings.
(I.98)

She knows that what he claims as love is only lust:

He said: 'I am your faithful lover'
And touched my dress.
How unlike an embrace
Is the touch of those hands.

That's how one strokes a cat or bird,
Or looks at slender horsewomen.
There's only laughter in his quiet eyes
Beneath the light golden lashes.
(I.99)

But she is trapped by her own weakness ('Thank God, for you are alone for the first time with the man you love', I.99), and knowing that the unknown murmur from the trees, telling her that her lover has brought her only pain, speaks the truth, she cries in defence:

You are cunning and evil,
You are quite without shame.
He is quiet, tender and submissive,
In love with me for ever.
(I.88)

In the Wandering Dog where the walled-up windows shut out completely the outside world, all of them, not just the girl who is dancing, seem to be in Hell, or at least cut off from all that is good and pure and real. From this world the poet looks back nostalgically to the time of her lost innocence:

Instead of wisdom—experience, a tasteless,
Unquenching drink.
And youth was like a Sunday prayer . . .
Am I to forget it?
(I.120)

and again:

To become a girl of the sea shore again,
Put shoes on my bare feet,
Wind my braid in a crown round my head
Sing with emotion in my voice.

Stare out at the dusky domes
Of the church at Khersones from the porch
And not know that from joy and fame
Hearts can decay hopelessly.

(I.107)

If it is a sign of hope that the poet can find the strength to survive the torments and trials of love by abandoning or being abandoned by the beloved and leaving his house, her home, this does not mean that her lot is a happy one. Suffering, which in earlier poems was simply stated, is in *Rosary* questioned, rebelled against, and sometimes balanced against a new element in the poet's life: fame. 'Fate sings a long flattering song about fame' (I.96), Akhmatova writes in the poem 'You gave me a hard youth'. In another we find:

Too sweet is the drink of the earth,
Too strong are the nets of love.
Let children read my name
One day in their books at school

And learning the sad tale,
Let a sly smile cross their faces.
If you can't give me love and peace,
Then give me bitter fame.

(I.103)

Suffering is made bearable by the hope that there is some reason behind it all, as yet impossible to grasp except in the simple faith of the village woman:

Pray for the beggar, for the one who is lost,
Pray for my living soul,
You who are always sure of your path,
Who can see the light in the hut.

(I.92)

Akhmatova ends this poem, written in Florence in the second year of her marriage, with the question: 'Why does God punish me every day, every hour? Or is it an angel pointing out a light we cannot see?' (I.92). The home of the homeless is the house of God. It is for others to bring up children:

> You will live and know no harm,
> Rule and judge,
> With your quiet girl you will
> Bring up sons.
>
> May your life be a success,
> You be esteemed by all,
> Don't find out that through my tears
> I've lost count of days.
>
> There are many of us homeless
> Our strength lies in that
> For us the ignorant and blind
> God's house is bright.
>
> And for those who are bent down,
> Altars burn,
> And up unto God's throne
> Our voices rise.
>
> (I.106)

Sometimes death is seen to be the only solution to an unbearable situation: 'You know . . . I am praying to God for death' (I.107), she writes in one poem. In another she is actually dying. Tormented by the problem of life after death, she begs that memory be left her, as then she will be able to survive Hell. Death is made bearable by a visit from the beloved. Real death, with its withering of the body, is contrasted with her previous idea of what it was. She asks the beloved not to force her to suicide: 'Don't drive me under the airless arch of the bridge where the dirty water grows cold' (I.109). Death and poetry are sometimes intertwined: she asks who will write her poems if she dies, and once more it is not only her own death that concerns her.

In three poems in *Rosary* we find mentioned the death of a young man. It is 1913 and in one case, at least, there is no doubt that the poem refers to the suicide of Knyazev. In 'Voice of Memory', dedicated to Ol'ga Glebova-Sudeykina, she asks her friend who is staring at the wall if she sees before her the man who killed himself to escape the prison of his love for her. But the answer is 'No. I see only the wall and on it the dying fires in the sky' (I.104). Elsewhere it would seem that she, who perhaps loved and was not loved in return, takes upon herself the guilt which Sudeykina, her 'double', refuses to bear. She describes a boy suffering the pain of first love:

> The boy said to me: 'How it hurts!'
> I felt such pity for him.

Such a short while ago, and sorrow
Was hearsay and he content.

And now he knows it all no worse
Than the oldest and wisest of you.
                                    (I.108)

Elsewhere she says: 'Forgive me happy boy that I brought you death ...
I did not know how fragile the throat is under its blue collar' (I.111).

Many of Akhmatova's poems grew out of circumstances which they
precisely record. This does not mean, of course, that the poems must
always be taken literally; but if Akhmatova mentions a concrete detail,
more than likely she is referring to something immediately identifiable
by anyone present at the time. To presume that none of the details in her
poems is imaginary is perhaps dangerous, but that is certainly better
than presuming that such details are casually chosen merely for their
aesthetic effect. What must be remembered, however, is that individuals
whom Akhmatova knew are often merged in her poems—they become
in a sense each other's doubles, as Ol'ga Glebova-Sudeykina in the
'Poem without a Hero' is one of hers. Her use of doubles does not
signify an inner confusion between two persons (for which she once
censured the poet Ol'ga Berggol'ts) but, at a deeper level, has to do perhaps with a recognition of complementary types and also with the historical roles she and her contemporaries were forced to play.

In the strange poem 'I have come to take your place, sister' there is
again a suggestion of the double—two people who may yet be one—
recalling the two girls of 'By the Sea Shore' or the description there of
the Muse's visitation to the young child of the sea. But here the one who
has grown deaf and dull through sorrow is replaced by the great fire.
The coming of the other, who calls herself her sister and carries a flute,
means to her the coming of death:

> You have come to bury me.
> Where is your spade, where is your shovel?
> You have only a flute in your hands.
> I will not cast any blame upon you,
> For is it a pity then that long ago sometime
> My voice became silent for ever.
>   (I.94)

She recognizes that to reach this place the newcomer must have travelled
a hard road. Having given up her place and her clothing, she goes away,
groping, still imagining herself lit up by the light of the fire with the
tambourine in her hand. Grief, it seems, has been the cause of spiritual

death (for she goes on living)—the giving up of her special position as a poet because sorrow has silenced her voice and made her no longer fit for the task:

> Your hair has grown grey. Your eyes
> Have grown dull and misty through tears.
>
> You no longer understand the birds' song,
> Notice the summer lightning or the stars.
>
> For long now the tambourine's not been heard
> Yet I know you are frightened of silence.
>
> I have come to replace you, sister,
> By the high fire in the woods . . .
>
> (I.94)*

Another poem written in 1913, published in *White Flock*, treats the state or situation of dumbness, but here it is not the pagan Muse or sister who brings relief, but the fiery touch of God on the poet's closed eyelids. And it is a 'miraculous dumbness' to which God's touch comes as a blessing, quenching 'the dull thirst for song' and restoring the link between God and the mortal being bound by earth's laws. Pushkin in his poem 'The Prophet' had written:

> Suffering from thirst of the spirit
> I dragged myself through the dark desert
> When a six-winged seraph
> Appeared at a crossing of the ways;
> With fingers light as a dream
> He touched my eyes . . .

Akhmatova writes:

> So I, Lord, am prostrate:
> Will the heavenly fire touch
> My lowered lashes
> And my miraculous dumbness?
>
> (I.122)

If this is a prayer—that, as she cannot be released from her thirst for song while she is on earth, this compulsion may be transformed, so that

---

* In October 1939, Akhmatova's friend Lidiya Chukovskaya mentioned to the poet that she could not understand this poem. Akhmatova answered that it was the only poem she had written that she herself had never been able to understand. But in retrospect, it seems to prefigure a theme which appears in Akhmatova's poetry after 1940, particularly in the 'Poem without a Hero' (not yet begun in 1939), in which the pagan Muse or *Poema* saves and revives the poet forced into silence.

she becomes like Pushkin's Prophet able to 'burn the hearts of men with the Word'—she does not say so explicitly. Poetic inspiration for Akhmatova had always been a gift, whether as a ring from the moon or a visitation from the Muse. Here it is seen as the touch of the hand of God, providing the link between Him and mortal man, who by himself cannot rise to His Throne. The poet is thus the passive instrument dependent on the grace of God, the Word, the living link between heaven and earth. Her 'dumbness' is 'miraculous', because it is the recognition that the Word is God's and not hers, which makes it possible for her to receive it with closed eyes in faith.

Akhmatova does not here do more than imply that God's touch will allow her to rise up towards Him. She does not, as Pushkin does, go on to talk of the effect of the Word on other men. Perhaps she is relying on her poem recalling Pushkin's to many readers. Elsewhere it is the fact that the voices of the homeless wanderers rise 'up unto God's throne' (I.106) which gives them strength and makes sense of their existence. But in 'I have come to take your place, sister' there is also a tentative suggestion that the poet's role is more than the passive acceptance of God's Word, for she who can no longer sing must be replaced by the fire. In this replacement there is, of course, also a deliverance, particularly if the two sisters are considered as one. Instead of a shovel to bury the dead, the newcomer carries a flute. But although she has reached that place 'by a hard road' there is still the same division as in 'By the Sea Shore'. The two sisters, or halves, remain separate, the pagan Muse simply taking over from the one worn out by grief.

But by linking the pagan Muse with the Christian pilgrim woman, however tenuously, and poetry with prayer, Akhmatova is precipitating a further conflict. For if the strength of the homeless wanderer lies in the voice rising to the throne of God, then to sacrifice her gift of poetic inspiration is to cut herself off from Him. The only response the poet has found to the torment of love, except for that given in the poems about Petersburg quoted earlier, is in leaving her home and writing poetry. But she has by no means freed herself finally from the power wielded over her by the man she loves, or her own desire to be an ordinary woman. The overwhelming mood of *Rosary* is of suffering and grief, of a woman abused and deserted, forced back out of necessity, not desire, to discover her own source of strength: poetry/prayer with its bitter-sweet accompaniment of fame. And this solution is not easily available to all the heroines that make up the poet—for instance, the sophisticated Akhmatova with her elegant fringe and tight skirt, taking part in the bohemian night life of the capital and looking back with nostalgia to the pure life of her childhood.

Rosary does not rely, as does *Evening*, upon variation in the presenta-
tion of its subject matter, which covers a much wider range. The use of
several heroines is now less a formal necessity than a reflection of the
multiple and disjointed facets of the poet's personality. There are signs,
in *Rosary*, that integration between the two extremes of 'By the Sea
Shore' is beginning to take place. Akhmatova can no longer write as she
could in 1911 of 'grey-eyed boys like you who live gaily and die easily.'[35]
She is no longer the child who could laugh at someone's love because she
was waiting for her prince. In Ol'ga Sudeykina, who stares at the wall
but does not see the image of the man who killed himself out of love for
her, Akhmatova has seen a reflection of the blind, unconscious selfish-
ness of that child, who never realized in her pagan innocence what
Gumilyov's suicide attempts out of love for her really meant. Now she
knows that the child of the sea shore 'comforted badly' the grey-eyed
boy (I.351). It is this understanding that had made it possible for her to
write 'By the Sea Shore'. Previously there had always been someone else
to turn to, the option of going north to live with the grey-eyed boy had
remained open. Now as her marriage collapsed around her, Akhmatova
knew that this had been tried and had failed.

II

1914-1924

You will hear thunder and remember me,
And think: she wanted storms . . .

News of the declaration of war in July 1914 affected Akhmatova profoundly. 'We grew a hundred years older,' she wrote, recalling this day. 'And it happened in an hour' (I.158).

Yet, in her quiet way, she seems to have been waiting for the 'True Twentieth Century' to begin. Having borne perhaps from early childhood an obscure foreknowledge of the tragic times ahead, she felt on one level a kind of relief at this break in what she later described as the unreal 'torture of happiness'.[1] Before the war, in the spring of 1914, she had written: 'covering my face as if before eternal separation I lay and awaited what yet had to be called torture' (I.124). Perhaps this had nothing to do with the disasters that were to follow, but another poem, 'To My Sister', written at Darnitsa just before the war, seems very close to her later prayers that she and her gifts be sacrificed in order to bring peace again to her tortured country:

> . . . The seer looked at me and said
> 'You are the bride of Christ!
> Envy not happy people's success,
> For you a place is prepared.
>
> Forget your parents' house,
> Be like the heavenly lily.
> Sick, you will sleep on straw
> And come to a blessed end.'
>
> He must have heard from his cell
> How I sang on my way home
> Of my inexpressible joy,
> Wondering and rejoicing greatly.
>
> (I.131)

On the eve of the war, in Kiev, she wrote of her 'path, sacrificial and glorious' (I.127), and again that summer, 'I don't need small happiness' (I.131).

When war was declared, Akhmatova shared none of the initial patriotic excitement about it. Instead she saw Petersburg filled with soldiers and armaments as a 'wild camp' (I.194) and 'covering her face with her hands', prayed to God 'to kill her before the first battle' (I.158).

Gumilyov volunteered as soon as possible and just over a month later left for the front. From there he wrote to Akhmatova of the reality of war as opposed to how it is described in fiction: '. . . the wounds are somehow such strange ones and they don't get wounded in the breast or

42

the head as described in novels, but on the face, the hands, the legs. A bullet smashed the saddle beneath one of our lancers just the second he rose in a trot; one second earlier or later and he would have been wounded.'[2]

In the same letter he mentions her poem 'By the Sea Shore' and her promise to finish it and send it to him. The poem was published in the magazine *Apollon* early the following year. Another poem of hers, also published in 1915 in a collection called *The War in Russian Poetry*, came to seem as much about the future as 'By the Sea Shore' is about the past. It was in fact frighteningly prophetic of all that was to happen to her.

> Give me black nights of sickness,
> Of choking, sleeplessness and fever,
> Take my child and my lover,
> The mysterious gift of song—
> Thus I pray at Your liturgy
> After so many exhausting days
> So that the storm-cloud over dark Russia
> Becomes a cloud in light's glorious rays.
>
> (I.152, 392)

Later she altered 'black nights' to 'long years' and 'bitter years'.

Despite its popular success, *Rosary* had received only a semi-favourable, rather superficial, critical reception. It was taken as an example of the Acmeists' lack of originality and Akhmatova was criticized for limiting herself to the single theme of love and for being interested in little beyond herself and her own moods (although Bryusov in his review hastened to assert that this did not change the fact that she was a master within her own narrow limits). Ivanov-Razumnik urged her, as many later critics of her poetry were to do, to come out into' the wide open spaces of life', saying that to do this she would have not only to want to do so, but also to undergo inner change.[3]

In 1915, however, appeared three articles—by D. Usov, A. Gizetti, and N. Nedobrovo—which considered Akhmatova's poetry in greater depth.[4] Those by Gizetti and Nedobrovo remain among the most interesting studies of the poet's early work. Akhmatova told many people that she considered the article by Nedobrovo, her close friend, to be one of the most accurate things ever written about her, remarkable for the way he was able not only to assess what she was, but also to understand what she would become.

Gumilyov, in his careful and considerate review of *Rosary* in 1914,[5] had mentioned that Akhmatova in her poetry gave a voice to things previously without one. Nedobrovo also emphasized the importance of this, noting as well that for a poet like Akhmatova, writing poetry is a life-saving necessity. Although she treated the theme of tragic love, he said, her voice was never weak or sentimental and the extent of her suffering was brought about by her desire to experience the extremes of emotion. He counselled Akhmatova to follow Pushkin when he says 'Go where your secret dreams lead you', and it seems possible that, in the difficult times which were to follow, this advice from a friend of her youth was something she could hold on to, helping her to remain true to herself. That it was Pushkin's advice Nedobrovo told her to follow is also important, for the study of Pushkin and Pushkin's fate became for Akhmatova a source of strength.

In May 1915 Akhmatova went to Moscow for a short while to see Gumilyov, who was in hospital there. She spent the summer as usual with her small son and her husband's various relatives at Slepnyovo where, that summer and the following year, she wrote most of her third book of poems, *White Flock*. Her father's death in August 1915 brought her to Petersburg; she herself was at this time extremely ill with tuberculosis. She spent a few weeks in the autumn in a sanatorium near Helsinki, and most of the winter flat on her back. She was told that it would be dangerous for her to spend another winter in the north until she was better.

In February 1916, in Tsarskoe, Akhmatova met the artist Boris Anrep, a close friend of Nikolay Nedobrovo, who had written to him so much about her. Anrep had returned from London and Paris to take part in the war. He came to see her again that April on leave and brought her an altar cross he had found in a ruined church. When at the end of the summer she was forced to go south for her health, she took this cross with her. The details of her meetings with Anrep and their parting can be guessed at only through her poems. A large part of *White Flock* is dedicated to him and one poem, 'Little Song', is an acrostic on his name. Like a few others with whom Akhmatova's intimacy must be measured in depth, not in the frequency or length of their meetings, Boris Anrep remained an important person in her life, although she had news of him only two or three times after 1917, and did not see him again until 1965.

Yet of all the poems about love in *White Flock*, the one in which the poet's voice resounds as most truly her own, albeit harshly, is that dedicated to Nikolay Nedobrovo, through whom she had met Anrep. Nedobrovo without doubt loved Akhmatova and understood her work probably better than anyone else she was to meet. Of him, in a poem of 1915 beginning, 'For a whole year we have been inseparable', she wrote:

He is so quiet, does not ask for caresses,
Only looks at me for a long time
And with an angelic smile suffers
The terrible raving of my delirium.

(I.141)

Akhmatova's love for Anrep and her inability to love in the same way
this man who was her dearest friend was always a source of grief and guilt
to her, and drew from her one of her finest and most pitiless poems:

There is a sacred line in human intimacy
That love and passion cannot cross—
Though in uncanny quiet our lips merge
And the heart is torn apart by love.

Here friendship is powerless and years
Of lofty and fiery happiness,
When the soul is free and a stranger
To the slow languor of voluptuousness.

The mad seek to approach it, but
On reaching there are struck with sadness . . .
Now you see why my heart
Beats no faster beneath your touch.

(I.143)

In the south Akhmatova stayed for a while with her mother and
brother near Sebastopol, then lived by herself in a rented room in the
city. In December 1916 she stayed at Bel'beks as the guest of Yuniya
Anrep, Boris Anrep's estranged wife, who was probably then at home on
leave from her work as a nurse in the war.* To Yuniya Anrep Akhmatova
dedicated a poem reflecting the changes that had taken place in her life
since the beginning of the war two and a half years before:

Has my fate really changed completely,
Is the game truly at an end?
Where are those winters gone when it
Was six in the morning when I went to bed?

In a new way now, peacefully and strictly,
I am living by the wild sea shore.
Already I cannot bring myself to say
An idle or a tender word.

* Akhmatova apparently knew Yuniya through Nedobrovo, as Boris Anrep was
surprised to learn later that the two had ever met.

How is it that soon Christmas will be here.
The green of the steppe is so moving.
The sun shines and the smooth shore is lapped
By what would seem to be warm waves.

Languishing exhausted from happiness,
With inexpressible agitation,
I dreamt of quiet such as this
And this is the way I imagined
The soul's wandering after death.

(I.163–4)

That autumn at Bakhchisaray, Akhmatova had seen Nedobrovo for what was to be the last time; he died of tuberculosis in 1919. In January 1917 she was pronounced fit enough to go north. She went to Petrograd and from there with Gumilyov to see their son, who was living at Slepnyovo with his grandmother. In Petrograd again, on the eve of the February revolution, the break between her and Gumilyov became final and she did not return to their house in Tsarskoe Selo. From this time on until the very end of her life, when she was given a small *dacha* in the writers' colony at Komarovo for her use during the summer, Akhmatova regarded herself as homeless, as someone living always in other people's houses. At the same time she was glad to close the door of the house in Tsarskoe behind her. For she had always felt there was something horrible lurking there, a feeling which she later interpreted as a premonition of Gumilyov's tragic death.

2

From January 1917 until the autumn of 1918, Akhmatova lived with the Sreznevskys at 9 Botkinskaya Street.* During this period she saw a great deal of Osip Mandel'shtam. As she later recalled,

Mandel'shtam often came to see me and we drove in horse-drawn cabs (*izvozchiki*) over the incredible ruts in the roads that winter of revolution, between the famous bonfires that burnt almost until May, to the rumble of guns carried from somewhere unknown. We drove like this to poetry recitals at the Academy of Arts, where there were evenings in aid of the wounded and where we both performed several times. . . . (II.174)

In 1917 Akhmatova wrote a poem which made a profound impression on her fellow-countrymen, and which is still quoted in the Soviet Union, though usually without the first eight lines:

* The address is that of a hospital, but Akhmatova was living 'not', as she later wrote, 'in the lunatic asylum, but in the flat of the senior doctor Vyacheslav Sreznevsky, the husband of my friend Valeriya Sreznevskaya' (II.174).

When in suicidal anguish
The nation awaited its German guests
And the stern spirit of Byzantium
Had deserted the Russian Church;
When the capital by the Neva
Had forgotten its majesty
And like a drunken prostitute
Did not know who would take it next,
I heard a voice call consolingly.
It was saying: 'Come to me here,
Leave your remote and sinful country,
Leave Russia behind for ever.
I will wash your hands of blood
Take the black shame from your heart
And cover up with another name
The pain of insult and defeat.'
But with indifference, peacefully,
I covered my ears with my palms,
So that these unworthy words
Should not sully my mournful spirit.

(I.378)

One person deeply moved by this clear statement was the poet Aleksandr
Blok. Korney Chukovsky says that Blok quoted this poem to him, and
added: 'Akhmatova is right—to speak like that is disgraceful. To run
away from the Russian revolution is shameful.'[6]

Akhmatova was at the height of her early fame. The painting by
Al'tman reproduced in the magazine *Apollon* early in 1916 made her easy
to recognize. Her striking looks, her bearing, and her famous shawl gave
her a further distinction for those who knew and loved her poems. An
article of 1916 called 'The Overcoming of Symbolism', by the young
critic Viktor Zhirmunsky,[7] for the first time took Acmeism seriously as a
literary phenomenon, studying in considerable depth the work of
Gumilyov, Mandel'shtam, and Akhmatova, and finding Akhmatova the
most typical representative of the poetry of what was still called the
'younger generation'. When *White Flock* was published, towards the end
of 1917, Zhirmunsky noted in it a distinct movement in the direction of
classical form.[8]

Not surprisingly, in that volume it is through the mouth of the village
woman or pilgrim that Akhmatova is able to express her deepest feelings
about the war. She sees it as a wounding of the body of Christ and uses
imagery related to that of early Russian folk poetry, showing sensitivity
to the land as to something alive. When not making use of this persona,
she approaches the subject with greater difficulty as if finding it almost

impossible to express her grief and horror. Her first reaction is to cover .her face with her hands and ask God to take her as a sacrifice, but this is not allowed. As a poet she has a duty to perform and God's command is that her memory, emptied of passion and song, become the 'terrible chronicle of news of the storm' (I.158).

One of the ways she can express what has happened is by contrast:

> We thought we were paupers, had nothing at all
> But when we lost one thing after another
> So that every day
> Became one of remembrance—
> We began to compose songs
> About God's great generosity,
> About the wealth we once had.
>
> (I.138)

Another approach is so subtle that at first we may not realize she is talking not only of the late spring snow killing the young birds, but also of the war mowing down her young contemporaries:

> On the fresh turf the transparent shroud
> Lies and thaws, unnoticed.
> The cruel, cold spring is murdering
> The swollen buds.
> This untimely death is so terrible
> I cannot look at God's world.
> I feel King David's grief, his regal bequest,
> Passed down for a thousand years.
>
> (I.155-6)

She seems once more to have been brought to that state of despair reached earlier on a different level in *Evening*, when the girl driven mad by suffering, searching for a place for a grave, is warned by the monk that Paradise is not for sinners.

Covering her face with her hands, refusing to look at God's world, cannot for Akhmatova be more than a temporary state. Central to her beliefs is the knowledge that she must find a solution to her dilemma through life, not by avoiding it. To block out the sight of war or to wish for death is a reaction to what seems more than she can bear, but she cannot remain in that position for long. She cannot 'escape' into religion as her critics were to claim she had done, because she feels that her belief should be sufficient to make it possible for her to 'look at God's world' and if it is not, then it is she who is at fault. That she cannot yet look and that she feels death should not be grieved over, produces a feeling of suffocation when she tries to find comfort:

You will receive no more news of him,
Not hear of him again.
In a sorrowful Poland embraced by fire
You will not find his grave.

May your spirit be quiet and peaceful,
Already it isn't a loss:
He's a new warrior in God's army
Do not grieve over him any more.

And it's sinful to cry and sinful to suffer
In the dear family house.
Think you can already pray
To him, your intercessor.

(I.135)

It is as if there is a split between what her head tells her and what her heart feels. The result is a sort of numb paralysis.

Akhmatova's prayers to be taken as a sacrifice are a sincere attempt to find a way out of this impasse. They develop from her initial desire to be killed before the first battle, which could perhaps be seen as an escape, to the courageous prayer that she may take upon herself some of the world's suffering and thus lift the burden weighing down her country. But in her horror at the tragedy of war, she has forgotten that there is one thing she has learnt already, which she must never sacrifice whatever the cost: her 'secret gift of song' (I.152).

Perhaps too the fact that she is prepared to include her child in the sacrificial offering underlines once more her failure as a mother. In the very few poems referring to children and motherhood written at this time the negative aspect is emphasized. 'Sleep my quiet one, sleep my boy, I am a bad mother', she sings in her 'Cradle Song' (I.195). And the gypsy woman when asked where her child is answers:

'The lot of a mother is a bright torture,
I was not worthy of it.
The gate opened to white Paradise
And Magdalena took my little son.'

(I.135)

The general mood of *White Flock* is not, however, one of despair. Once more the poet draws strength from her understanding that love transcends time and space. This world of love exists on some other plane. As the soldiers march by, the heroine searches for a white house:

. . . play soldiers,
I'll look for my house,

I'll know it by its sloping roof
By its eternal ivy.

But who has taken it away
Put it down in other towns
Or taken for ever from memory
The road that led to it . . .
(I.133)

Sometimes this other world is different—the 'simple life' that seems to have disappeared with the war. But, as Akhmatova was to say again so firmly much later, she has no desire to exchange her life for that one, however attractive it may seem:

Somewhere, after all, that simple life goes on,
A world, transparent, warm and happy . . .
A young man chats with the girl over the fence
Towards evening and no one but the bees
Hears this most tender of conversations.

Our life in contrast is harsh and splendid
And we honour the rites of our bitter meetings,
When with a swoop the reckless wind
Breaks off a sentence just beginning—

For nothing would we exchange the splendour
Of our granite city of fame and misfortune,
The sparkling ice of its wide rivers,
Its sombre, sunless gardens
And the barely audible voice of the Muse.
(I.149)

The image of St. Petersburg is used as well elsewhere to evoke the harsher aspects of the poet's fate. It is the 'stern dark city of many waters' (I.128); 'the dark city by the stormy river . . . quiet and foggy' (I.126).

Akhmatova, however, had not yet reached the stage where she could use her gift to inspire people and strengthen them, as she was able to do in the Second World War. Although it is wrong to say that she avoided mention of the war in her poems, her approach was, as always, a personal one. As for many of her countrymen, the reasons for the war did not seem to her clear-cut, but the result, the death of her contemporaries, was only too painfully clear. It is not surprising, therefore, to find that despite the war by far the greater number of poems in *White Flock* deal with what had up till now been the poet's central obsession, the theme of love. Again we find the nostalgia for lost innocence before marriage, and the reflection of the beloved's casual cruelty. Love is referred to as something causing 'sickness', something to be 'cured' by 'the ice of non-love' (I.132). Here also are a few poems concerned with the death of love in marriage and its betrayal by the poet, and three poems concerned with death itself in relation to love—not surprisingly, considering that at this time Akhmatova was seriously ill with tuberculosis. Death is seen as a pleasant thing, 'a green paradise of peace for body and soul beneath the shady roof of the poplars' (I.138), and as something bringing one closer to a real understanding of what is important: to do harm to no one.

Most of the love poems in the book have, however, a quite definite theme that could perhaps be regarded as the resurrection of the prince or tsarevich. Written mainly in 1916 and 1917, after Akhmatova's meeting with Boris Anrep, they describe the arrival of the true, long-awaited lover, a 'bridegroom' from whom parting can never be separation. There is an immediate connection with the child waiting by the sea for the prince and the girl searching for her 'white house' while the soldiers 'play'. But this theme also extends into the future, to the 'Poem without a Hero', where the Akhmatova of 1913 is actually awaiting a 'guest from the future' (II.104). So it is not surprising to discover that one poem definitely forming part of this group in *White Flock* dates from 1915, before the poet's meeting with Anrep.* In it she says:

> You have come ten years too late—
> I'm glad to see you all the same.
>
> Sit down here closer to me
> And cast your happy eyes this way:
> See, here's the blue copy-book
> With the poems I wrote as a child.
>
> Forgive me for living sorrowing,
> For not rejoicing enough at the sun.
> Forgive me, forgive me that I took
> Too many others to be you.
>   (I.142–3; variant I.390)

Some of the poems from 1916 on reflect the hesitation and excitement experienced before the arrival of the long-awaited one. 'Now it's high time for my lover to return from beyond the sea,' she writes (I.155). She

---

* Anrep told me that he and Akhmatova had met before February 1916, but that this was their first 'meeting'. It is possible of course that a meeting which took place the year before had had a meaning for Akhmatova.

is happy that only a few more days are left to wait. Looking back later
she remembers:

> Everything promised him to me:
> The sky's edge of dim vermilion,
> The sweet dream just before Christmas,
> The many sounds of the Easter wind . . .
>
> (I.157)

Far less arrogantly sure of herself now than the young sea-princess was
earlier, she writes: 'I couldn't believe that he would be friendly' (I.157).
Life before the arrival of the beloved now has the quality of a dream and
he will make up to her for all she has gone through:

> I know that you are my reward
> For years of pain and work,
> For never giving myself up
> To the comforts of this earth,
> For never saying to the man
> I loved: 'I love you so,'
> Because I've forgiven everyone
> You'll be my angel now.
>
> (I.155)

In another poem written in 1916, but not published until later, in
Plantain (1921), the true lover takes her ring, but it seems to be his
right, as it was not for the earlier Don Juan figure. Parting from the true
lover is not separation or, if it is, this is because they are wrongly
behaving as if they were mortals. But, as others need bread, she needs
news of him: not for 'passion, not for a game, but for the sake of great
earthly love' (I.177).

In two poems, one written in 1915 and the other in 1916, the search
for the tsaritsa is seen from the point of view of the tsarevich. In one he
wanders through fields and villages asking where she is, 'where is the
happy light of those grey stars, her eyes' (I.144). In the other poem,
printed in *Plantain*, there is again a reference to the ring. The heroine
at first denies that she is the one sought after. Sitting by the sea where
the splashes from the green waves are salty like her tears, she recalls the
spring when it happened:

> The nights became warmer and the snow thawed.
> I went out to look at the moon
> And a strange man asked me quietly,
> Whom I met among the pines,
> 'Are you the one I've been searching for,
> The one for whom since a child

As for a dear sister
I've grieved and rejoiced?'
To the strange man I answered: 'No!'
But as light from heaven lit up his face,
I laid my hands in his
And he made me a present of a secret ring
To protect me from love's charms.
And he pointed out four things
That would be where we met again
The sea, the round bay, the tall lighthouse
And most important—the wormwood . . .
Let my life finish as it began
I have said what I know: Amen!

                                        (I.175–6)

The connection between this later visitor and the tsarevich of her childhood is clearly underlined and at the same time connected with poetic
inspiration, the gift of the ring.

The Muse and the writing of poetry is a theme of considerable importance in *White Flock*, sometimes as the subject of a whole poem, elsewhere in relation to the love theme or to the changes that had taken
place in the poet's life and the life of her country since the advent of war.
Her desire is to sacrifice 'all' for her country, including her gift of song.
Yet the conflict between this desire to 'give away the ring', either to
the beloved or, as here, for the greater cause of stopping the senseless
killing of war, and the recognition that the ring, her gift of poetry,
is still not only a source of strength, but also a link with God, is
unresolved.

Some poems in *White Flock* extend a theme expressed in *Rosary*,
in 'I have come to take your place, sister'. In one poem, written in
1915, Akhmatova compares herself to a wounded crane hearing the call
of the others to fly away—for, no longer able to sing, what reason has she
for existence? In another the Muse has simply left because 'there is a
grave here, how can you still breathe?' In this poem (I.152) the poet
wants to give the Muse a white dove but finds the bird has already flown
after her beautiful 'guest'. The white dove seems to be another link with
that 'other world', in fact from the title of the book we could take each
poem to be a bird of the 'white flock'.* In the hard world of St. Petersburg during the war, again the voice of the Muse is 'barely audible'
(I.149) and in Sebastopol in 1916 she lies without strength on the poet's
breast.

Yet the poet's strength is the song that comes miraculously out of

* It could also be connected with the image of the swan, and is a point where the
imagery of folklore intersects with that of Christianity.

grief and melancholy, and poetry brings the release from pain. It is the Muse who leads her, the blind one, and finishes off her incomplete page. Fame is no longer seen as a compensation for anything; here it is just 'smoke' (I.174), a 'trap where there is no joy or light' (I.146). Even if Akhmatova seems at times prepared to sacrifice her gift of poetic inspiration, it is when firmly accepting herself as a poet that we see her strength and her unquestionable authority:

> No, tsarevich, I'm not she
> Whom you wish to see in me
> And for long my lips
> Have prophesied, not kissed.
>
> Don't think that in delirium
> And tortured by pain and grief
> I loudly court disaster:
> It is my profession.
>
>   (I.146)

From this position of strength she can even carry the weight of someone else's guilt and can say: 'I will answer for your sin before God, my darling' (I.146). If earlier she had understood how her words rising to the throne of God linked heaven and earth, now, like Pushkin, she understands that this is a two-way motion. She can write for 'us' and this is for those who are poets. She may fall from this position of strength try once again to sell herself for an easier, more ordinary, earthly happiness, but as a poet she knows her worth and her power:

> If we lose the freshness of words,
> The simplicity of feeling,
> Is it not like an artist losing his sight,
> An actor—his voice and movement,
> A splendid woman, her beauty?
>
> But don't try to keep for yourself
> What has been the gift of Heaven:
> Our lot as we ourselves know
> Is to squander, not to save.
>
> Go alone and heal the blind,
> And in the difficult hour of doubt,
> See your disciples jeer and gloat
> And know the indifference of the crowd.
>
>   (I.144)

3

In an article published in the Petrograd newspaper, *New Life*, in December 1917, the critic and psychologist D. Vygodsky wrote:

In present-day poetry one can observe two streams, two directions. In one we find the attempt to resurrect classical accuracy of expression and artistic perfection of form, which has found its best expression in the poetry of Akhmatova and Mandel'shtam. The other, at whose base lie Futuristic theories, is at the moment represented by Mayakovsky. And almost all young poets, expressing their own individuality to a greater or lesser degree, move consciously or unconsciously in one or other of these directions.

As fifteen years ago everyone was writing like Bal'mont, so now they are writing either like Akhmatova or like Mayakovsky.[9]

Akhmatova was thus already beginning to be considered as someone connected with the past. In a cultural atmosphere such as that of postrevolutionary Russia, which had its gaze firmly set on the future, this could not but bode ill.

The literary night life of before the war was fast disappearing. Akhmatova herself was to write far fewer poems during the next three years. In 1917 she had written 'Now no one will listen to songs, the days that were foretold have come to pass' (I.185). But this prophecy was not borne out by events, for in fact during the bleak years immediately following the revolution, poetry was extremely popular. Akhmatova's reasons for not writing are more likely to be found in the personality of the man who became her second husband, Vladimir Shileyko.

Among those of her friends who were amazed at the news of her impending marriage to Shileyko was Salomea Nikolaevna Andronikova, who heard about it that winter, when a friend from Petrograd came to Baku where she was staying with her mother, prevented from returning north by the outbreak of civil war. Princess Andronikova had last seen Akhmatova in May 1916, and this development in her friend's life seemed so incredible that she thought it might be a reaction to the unstable climate of revolution. But Akhmatova had known Shileyko for a long time. A well-known assyriologist as well as a poet, he was said to have deciphered an ancient Egyptian text when still a boy of thirteen or fourteen. Akhmatova said later that she had thought it would be interesting to be of use to a great scholar. Perhaps she felt that this might solve the problem of marriage for her, as she would be able to contribute her intellectual gifts to her husband's world and yet not be competing in it as she had been when married to Gumilyov.

But Shileyko wanted a wife, not a poet, and burnt her poems in the samovar. From the beginning she describes her love for him as hardly a happy one. In a poem of 1917 she wrote:

> You are always secretive and new,
> And I, more obedient every day.
> However, strict friend, your love
> Is a testing by fire and steel.
>
> You forbid me to sing and smile
> Long ago you forbade me to pray.
> Only keep me by your side,
> I don't care about anything else.
>
> Thus a stranger to earth and sky
> I live and no longer sing,
> As if you've taken my free soul
> Out of Hell and Paradise.
>   (I.186)

Again, in April 1918, she wrote:

> Why do you keep punishing me,
> I don't know what I've done wrong.
>
> If you have to—then kill me,
> But do not be hard.
> You do not want children from me
> And you do not love my poems.
>   (I.186)

and that July:

> From the enigma of your love
> I cry out as if from pain.
> I've become yellow and have nervous fits
> Can hardly drag my feet along.
>   (I.187)

In April 1918 Gumilyov, who had been in Paris and London, returned to Russia. Akhmatova asked him for a divorce. That May they went to Slepnyovo to visit their son, Lyova, who was now six. This was to be their last meeting.

The divorce came through in August. In the autumn Akhmatova and Shileyko were married and left for Moscow, hoping that it would be possible to live there. They were not successful in finding more than temporary accommodation, and soon went back to Petrograd. Before the revolution Shileyko had worked as tutor to the boys of the Sheremetev family who lived in the huge Fontannyy Dom—the 'Fountain House'—

on the Fontanka canal, and it was here that he and Akhmatova now returned to live. This was Akhmatova's first connection with this great house, with its coat of arms bearing the words '*Deus conservat omnia*', in which she was to live for many years.

Shileyko's room was in what had previously been the servants' quarters. It was large and difficult to heat. In 1919 there was no wood to burn and very little to eat. Sometimes there was frost even inside the room. It was at this time that Akhmatova wrote:

> In what way is this century worse than the others?
> Can it be that in the frenzy of grief and fear
> It fingered the very blackest of ulcers
> But was not able to bring it healing.
>
> In the west the winter sun still glows
> And the city rooftops shine in its rays,
> Here Death is already marking crosses on the doors
> And calling to the crows and the crows are flying.
>
> (I.188)

No poems by Akhmatova are dated 1920. For several months that year she worked and lived in the Institute of Agronomy because its employees were given firewood. Akhmatova describes the city in 1920 in her memoir of Mandel'shtam:

All the old Petersburg signboards were still in place, but behind them there was nothing but dust, darkness, and yawning emptiness. Typhus, hunger, executions, darkness in the flats, damp firewood, people so swollen as to be unrecognizable. In Gostinyy Dvor* one could pick a large bouquet of wild flowers. The famous Petersburg wooden paving was rotting. From the basement window of Kraft's one could still catch the smell of chocolate. All the cemeteries were in ruins. The city had not simply changed, it had in fact turned into its opposite. But people loved poetry (mainly the young) almost as much as now [i.e. 1964]. (II.172)

Shileyko continued to appear in Akhmatova's poems.† 'My husband is an executioner and his home a prison' (I.211), she wrote in 1921, and in 1922:

> Why do you wander about aimlessly,
> Why do you stare, without taking breath?
> You must have understood that one soul
> Is soldered hard on to two of us.
>
> (I.216)

---

* The department store.

† Akhmatova told Lidiya Chukovskaya that the one poem actually dedicated to Shileyko (I.220) had no connection with him, but that she had found it necessary to put that dedication on it to end the gossip. It seems possible that people were wrongly connecting the poem with Gumilyov.

and

> He whispers 'I do not regret
> Even that I love you so
> But you must be completely mine
> Or I will have to kill you.'
> (I.218)

But in the summer of 1921 she had succeeded in freeing herself from his domination:

> I swear by the garden of the angels,
> I swear by the miraculous icon,
> By our burning nights' delirium
> That I will never return.
> (I.204)

With her freedom from Shileyko Akhmatova's creative impulse returned. After the silence of 1920 at least twenty-five poems date from 1921. Akhmatova was staying with her friend Ol'ga Sudeykina on the Fontanka (no. 18). It was most likely at this time that she lived with the composer and musician, Artur Lourié, whom she later referred to as one of her 'husbands'. It seems that here there was again some sort of triangle: Akhmatova–Lourié–Sudeykina. Not long after both Sudeykina and Lourié emigrated. In 1962, Lourié wrote about those far-off years:

> I recall how I tried to drag her away from there long ago, she was stubborn and did not want to come to Paris, where I was urging her to go. Ol'ga agreed at once and followed very shortly after me. We lived together, the three of us, on the Fontanka and the *Poema* ['Poem without a Hero'] tells of this in a coded way. That is its main theme. . . . Anya is now seventy-three. I remember her at twenty-three. . . .[10]

In August 1921 Aleksandr Blok died at the age of forty-one. Barely a fortnight later Gumilyov was arrested and shot for alleged complicity in an anti-Bol'shevik conspiracy, the Tagantsev affair.* A new note, that of fear, begins to creep into Akhmatova's poems. At the time of Gumilyov's death she wrote:

> Fear picks out objects in the dark
> And guides the moonbeam to an axe.
> Behind the wall is an ominous noise—
> What is it: rats, a ghost, a thief?

---

* After the Kronstadt rising a certain Professor Tagantsev at the University in Petrograd was accused, with a number of others, of counter-revolutionary activity; Gumilyov was one of some sixty men and women said to have been executed at the time by the Cheka.

. . . .

Better to lie against the bare boards
Of a scaffold raised out on the green square
And to the cries of joy and the groans
Pour out red blood to the end.

I press the smooth cross to my heart:
O God bring back peace to my soul.
The sickly sweet smell of decay
Is given off by the cold sheet.
25 August 1921. Tsarskoe Selo*
(I.206)

On another poem written at the time she changed the date, making it 1914 to avoid referring obviously to Gumilyov.

You are no longer among the living,
Cannot stand up from the snow.
There were twenty-eight with bayonets,
Five bullet wounds.
What a bitter present
I sewed for my love.
How the Russian earth
Loves the taste of blood.
(I.208)

The autumn became for her the personification of her grief: 'Tear-stained autumn like a widow in black clothes . . .' (I.211). In December she went to see her son who was living with Gumilyov's mother as before. The horror of returning to a place she had known with her husband now, at a time of Christmas festivities, is expressed in the poem 'Bezhetsk':

There stern memory now so mean
With a low bow opened its rooms for me;
But I did not go in, slammed that terrible door;
And the town was full of gay Christmas sounds.
(I.214)

4

The year 1921 had seen the publication of *Plantain*, a tiny book about three inches by six, which contained poems written between 1917 and 1919; these were then included in a larger collection, *Anno Domini*

---

* This date, thought to have been that of Gumilyov's execution, is written in Akhmatova's hand by this poem in Anatoly Nayman's copy of her book.

MCMXXI, published early in 1922. The latter was not just a haphazard collection of single lyrics, but a carefully compiled selection in which the order, the divisions, and the epigraphs were as important as the poems themselves. It is unfortunate that the integrity of Akhmatova's early collections has been lost in later collected editions, for the way a poet who writes mainly short lyric poems puts them together into a book is extremely important. It is the creation of a larger unit with its own different rules. Looking at the early collections in their original form it is obvious, for instance, what the Formalist critic Eykhenbaum meant when he called Akhmatova's poetry a 'lyric novel'. Although in the twenties the place of the epigraph is still small in relation to the poems, in *Anno Domini* we see Akhmatova making it an integral part of the whole work, as she was to do in the 'Poem without a Hero'. Isolated by the revolution both from most of her close friends and from the mainstream of literature, she may have seen it as a way of showing that she moved in the company of other poets, in a world not bound by time or country. By choosing an epigraph from Gumilyov for the last part and by opening the book with the poem 'Bezhetsk', she gave the reader little choice but to bear her late ex-husband in mind when considering *Anno Domini*. Her public, knowing of Akhmatova's marriage to Gumilyov and not of her marriage to Shileyko—or if they did, not that it had ended—would naturally assume that the jealous husband was Gumilyov and her guilt entirely to do with his death. As Eykhenbaum pointed out, one of Akhmatova's poetic tricks is to make us feel we have been allowed to read an intimate diary; it is only after careful consideration that we realize how very impersonal this 'personal' diary is.

The poems in *Plantain* and *Anno Domini* cover the period from the end of the war on through the February and October revolutions and the civil war. To say, as her critics later did, that nothing about these great historic events can be found in Akhmatova's poetry is simply not true. Nor can it be held that her response to the revolution was entirely a pessimistic one. It was an honest one and she managed to keep it so by dealing, as always, only with her own experience. Working outward from herself, she attempted where possible to set her experience and understanding in the framework of something larger.*

In a poem written in 1923 we find Akhmatova using contrast to express the horror of war by setting it against a picture of complete peace:

---

* At least two poems written during this period can be taken as examples of where she does not succeed in doing this: 'Your arrogant spirit is clouded over' and 'You apostate: beyond the green island'. The result is rather like eavesdropping on a private conversation.

The stronghold of Erzurum had fallen.
Blood had flooded the neck of the Dardanelles,
But in this park no sound was audible,
Only a rusty weathervane creaked far off.
But in this park sullen and silent
The moon shines and the snow is diamond white.

(I.341)*

A poem written in the summer of 1917, 'The river flows slowly along the valley' (I.84), might seem at first to have absolutely no connection with what was happening. But noting the date, the words 'And we are living as they lived in Catherine's day / Going to church and waiting for the harvest' can be appreciated in their full irony.

Another way of expressing the greater emotions of the country at war was by voicing the sorrow of the mother. In the poem 'Why then did I carry you', the reference to the youth's death is set apart from herself. We do not even know if it is the heroine's son who has died. More likely it is simply a mother's question: why do we bear children and bring them up only to have them die in war? The tone is quite impersonal:

Why then did I carry you
Long ago in my arms
Why then did strength glow
In your blue eyes!
You grew up tall and slender
Sang songs and drank Madeira
Took your torpedo boat
To far-off Anatolia.

At Malakhov Kurgan
They shot an officer
He'd looked at God's world
One week short of twenty years.†

(I.169)

Years later she was to write in 'Poem without a Hero' of the days when they brought up children for 'execution / At the block, or back to the wall, / ... for the prisons.'

When other people had at the beginning of the war been excited at the prospect of glory, Akhmatova had seen St. Petersburg as 'a city of sorrow and anger' (I.194). The revolution seemed equally terrible:

---

* This poem remained unpublished until 1946.
† The poem may in fact have been inspired by the news (later proved false) that Akhmatova's younger brother had been shot at Malakhov Kurgan in the Crimea at a mass execution of White officers during the civil war.[11]

And all day, frightened by its own groans,
In deathly anguish the crowd has tossed,
While over the river on banners of death
Sinister skulls smile evilly.
Is it for this that I sang and dreamed,
My heart has been torn in two,
As after a volley of shots it's silent,
Death's sent its scouts out on patrol.

(I.184–5)

It was at this time too that Akhmatova wrote that most gloomy and despairing poem comparing her country, where white death was marking houses with a cross as in the time of the plague, with the west where the sun was still shining.

But through what seeméd on the face of it to be the destruction of everything, Akhmatova sensed that something extraordinary was in the air. In this she may have been closer to the Symbolists' expectation of a new era than to that of the Marxists; one of her poems shows the 'miraculous' coming to birth amidst the dirt, death, and hunger as clearly, if not so violently, as Blok did in 'The Twelve':

Everything is plundered, betrayed and sold,
The wing of black death has passed by;
Everything is swallowed up in hungry grief,
Why does it seem bright?

By day the fantastic wood below the town
Is sweet with the breath of cherries;
At night the depths of the transparent July skies
Glitter with new constellations

And the miraculous is drawing so close
To the dirty, ruined houses . . .
Known to no one, no one at all,
Yet awaited by us for centuries.

(I.201)

It is perhaps understandable that in 1918 Akhmatova married a man whose stern demands upon her must have seemed at the time proof of his strength, something she could hang on to as her world crumbled leaving what she wrongly felt was one in which no one would be interested in 'song'. Of the love poems in *Plantain* and *Anno Domini*, approximately half are concerned directly, using vivid descriptions of the jealous, passionate 'dragon' who has her in his power, with the problem of freedom in love; others deal with it indirectly. At first her loss of freedom is because she is captivated by the beloved—in love with him. The heroine has left her child and wanders in a foreign capital in the hope of catching a glimpse of him. It is a 'testing by fire and sword', yet she can cry: 'As long as I don't have to part from you the rest is unimportant' (I.186).

This picture of a harsh man holding the heroine in his power is not new in Akhmatova's poetry. In *Evening* there was an earlier and less ferocious version of the character in the shepherd boy who laughingly suggested to the girl that they would meet in hell. Closer perhaps to the present 'hero' was the guest in *Rosary* who never took his eye off the heroine's wedding ring as he asked: 'Tell me how people kiss you, tell me how you kiss' (I.133) and who she knew gloated over the fact that while he had no need of her she had not the strength to deny him anything. He is not unlike the killer of the white bird, but there is an important difference: for even if we take the white bird to signify the heroine's individuality, her ability to be a poet, we cannot deny that its killer tells her to 'write poems' (I.125). The 'dragon' will not let her do that.

In the poems of *Plantain* and *Anno Domini* this character's love is paid for in very large currency indeed: the heroine's poetry, her smiles and her prayers. On top of this he punishes her. Everything she has to offer as a poet and a woman: her poems, children, he does not like. Love becomes torture:

> But claw, claw, more frenziedly
> At my consumptive breast
>
> So that blood spurts out of my throat
> More quickly on to the sheet,
> So that death plucks from my heart
> The cursed intoxication.
>
> (I.187)

The 'dragon' wants to reform her so that she 'becomes better than everyone else' (I.203) and his method is the whip. He wanders about restlessly, for sharing one soul causes discomfort. Hurting the one he loves only hurts himself. Jealous, he whispers he will kill her if she will not be his alone.

Even if we do not connect these descriptions with Shileyko—and there seems little doubt that he played a role in the development of this character—inevitably we find a reflection in Akhmatova's poetry of the escape from the domination of the 'dragon'. After all, had he been successful in teaching obedience to his whip, there would have been no poems describing him. When the time comes to deny this love the recantation is as violent as the expression of it has been. And, as if in answer to Gumilyov's voice from beyond the grave ('Distant Voice'), the poet accepts that she is like one who poisoned the stream for others only to stumble upon it herself and drink her death. For how in days past could she have been jealous when in fact she had no rivals, had failed to understand that their relationship was on a different level:

> It is not true, you have no rivals.
> You are not for me an earthly woman,
> But the consoling light of the winter sun,
> The wild song of the homeland.
>
> (I.374)

Shileyko's possessive jealousy, his desire to have *all* of her, has made her realize that jealousy and possessiveness have nothing to do with love. Gumilyov had told her that he needed to travel to Africa to develop and deepen his own personality and this 'escape' from her was not a sign that he did not love her. He had also insisted that his affairs with other women had nothing to do with their own special relationship, but Akhmatova had felt that they did and she had separated from him. Now she herself has realized that not to allow the beloved full freedom is to deprive him of 'wings'.

In contrast to the 'dragon' we find also in the poems of these years the image of the 'true lover' who came and was recognized but left. He is her 'angel' who will find her sadly changed when he returns, for she is 'no longer beautiful, no longer the one who confused him with her song' (I.217). It is to him, also a wanderer, that she describes her prison. Perhaps it is the memory of this 'angel' that gives her strength to leave it. She is also grateful to the kind friend who opens his door to her when she escapes* but laughs at him for thinking she could possibly be 'obedient to him' for she is 'obedient only to the Will of God'. Her home is a prison and coming to him was something different. This captivity is 'bright' and so with complete freedom she can say as he bids her farewell, 'Goodbye my quiet one, I will always be fond of you because you let the wanderer into your house' (I.211). Thus her strength and peace of mind are found once more when she accepts her role as the pilgrim-wanderer. Also, as she disentangles herself from the powerful attachment to the 'dragon', the Muse is there with comfort:

> Somehow we managed to separate
> To put out the hateful fire.
> Eternal enemy, it's time to learn
> How truly to love someone.

* Possibly referring to Artur Lourié.

I am free. Everything's amusement.
At night the Muse will fly to comfort me
And in the morning Fame drag herself here
To sound her rattle in my ear.

(I.205)

Free, she can see that the agony she endured was not a necessary part of their love, and no longer a slave, she herself has no need of slaves.

Poems referring to the 'true lover' running parallel chronologically with the theme of the 'dragon', merge later with poems reflecting Akhmatova's grief at the death of Gumilyov. At Slepnyovo in the summer of 1917, four years before this tragedy, she had written:

I don't ask for caresses or love's flattery
With my foreboding of inevitable doom,
But come and look at the paradise where we
Together walked blessed and innocent.

(I.183)

Perhaps this was nostalgia for her early happiness with Gumilyov, perhaps she was thinking of Boris Anrep. Grief at the death of the beloved is complicated by guilt:

Stubborn, I wait to see what happens,
What will happen to me, as in a song?
He will knock on the door with assurance
And happy, ordinary, as before,

He'll walk in and say 'Enough,
I too, you see, can forgive.'
It will not be terrible or painful . . .
No roses, no archangel's powers.

So in a frenzy of confusion
I protect my heart,
Because I cannot imagine
Death without this moment.

(I.208)

Again, without the date (August 1921) this could be simply another poem about love, an extension of, say, 'She clasped her hands under the dark veil' (I.64) from *Evening*. But the knowledge (from outside the poem) that the beloved is dead and can never return to forgive lends it a completely new dimension. There is a link too between the guilt expressed in this poem and that experienced in her relationship with Nedobrovo and with the young boy, Knyazev, whose love was not returned and who committed suicide. Guilt before the dead must be carried with one through life—a theme that was to become important in 'Poem without a Hero'.

The memory of happiness which in 1917 she could ask the man she loved to share with her, now makes her grief at his death all the more terrible. Only by once more taking refuge in the language and imagery of the pilgrim-wanderer can she set this death in a larger context. It also results in the entry of a new emotion into her poems—fear. She 'comforts' herself with the story of Bluebeard; describes a house where she can sense that something horrible has happened. She is also horrified by her own earlier prophecies of doom (Mandel'shtam had called her Cassandra):

> I called down doom upon my friends
> And they died one by one.
> Oh grief, my words prophesied
> Those graves.
>
> (I.209)

The powers of a witch to see other people's dreams and to prophesy, which she had enjoyed earlier, now seem to make her partly responsible for what is happening. Here it is not a question of guilt over not having done something she could have done, such as forgiving someone before his death. It is something much larger: a feeling of complicity in the evil manifest around her, from which she can only be freed by accepting it in the details of her own behaviour. It is not the guilt of the upper classes towards the poor, but the beginning of what is still a semi-conscious acceptance of the guilt borne by humanity at large for the treatment accorded man by man. It is this acceptance of guilt which in time gives Akhmatova the right to judge others, but makes her judgement of her fellow-countrymen so easily misunderstood by Russians living abroad and by foreigners. For although she judges looking down 'as from a tower', she includes herself among the people she sees walking below.

5

Plantain and *Anno Domini MCMXXI* were the last volumes of Akhmatova's poems to be published until 1940. For the next couple of years, however, her work continued to appear in magazines and journals. In September 1922 in one of these poems she defined what she considered to be her position for the people of her country.

She emphasized that the poem was written not just to a small group of friends by entitling it 'To Many People'; an allusion to having been

given 'the best of your sons' can only refer to Gumilyov. Following his
death, Akhmatova had learnt of his great popularity when letters began
to arrive from all over Russia, telling her how much his poems were
loved and asking among other things whether she knew where he was
buried.* She was sad that he had never known his work was so much
appreciated, because it had only begun to be widely read during the
years of the war and the civil war, when communications were disrupted.
'To Many People' may have been a kind of direct answer to these letters.
It was also a reaffirmation that she would never emigrate. She had, however, gone considerably further than in 1917, when she had written
'When in suicidal anguish', for now she identifies herself completely
with the people to whom the poem is addressed.† She is their 'voice' and
although she may long to be forgotten, she realizes that this is like the
soul longing to be free of the body:

> I am your voice, the heat of your breath,
> I am the reflection of your face,
> Useless wings flutter uselessly
> For anyhow I'm with you to the end.
>
> That's why you love me so greedily
> In my sin and helplessness;
> That's why with no regrets you gave
> Me the best of your sons;
>
> That's why you have not even asked
> For a single word ever about him
> And have filled my ravaged home
> With the fumes of praise.
> They say that one cannot be more close,
> Cannot love more irreparably . . .
>
> As the shade wishes to leave the body
> As the soul wishes to part from the flesh,
> So is my wish now to be forgotten.
>   (II.137)

* Irina Nikolaevna Punina recalls being taken as a child by Akhmatova to the place
where Gumilyov had been shot, and was presumably buried. There is however no
marked grave. N. Mandel'shtam also mentions walking with her husband and Akhmatova over various places rumour had it that Gumilyov was buried (*Hope Abandoned*,
London and New York, 1974, p. 144).

† Although it had a profound effect on her public in 1922, 'To Many People' was
never included in a collection of Akhmatova's poems, and disappeared so completely
that in 1966 it was still unknown to so precise and devoted a collector of the poet's
work as Lidiya Chukovskaya; it was Akhmatova who drew it to her attention, com-
plaining that it had been excluded from her collected works.

But although Akhmatova may have defined for herself and her readers her relationship with them and what she felt to be her function in post-revolutionary Russia, she was soon to be cut off from that public. Symbolism with its other-worldliness might have been thought less compatible with a revolutionary literature than Acmeism, with its emphasis on the here and now, but the opposite turned out to be the case. Aleksandr Blok's poem 'The Twelve' had linked the revolution with an idea, current among the Symbolists, that the twentieth century was to see the Second Coming. This, coupled with Bryusov's willingness to compromise himself for the sake of his position with the new regime, Gumilyov's execution, and Gorodetsky's loud and cowardly refutation of Acmeism, opened the way for a new interpretation of Symbolism showing it in a not unfavourable light. Acmeism, which had been contrasted with it, and Akhmatova suffered accordingly.

Blok's death in 1921 made it possible to speculate that he might have written more poems like 'The Twelve'—even though this did not entirely accord with what was known of the poet. Unwittingly, as far as concerned Akhmatova, Blok had himself added fuel to the flames in an article written in April 1921, a few months before his death. 'Without Divinity without Inspiration', published posthumously in 1925, was a savage attack on the new 'school' of Acmeism, especially on Gumilyov, whom Blok accused, little knowing how the word was later to be misused, of 'foreignness'. Akhmatova was the one poet exempt from this attack, but Blok's reasons for not considering her a typical Acmeist were hardly likely to appeal to those trying to create a new, 'positive' revolutionary literature. 'I do not know whether she considers herself an "Acmeist" ', Blok wrote; 'in any case "the blossoming of physical and spiritual powers" is certainly not to be found in her weary, morbid, feminine, self-absorbed style.'

For the other poets of Acmeism Blok showed no mercy:

Gumilyov and some other no doubt talented 'Acmeists' are drowning in the cold swamp of soulless theories and all kinds of formalism. They are sleeping a sleep without dreams from which they cannot be awakened. They have not and do not want to have the slightest notion about Russian life and about life in the world in general. In their poetry and, it follows, in themselves, they hush up what is most important, the only thing of real value: *the soul*.[12]

Nadezhda Mandel'shtam, Osip Mandel'shtam's widow, talking of the position of the Acmeists after the revolution, says: 'They brought something with them that provoked blind fury in both literary camps: Vyacheslav Ivanov and his entourage, as well as the Gorky circle, met them with hostility. . . . M [Mandel'shtam] always said that the

Bol'sheviks preserved only those who were passed on to them by the Symbolists.'[13]

With the deaths of Blok and Gumilyov, the debate between Acmeism and Symbolism came more or less to a close. Thereafter criticism in the Soviet Union reflected more and more the split between the 'Akhmatova faction' and the 'Mayakovsky faction' which Vygodsky had noticed among the young poets as early as 1917. The Futurists, with Mayakovsky bursting with an energy he was prepared to harness to the creation of a glorious new world, seemed more in tune with the emotions that had created the revolution and were trying to recreate the country, than the quiet poems of a woman intent on examining and discovering truth in what seemed to be a very personal way. The emigration of large numbers of intellectuals during the early twenties and the appearance of their critical articles in Russian journals abroad, did nothing to help the situation. Though she had clearly stated that she considered leaving the country to be something shameful, the émigrés continued to regard Akhmatova as 'one of them', which for those of her countrymen who had not left served only to emphasize her connection with the past.

On 20 September 1921, Korney Chukovsky had given a lecture at the House of Arts in Petrograd entitled 'Two Russias'. Calling for a synthesis of what he termed the Russia of Akhmatova and the Russia of Mayakovsky, both of which he claimed to love equally, he none the less unintentionally (and very much to his regret later on) succeeded in crystallizing their differences.

Chukovsky pointed out in his lecture many things that were to be used against Akhmatova by those who wished her to be silenced. He described her as a nun who crosses herself as she kisses her beloved; as the last and only poet of Orthodoxy; as a woman of Novgorod of the sixteenth or seventeenth century. He noted that 'the eternal Russian temptation to self-disparagement, humility, meekness, poverty, that attracted Tyutchev, Tolstoy, Dostoyevsky' fascinated her and that she was above all the poet of love without hope. 'I love, but I am not loved; I am loved, but I do not love—this is her main speciality. In this no one has yet been able to surpass her. . . . She was the first to reveal that to be unloved was a subject for poetry.'

Chukovsky contrasted Akhmatova's quiet subtlety with Mayakovsky's inability to recognize anything less than a shout. If Akhmatova notices minute details, Mayakovsky cannot even see anything small. He knows no number under a million. His poetry is not intimate but written for crowds: 'He is the poet of the thundering and rumbling, of all kinds of roaring and screaming. . . .' But Chukovsky felt that, however strange

Mayakovsky's vocabulary and rhythms might seem, literature would, in the near future, follow along the same path:

Akhmatova and Mayakovsky are as hostile one to the other as the epochs which gave them birth. Akhmatova is the careful heir to all that is most precious in Russian pre-revolutionary literary culture. She has many ancestors, Pushkin and Baratynsky and Annensky. In her we find that refinement of spirit and charm which is the result of centuries of cultural tradition. But in every line, every letter of Mayakovsky we find the birth of the present revolutionary age. In him we can find its beliefs, can hear its cries, see its failures, know its ecstasies. He has no ancestors and if strong in anything, is strong in posterity. Behind her stand the many splendid centuries of the past, in front of him the many centuries of the future. She has the Old Russian belief in God, preserved from days of old, he is blasphemous and sacrilegious, as befits a revolutionary bard. For her, the most sacred thing of all is Russia, her country, our land. He, as befits a revolutionary bard, is an internationalist, a citizen of the planet. . . . She is the solitary quiet one, eternally in seclusion. . . . He belongs to the square, the meeting, he is part of the crowd, he is the crowd.

Thus despite Chukovsky's call at the end of his lecture for a merging of these extreme positions in order that literature might proceed, he had so effectively labelled Akhmatova that although she was only thirty-two years old, she was henceforth considered by many to be so much a part of the past as to have no possibility of development, no link with the post-revolutionary literary life of her country.

Chukovsky's talk was published the same year, under the title 'Akhmatova and Mayakovsky', in the first number of the journal *The House of Arts*,[14] which also contained a prophetic article on the future of Russian literature, 'I Am Frightened', by Evgeniy Zamyatin. 'I am frightened,' wrote Zamyatin,

that we will have no true literature so long as people look on the Russian demos as a child whose virginity must be preserved. I am frightened that we will have no literature until we have cured ourselves of a sort of Catholicism which no less than its predecessor fears every heretical word. And if this sickness is incurable—I am frightened that Russian literature will only have one future: its past.[15]

The people of the Soviet Union were soon to be 'protected' from Akhmatova. In order to give it wider circulation, Anatoly Lunacharsky, Lenin's Commissar of Education, reprinted the whole of the final section of Chukovsky's article in the magazine *Press and Revolution*.[16] (He likened its original appearance in *The House of Arts* to coming on some interesting antediluvian flora that had been preserved in isolation.)

Lunacharsky disagreed with Chukovsky, not in his choice of Akhmatova as a representative of the old world, but with the choice of Mayakovsky as a representative of the new. On 19 January 1922, in a speech devoted to the 'cleaning up of modern poetry', Mayakovsky himself found that his demands for a revolutionary literature made it necessary to exclude various writers from it:

> Anna Akhmatova's indoor intimacy, Vyacheslav Ivanov's mystic poems and Hellenistic themes—what meaning have they for our harsh and steely age?
> But how can we suddenly say writers like Ivanov and Akhmatova are worthless? Of course, as literary landmarks, as the last remnants of a crumbling order, they will find their place in the pages of histories of literature, but for us, for our age, they are pointless, pathetic and comic anachronisms.[17]

The Futurists had often spoken of throwing overboard all the great writers and artists of the past: Pushkin and Dostoyevsky, Raphael and Michelangelo. But this public condemnation by Mayakovsky of a contemporary poet whose work he admired and read almost every day in private,[18] was symptomatic of the sickness affecting Soviet literary criticism which caused men and women of the highest ideals to mistrust their own intuitive judgement. Mayakovsky did not and could not realize that his love for Akhmatova's poetry was in itself proof that she had not buried herself in what he called 'the abyss of the irrelevant, distant, and alien'. Only many years later when critics noted her remarkable survival were they forced to admit that even her early love poetry reflected emotions common to much of humanity and was not merely a museum curiosity.*

Another symptom of the disease affecting Soviet criticism could be seen in an article of 1922 about the literary life of Petersburg by the visiting Moscow critic G. Gorbachev.[20] Gorbachev deplored the fact that, in contrast to the Futurist and Imagist poets of Moscow, who had their books printed as cheaply as possible, the Acmeists of Petersburg had theirs printed carefully and expensively on beautiful paper. To back up his view that *Anno Domini* contained 'nothing new either in subject matter or form except for hostile references to the present day', Gorbachev proceeded to quote the first line of Akhmatova's poem 'Everything is plundered, betrayed and sold', omitting to point out that the poem continues, 'The wing of black death has passed by; / Everything is swallowed up in hungry grief, / Why does it seem bright?' In Gorbachev's article the word 'new' already has a definite connection with 'revolutionary'.

* 'Tell me, please,' wrote a young boy to Korney Chukovsky in the 1960s, 'can I, a schoolboy, consider A. A. Akhmatova to be my favourite poetess? I have to defend her poetry so often that I am hoarse, if not almost in tears.'[19]

But in the early 1920s it was still possible for non-Marxist schools of literary criticism such as Formalism to exist and, as Marxist criticism had not yet hardened into dogma, for many differences of opinion to be found within that school. The extremely varied attitudes to literature prevailing at the time could still be freely expressed and argued about in literary journals and papers, and are reflected in the reviews of *Plantain* and *Anno Domini* and in other writing about Akhmatova published between 1921 and 1925. One group of critics was concerned with defining the function of literature in a revolutionary society, another interested in studying Akhmatova's poetry as a literary-linguistic phenomenon. A third group, closely linked with the second, consisted of those publishing abroad. From this point dates what might be called the émigré approach to Akhmatova, though much of what was written at first by people who had only just left Russia, differed very little from what was published there.

Although the critical views of Chukovsky, Mayakovsky, Lunacharsky, and Gorbachev were to have profound effect on Akhmatova's future as a writer, it was criticism by the other group, which included the 'subjective' critic Aykhenval'd, the Symbolist Bryusov, and Formalists such as Shklovsky, Eykhenbaum, and Vinogradov, that at first predominated. Eykhenbaum and Vinogradov both produced detailed critical studies of the poet's first five books, Eykhenbaum hoping thus to elucidate some of the problems of contemporary poetry, Vinogradov to discover the secrets of contemporary poetic language. One of the things Eykhenbaum noted was Akhmatova's use of the intonations of everyday speech in contrast to the musicality of Symbolism. He saw the severe, clerical-Biblical, Byzantine language of her later poems as a means of escaping from these limitations, and in this connection he made the famous and later much misused observation: '. . . Here already we can see the beginnings of the paradoxical, or more correctly, contradictory, double image of the heroine—half "harlot" burning with passion, half mendicant nun able to pray to God for forgiveness.'[21]

In complete contrast to the studies of the Formalists was the controversy raging round Akhmatova in the magazines *Young Guard, Red Earth*, and *On Guard*, occasioned by two well-known Bol'sheviks having declared their belief in the value of Akhmatova's work. In the Moscow newspaper *Pravda*, the official organ of the Party, N. Osinsky (Obolensky) had stated in 1922 that he felt that since the death of Aleksandr Blok, Akhmatova was the greatest living Russian poet.[22] By itself, this would probably not have caused much commotion in the Marxist camp, but in February 1923 an article by Aleksandra Kollontay took the matter a great deal further. Kollontay, a colourful figure close to Lenin, famous among other things for being the world's first woman ambassador, believed that socialism meant above all sexual freedom and fulfilment for women. In her article, 'About the "Dragon" and the "White Bird" ', published as part of her 'Letters to Young Workers' in *Young Guard*,* Kollontay explores the reason for Akhmatova's strong appeal to young working women despite the fact that the poet is not a Communist, and concludes that this is because Akhmatova expresses the suffering of a woman in the face of man's refusal to love her for her individuality and not only for what she shares with the rest of her sex. This, Kollontay says, is the beginning of woman's attempt to find her place in the new culture. Kollontay sees the 'white bird' of Akhmatova's 1914 poem (which her lover kills to stop it singing of former days) as all that is individual and important in a woman. The 'dragon' of a 1921 poem connected with Shileyko is that which in a man seeks to destroy it.[23]

Kollontay's article was attacked in the April–May edition of *Young Guard* by V. Arvatov, who considers that Akhmatova's poems are liable to 'develop neurotic emotions and attitudes of the submissive martyr in young working women' by making these seem aesthetically pleasing. He denounces her work as 'narrow, petty, boudoir, home-and-family poetry: love from the bedroom to the croquet lawn.'[24] P. Vinogradskaya, writing in *Red Earth* later that year, is even more savage: 'Akhmatova knows nothing about the woman who works and she does not compose songs about her. Akhmatova's women are capricious changeable beings, boudoir toys, who have come into this world only for the amusement of men.' Kollontay, Vinogradskaya feels, must be out of her mind to send young workers to Akhmatova for a solution to their problems:

Why, there is nothing in her except love, nothing about labour, about the collective. . . . Love for her only exists when interwoven with thoughts about God and with the thirst for the life of the other world. She cannot call our women to active participation in construction, but only to God, to dear little God with his angels. Except for God and love she cannot see anything further than the tip of her nose.[25]

In his book *Literature and Revolution*, published that same year, Leon Trotsky also mentions 'Akhmatova's God', describing Him as:

. . . a very comfortable and portable third person, with good drawing-room manners, a friend of the family from time to time fulfilling the role of a doctor specializing in women's ailments. How this personage, who is no longer in his first youth, burdened with personal, often quite troublesome errands from Akhmatova, Tsvetaeva, and others, still manages in his free time to deal with the fate of the Universe—is simply more than the mind can grasp.[26]

---

* With the article was printed a note to the effect that the editors of the magazine were not in agreement with all the ideas expressed.

Armed with quotations from Plekhanov, Trotsky, Arvatov, and the nineteenth-century critic Belinsky, G. Lelevich now sailed into the attack in the pages of the magazine *On Guard*. Taking as his starting point the fact that Osinsky had called Akhmatova Russia's greatest living contemporary poet, he proceeds to define the qualifications for this title and then demonstrates, not surprisingly, why no one in his right mind could possibly consider Akhmatova suitable. Effecting to see no distinction between the poet and her heroine, Lelevich decides on rather dubious evidence that Akhmatova has come from a 'nest of gentry' and that, lacking the courage to break out of her 'noble vault', she has 'escaped into mysticism'. The love she writes about, he says, 'is full of pain and suffering, not so much because it is not returned as because it is saturated with the wretchedness of nervous debility characteristic of a refined aristocrat of the *fin de siècle*.'

Lelevich was the first to use Eykhenbaum's scholarly and detached description of Akhmatova in a quite different and loaded way. She is, he says, 'not quite a harlot burning with passion, not quite a mendicant nun able to pray to God for forgiveness' because mysticism and eroticism are so closely intertwined in her poetry as to be no longer divisible. Defining what he feels to be Akhmatova's position in Russian literature, Lelevich concludes: 'Akhmatova's poetry is a small and beautiful fragment of aristocratic culture. . . . The circle of emotions open to the poetess is exceptionally limited. She has responded to the social upheavals, basically the most important phenomenon of our time, in a feeble and, at that, hostile manner. There is no broad sweep of vision or depth of understanding in Akhmatova's world.'[27]

Lelevich had made his point: there was no place for Akhmatova in a revolutionary Communist society. Having dismissed her as unworthy of serious attention in relation to contemporary Russian poetry, the Marxist critics moved on to other pastures. If Akhmatova was mentioned now it was in the context of pre-revolutionary poetry.

6

With Gumilyov, Blok, and Nedobrovo dead, Anrep in western Europe, with Lourié, Sudeykina, and many others emigrating, and critical opinion slowly but surely turning against her, the early twenties must have been for Akhmatova a particularly grim and lonely time. But perhaps her final attempt to deny her poetic gift in her brief but stormy marriage to Shileyko had in fact done much to temper her to withstand what was to follow. For we see her finding strength in this very aloneness. Her decision to remain in Russia despite her friends' pleas to her to leave had brought her to an important point. Somehow she was beginning to understand that she and her country, now undergoing so much suffering, were in some mysterious way bound together. Others could go but she could not. Her first decision not to leave, recorded as early as 1917 in 'When in suicidal grief', is repeated in 1921. The man who calls her to go is reprimanded for his affrontery ('We cannot meet', I.202). Her feelings about émigrés are clear:

> I'm not one of those who have left their land
> For enemies to tear apart.
> I don't heed their rough flattery
> And I will not give them my songs.

and yet, she continues:

> But I always feel pity for the exile
> As for the prisoner, or the man who is ill.
> Your road is dark, wanderer
> And bitter the taste of foreign bread.
>
> (I.215)

The strength of those who have remained behind lies in their acceptance of suffering:

> Here in the dense fumes of the fire
> Destroying what's left of youth
> We have not deflected
> One blow from ourselves.
>
> And we know in the final reckoning
> Each hour will be justified,
> But there is no people more tearless,
> Prouder or simpler than we.
>
> (I.215–16)

The 'I' has become 'we'. Only because this 'we' was not the one favoured by the Marxist critics the shift was largely ignored or taken to refer to a very small group of people. By choosing the titles 'To Many People' and 'To My Fellow-Citizens' for poems, Akhmatova emphasized that this was not so. But the former remained uncollected, and the latter poem, in which the poet says 'no one wanted to help us for staying behind' and not choosing 'winged freedom' (I.213), was cut out of almost all the copies of the second, fuller edition of *Anno Domini*, published in 1923, for political reasons.[28]

Those Russians who emigrated in the early twenties, and who did not know her personally, had an image of Akhmatova based largely on

Rosary, which was reprinted over and over again during those years, and especially on that second edition of *Anno Domini*, with Annenkov's drawing of her suffering face. Although it is possible on looking back at them to find in the poems of *Anno Domini* some reflection of what was going on in the outer world, to a person reading the book in Paris or Berlin in 1923, Akhmatova's decision to stay in the Soviet Union must have seemed more like a desire for martyrdom than a source of strength arising from a recognition that she had a part to play in Russia's chaos, suffering, and rebirth.

Anna Akhmatova, the tall, skinny poetess of the Wandering Dog, had begun to recognize herself as the instrument through which many of her fellow-countrymen were to be heard. But because her voice was both the voice of many and yet one which many would have stilled, she had to pay dearly for her position.

In the second edition of *Anno Domini*, she included a poem which must be one of the harshest and most pitiless ever written by the mother of a young child. At first one is tempted not to take it seriously, to see it as referring to someone else; after all, it is a woman talking to a man. But set in its context and in that of the poet's life it becomes far more than that:

> Do not torment the heart with earthly consolation;
> Do not cling to your wife or to your home;
> Take the bread out of your child's mouth
> And give it to a man you do not know.
> And be the humblest servant of the man
> Who was your desperate enemy
> And call the forest animal your brother
> And do not ask God for anything.
>
> (I.215)

III

1924-1941

Why there is nothing in her except love:
nothing about labour, about the collective.
P. VINOGRADSKAYA, 1923

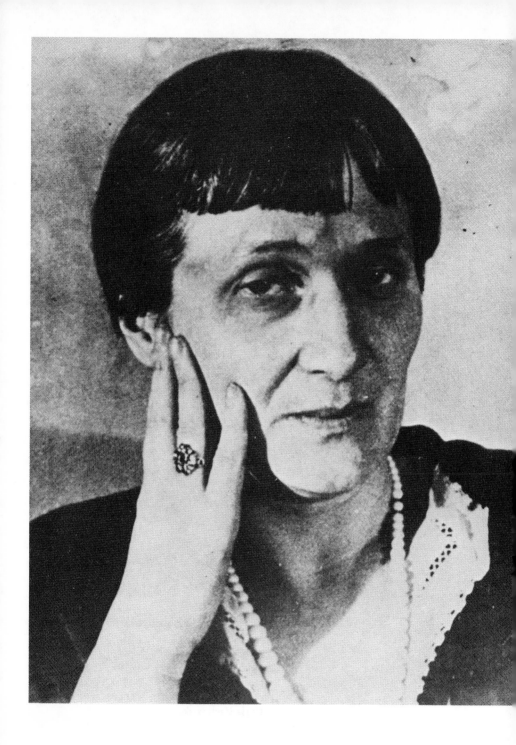

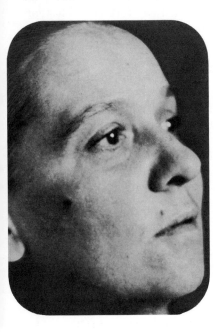

I

After *Anno Domini* the number of new poems published by Akhmatova dropped steeply. She was living in various places: with Sudeykina at Fontanka 18, at Kazanskaya 2, Fontanka 2, and then between 1924 and 1926 in Shileyko's flat in the house she called the 'Marble Palace' (*Mramornyy dvorets*) after he had left Petrograd to live in Moscow. Her previously published books continued, however, to be reprinted and, despite the articles in the Communist journals, her poetry remained extremely popular. In 1924 it was still possible for an evening to be devoted to her poetry in Moscow. In the opening address Leonid Grossman compared Akhmatova to Sappho,* and placed her first among Russia's women poets.[1]

But despite her stature and probably because of her popularity and the way she had been singled out by the critics, it was becoming increasingly difficult for her to publish. In 1925 a good selection of 32 of her poems appeared in the huge anthology *Russian Poetry of the Twentieth Century*, edited by I. Ezhov and E. Shamurin,[2] but these were probably the last to appear until 1940.† Later in 1925, according to Akhmatova, an unofficial Communist Party resolution banned any further publication of her work. Although the ban was never made public, for the next fifteen years none of her poetry was published in the Soviet Union.‡

Most of Akhmatova's close friends who had managed to survive the war, the revolution, and the years of hunger had emigrated. Cut off from her readers, deprived of the bohemian literary society that had once partly compensated for her 'homelessness', often ill, Akhmatova was forced once more back on to herself to find strength to continue to live in the country she loved and which she stubbornly refused to leave.

In the summer of 1924 Osip Mandel'shtam had introduced his young wife Nadezhda to Akhmatova in Leningrad.§ In the early spring of the following year the two women, both ill with tuberculosis,* stayed to-

* The Public Orator was to make the same comparison at Oxford in 1965.

† Svetlana Allilueva (*Dvadtsat' pisem k drugu*, London, 1967, p. 166) mentions being given this anthology in 1942 by A. Kapler; from it she learnt by heart poems of Akhmatova, Gumilyov, and Khodasevich.

‡ N. Mandel'shtam says that about this time the state, not knowing what to do with Akhmatova, provided her with an old-age pension which was about enough to keep her in cigarettes and matches (*Hope Against Hope*, London and New York, 1971, p. 124).

§ N. Mandel'shtam disagrees with Akhmatova about when they first met (*Hope Abandoned*, pp. 434–52).

* Akhmatova said later that the only reason she did not die as her sisters Rika and Iya had done from the terrible tuberculosis afflicting the Gorenko family, was because she also suffered from Basedow's disease, which holds T.B. in check.

gether in the same pension in Tsarskoe Selo. Akhmatova recalls this time in her memoir of Mandel'shtam: 'Both Nadya and I were extremely ill, lying in bed, taking our temperatures which remained high, and did not once go for a walk in the park which was right by us' (II.176).[3]

In Tsarskoe Akhmatova was visited almost every day by Nikolay Punin, the art critic and historian. Nadezhda Mandel'shtam found him clever but rough and unpleasant in manner. Now, however, he was extremely attentive. 'They are very nice when they are courting,' Akhmatova commented. But it was probably not until some time in 1926 that the poet left Shileyko's flat in the 'Marble Palace' and went to live with Punin in Fontannyy Dom. Because of the endless difficulties in obtaining or changing accommodation in those years, Akhmatova and Punin, Anna Arens, Punin's first wife, and Punin's baby daughter Ira all shared the same flat. Although Akhmatova and Punin had a separate room, the entire 'family' ate at the same table. During the day while Anna Arens was at work (she was a doctor), Akhmatova looked after the child. In the evening she and Punin often entertained guests. The atmosphere, as might be expected, was often extremely tense. In 1928 when asked by Mandel'shtam whether she was happy with this arrangement, Akhmatova answered that she was not. By 1929 things had become a little easier as Anna Arens began to accept the situation.

Unable to publish her poems, Akhmatova began to study in depth certain aspects of the life and works of Pushkin and to pursue her interest in the architecture of St. Petersburg. She assisted Punin in his work for the Academy of Arts, translating passages aloud to him from works in French, English, and Italian; she may also have helped write some of his lectures. In contrast to the period of her early fame, Akhmatova now found herself living in a milieu mainly interested in Futurism and modern art.

In 1928 Akhmatova and Shileyko were finally officially divorced. Punin, however, was never divorced from his first wife and although Akhmatova lived longer with him than with any other man, they were never legally married. By now the poet felt there was no need, as she put it, to register with the police the circumstances of one's private life; at this time in Russia marriage and divorce laws were in any case extremely flexible.

In the summer of 1927, still presumably recovering from her last bad bout of tuberculosis, Akhmatova had spent a month in a sanatorium where Stanislavsky recalls meeting her.[4] The following year her son, Lev Gumilyov, now sixteen, having been brought up in Bezhetsk by a grandmother who harboured little love for her daughter-in-law, came to live with his mother and Punin in Fontannyy Dom. Owing to the circumstances of his father's death, there had been difficulties in arranging for his further education. With the help of Punin's brother he obtained a place at the school where Aleksandr Punin was headmaster. From there he went on to study history at Leningrad University. It was also at this time that Akhmatova and Punin encouraged the young scholar and writer, Pavel Luknitsky, who was compiling a record of Gumilyov's life in connection with his poems.

On 25 August 1928, the seventh anniversary of Gumilyov's death, Mandel'shtam wrote to Akhmatova from Yalta, revealing that, despite all that had happened since to the three Acmeist friends of long ago, the bond between them had never been broken: 'I want to come home,' he wrote, 'I want to see you. You know I really can have an imaginary conversation with only two people: Nikolay Stepanovich [Gumilyov] and yourself. The conversation with Kolya has never ceased and never will . . .' (II.177–8). During the autumn of the following year, 1929, Akhmatova herself spent some time in the Crimea.

2

Although her name still turned up sporadically in Soviet criticism and memoirs after 1925, Akhmatova's literary career was usually dismissed as something over and done with. In 1929 in the *Literary Encyclopaedia* she was described as 'a poetess of the aristocracy who had not found a new function in capitalist society, but had already lost her old function in feudal society'. Her poetry is seen as a reflection of the culture of the nobility with their estates; her 'gloom', the result of belonging to a 'dying class'. The authors of the article quote Eykhenbaum's phrase 'half nun, half harlot', and rely heavily on him for the more technical part of their account. Despite everything they are forced to admit, however, that the poetess is very gifted.[5]

At the beginning of the thirties, according to Ivanov-Razumnik, the Writers' Publishing House in Leningrad received permission from the censor to publish a collection of Akhmatova's poems in two volumes. This was, however, to be edited and with a foreword and commentary by Dem'yan Bedny, a popular versifier beloved of the regime. Akhmatova, says Ivanov-Razumnik, 'categorically refused this honour, preferring to remain unpublished.'[6]

During this time of comparative domestic tranquillity there is little or no trace of Nikolay Punin in Akhmatova's poems. Instead she seems to be exploring more deeply the nature of poetic inspiration. In her isolation she looked for support to others who had known it, to Pushkin, to

Lermontov and Dante—poets who, like her, had suffered from their treatment by the state. Her poem 'The Muse', written in 1924, remains, despite all she wrote later, her most powerful description of what, for her, being a poet meant:

> When I await her coming in the night
> It seems as if my life hangs by a thread.
> For what do honour, youth or freedom mean
> When she comes visiting, her pipes in hand.
>
> And see—she's here. Throwing back her veil
> She looks attentively at me.
> I say: 'Did you dictate to Dante
> The pages of the "Inferno"?' She says, 'Yes.'
> (I.230)

Coming to terms with her fate is a painful process. A poem written in 1925 seems almost an ironic echo of 'The Muse':

> Oh had I known when, clothed in white,
> The Muse would visit my cramped abode,
> That my living hands would one day fall
> On to a lyre turned for ever to stone.
>
> Oh had I known when love's last storm
> Was rushing along playfully
> That, sobbing, I'd be the one to close
> The eagle eyes of the best of our youth.
>
> Oh had I known when wearied by fame
> I used to tempt magnificent fate
> That pitiless laughter soon would be
> The answer to my dying prayer.
> (II.138–9)

Not surprisingly, Akhmatova's study of Pushkin at this time was closely relevant to her own life. Thus in the essay 'Pushkin's Last Fairy Tale', published in 1933,[7] she explores Pushkin's difficulties with those in authority and the way he writes 'between the lines'.[8] She is also interested in his attempts to establish for himself some sort of normal social position as a historian and man of letters, and explores his censorship of his own work and his links with the culture of the west. In a later essay, 'Pushkin's "Stone Guest" ', she mentions Pushkin's tremendous early popularity which waned very suddenly when he refused to turn out replicas of his early works.

In the short 'A Word about Pushkin' Akhmatova makes her most pertinent comment on poets and those who try to curb their activity. The problem, she says, is not in the long run what 'they' did to Pushkin, but what Pushkin did to 'them':

> The whole epoch little by little (not, of course, completely smoothly) began to be called the time of Pushkin. All the society beauties, ladies in waiting, keepers of salons, cavalry officers' ladies, high-ranking members of the Court, ministers, generals and non-generals, began to be called Pushkin's contemporaries and then simply retired to rest in card indexes and lists of names (with garbled dates of birth and death) in studies of his work.
> He had conquered Time and Space.
> . . . In the rooms of palaces where they danced and gossiped about the poet, his portraits hang on the walls and his books are preserved, but their poor shades have been banished from there for ever. People say now about the splendid palaces and estates that belonged to them: Pushkin was here, or Pushkin was never here. All the rest is of no interest to them.   (II.275–6)

And Akhmatova 'quotes' Pushkin saying:

> You will not have to answer for me,
> You may still sleep quiet in your beds.
> Might is right, it's your children who
> Will curse you on my account.
> (II.276)

In the late twenties and early thirties Akhmatova must have felt specially close to Pushkin at the period when he was trying to find a way of living an ordinary life. As he had turned to the study of history, she approached his work as a scholar, and as he had been concerned at that time with his domestic life, so we find Akhmatova attempting once more to be a wife (to Punin) and a mother (to his daughter Ira and from 1928 to her son Lev). Happiness in her home life was, however, no longer something that Akhmatova attempted to buy with the dramatic sacrifice of her poetic gifts. Her life with Punin was more of an admission that even a poet had to come to terms with everyday existence, and was also perhaps a serious attempt to discover where the rewards of this sort of existence lay. Later, in 1940 when the experiment was over, Akhmatova spoke of this period, saying how crushed she had felt and how she had tried to move away from Fontannyy Dom as early as 1930. Yet at the end of her life she was proud she had made the attempt, even if it had ended in failure.

Akhmatova said repeatedly that she had never stopped writing poetry. Yet during these years of revaluation she wrote few poems. Once she told Lidiya Chukovskaya that she did not write poetry for thirteen years while with Punin in Fontannyy Dom. But when critics abroad later suggested that there had been a period of silence she was furious.* It is likely that she felt the battle against this 'shameful' silence (which her friend Nadezhda Mandel'shtam calls a 'crime against Man') was something no one outside Russia could comprehend, and that the weight and importance of a single poem written in the conditions of the thirties could in no way be compared to that of one written in easier days. Also any impression that her periods of writing coincided with the times when the state permitted her to publish implies an obedience on her part to the dictates of others, impossible because of the form her poetic inspiration took. Her only silence had been when for Shileyko's sake she had briefly tried to give up writing poems, and had failed. The period with Punin was quite different. Although she may not have produced much poetry, it was for her a period of retrenchment. Perhaps the house of Nikolay Punin was not the place for an experiment of the kind Akhmatova attempted. Punin's treatment of her and her position *vis-à-vis* his first wife were often humiliating. But although outwardly Akhmatova may not have seemed to rebel against it, she no longer, as she had with Shileyko, tried to win her happiness by complete surrender. Although she lives in her husband's house, she has 'hidden her heart' from him (I.234).

In three poems, probably written before she went to live with Punin, we see her exploring the world of famous women in history, as if here as well as in the lives of other poets might lie the secrets of her fate. The exploration was to continue in her later work with 'Cleopatra' in 1940 and 'The Last Rose', in which she links herself with Morozova,† Salome, Dido, and Joan of Arc. In the early twenties she drew her heroines from the Old Testament: Rachel, Lot's wife, and Michal, the daughter of Saul. In 'Rachel' Akhmatova emphasized how for Jacob the seven years' service for Rachel's hand seemed like seven days, but recalls how then Laban, her father, betrayed his trust and brought his eldest daughter, Leah, to Jacob's marriage bed. The poem leaves Rachel at the time when she should have been given to Jacob, crying alone in the night, cursing God and her sister and asking for death.

In the poem 'Lot's Wife' Akhmatova again seems to be refusing to

---

* Part of a long poem, 'Russian Trianon', written between 1925 and 1935, is mentioned in her list of 'lost works', and two 'lost' essays, 'The Fate of Acmeism' and 'The Last Tragedy of Annensky', probably date from these years. Other poems not 'lost' but remembered by friends and as yet unpublished may also date from this period.

† She recited this poem to Robert Frost in the summer of 1962. The seventeenth-century dissenter Morozova resisted the reformed ritual in the Orthodox Church introduced by the Patriarch Nikon; a famous picture of her being taken forcibly to Siberia was painted by the nineteenth-century artist Surikov. Akhmatova also talks of Morozova in connection with herself in the poem 'It seems no progress has been made'.[9]

accept God's judgement; Lot follows the messenger, but his wife's glance is drawn back:

> And the righteous man followed God's messenger,
> Huge and radiant, along the dark hill.
> But the voice of alarm spoke loud to his wife:
> 'It's not yet too late, you still can look back
>
> At the red towers of your native Sodom,
> At the square where you sang, the courtyard where you span,
> At the empty windows of the tall house
> Where you bore children to your dear husband.'
>
> She look back—and locked in the pain of death,
> Her eyes were no longer able to see
> And her body became transparent salt,
> Her quick feet rooted to the earth.
>
> Who will bewail this woman now?
> Does she not seem the least of the loss?
> Only my heart will never forget
> One who gave her life for a single glance.   (I.222)

But this may be not so much a refusal to accept God's world as a simple expression of the poet's compassion. Sympathy for Lot's wife was probably no more a justification of her action than Akhmatova's sympathy for the exile was a justification for emigration. But in this feeling for the woman who gives her life for a single glance back at her home, we see a change in Akhmatova's approach to the idea of home itself. Lot's wife does not look back at a place which has been a trap from which she has had to free herself or to some place where she has been a 'bad mother'. To know what it is to be homeless it is necessary to understand truly what the word 'home' means. In time, Akhmatova was to abandon her condemnation of all who had left Russia for the liberating understanding expressed in the 'Poem without a Hero', that the 'True Twentieth Century' had forced roles upon her and her contemporaries which they were obliged to play out to the end, but that they were all taking part in the same 'play'. In the *Poema* she writes of 1942:

> And the happy word 'home'
> Is known to no one now,
> Everyone looks through a foreign window.
> One in Tashkent, another in New York;
> And the bitter air of exile
> Is like poisoned wine.
>
>   (II.131)

It is as if her early homelessness had been too personal a thing to be linked with the homelessness of the émigré, who may not have been by nature a wanderer like herself. Her 'homes' had, after all, been a caricature of the word. It may have been partly because this word had gained new meaning for her, that she tried for so long to make a life with Nikolay Punin. Yet at the same time, the more clearly she understood what 'home' can really mean, the greater the pain of knowing that her fate was still to remain outside it. Akhmatova's emphasis in her essay on the 'Stone Guest' on Pushkin's fear of happiness may have been a reflection of that same fear in herself. 'Pushkin', she wrote, 'was frightened of happiness the way others are of pain. And just as he was always prepared for any kind of disappointment, so when faced with happiness he was terrified, that is, of course, at the prospect of the loss of happiness . . .' (II.267). Like Pushkin, Akhmatova had to learn to value what she could not have in order to understand the full weight of her loss.

In the third of the Biblical poems, 'Michal' (dated 1922–1961), Akhmatova depicts her heroine as torn between shame at being given as wife to a mere shepherd boy and physical desire for David. The women in these three poems, unlike the heroines of her early poems, occupy positions of profound historic and symbolic significance. They are women who will play a powerful role in the formation of a race, but who are forced to do this despite themselves.* Their suffering is due to lack of faith in the ultimate purposefulness of life, lack of trust in God. Their battle is with their desire which is in fact drawing them, although they do not realize it, to fulfil God's purpose. Michal's passion for David will leave her childless, yet she is to save his life and be the means by which he becomes son-in-law to the king. Rachel has to wait fourteen years for Jacob, but children are born to Leah and Jacob important for the future of Israel, and Rachel's reward is to be the mother of Joseph, who will bring them all through the seven-year famine. Akhmatova's heroines, blinded and torn by desire and by feelings of abandonment, thus become part of a larger whole.

They are also linked firmly to what had seemed at one time to be the poet's essentially private emotional experience. The Orthodox pilgrim woman used in the early poems as a means of setting personal experience against the larger structure of traditional village Christianity had had by her very nature to remain separate from the woman of passion ready to give up everything to be with her lover, the 'Akhmatova' of the Wandering

* Many years later, during the war, Punin was to write to Akhmatova about her own life: 'I thought then that this life was perfect not through will, but—and this seemed to me to be particularly precious—through its organic wholeness, that is, its inevitability, which seems somehow not to have anything to do with you. . . .' (See his letter quoted in full at p. 128.)

Dog. The split between the nun and the harlot, between Lena and her pagan sister, could never be resolved by the Christian pilgrim. But now Akhmatova can show that the Old Testament woman torn by sexual desire is not outside God's love and purpose (even though she may feel this to be the case) and that, despite herself, her desire is actually helping to fulfil that purpose. Even those who feel themselves damned are shown to be at that moment close to God.

The poet's choice of these women as heroines was not purely arbitrary. Akhmatova was not describing Rachel, Lot's wife, and Michal from outside, but looking through their eyes. In them she had found at least the suggestion of a way of looking at life which might begin to explain the riddle of her own existence. If she could use a heroine who drew together the disconnected facets of her own character, it could only be because she had herself undergone, or was undergoing, such a change.

3

When, in 1930, Akhmatova had made an abortive attempt to leave Punin, a friend had promised to find her a room elsewhere. But Punin had frightened him off, claiming that her staying was a matter of life and death to him. After this she continued to live with him at Fontannyy Dom, without the strength to leave except for short periods as when, on two occasions in the summer of 1931, she spent a month in the country looking after someone who was ill: first her friend Valentina Shchegoleva, then her young step-daughter Ira Punina.

In the autumn of 1933 the Mandel'shtams finally succeeded in getting somewhere to live in Moscow, and she went to visit them. Emma Grigorevna Gershteyn met Akhmatova then for the first time. She recalls her surprise at discovering how extremely close Akhmatova was to the Mandel'shtams, who had never mentioned her particularly. Mandel'shtam and Akhmatova were at that time reading Dante's *Divina Commedia* together in Italian. To her delight, another proof of their close spiritual ties, they discovered that they had begun to read Dante at the same time, each without being aware that the other had done so. Gershteyn also remembers the interest with which the 'Pushkinists' (Bondi and Vinokur in Moscow, Tomashevsky in Leningrad) regarded the work Akhmatova was doing on the poet and how they helped her with it.

At this time Akhmatova's extreme poverty was so apparent from her clothes that it was remarked upon when she visited Moscow. The artist Osmyorkin commented that it had a certain elegance of its own. She had one old cap and a light coat which she wore no matter what the weather.

When Valentina Shchegoleva died, she bequeathed her old fur coat to Akhmatova, and this the poet wore steadily up till the war. Very thin, with her hair in the famous fringe, however poorly dressed she managed to look striking, wearing scarlet indoor pyjamas at a time when it was still unusual for women to wear trousers. The group of friends whom she saw whenever she came to Moscow included Georgy Chulkov and his wife Nadya, Sergey Shervinsky, Sofiya Andreevna Tolstoy (the granddaughter of Lev Tolstoy and at one time wife of the poet Esenin), Nikolay Khardzhiev, the Mandel'shtams, and Viktor Ardov and his wife, the beautiful actress Nina Ol'shevskaya.

Nikolay Khardzhiev, who also came to know Akhmatova during the early thirties, recalls the first time he went to visit her in Fontannyy Dom. She was living in a room on the third floor with a beautiful blanket of old serf work on the divan. He noticed the drawing of her by Modigliani on the wall and put a piece of paper over a corner where the glass was broken so that it would not be damaged. Khardzhiev was struck by the poet's wit, intelligence, and sense of humour. He found her in some ways, however, like her poems which he disliked, being at the time only interested in the Futurists. Akhmatova told him it was pleasant to meet someone for a change who was not enamoured of her poems. Later, in Moscow, Khardzhiev met Akhmatova at the Mandel'shtams and noticed between the two poets what he called 'a kind of special inner connection —magnetism'.

One day in February 1934 as they walked together in Moscow, Mandel'shtam said to Akhmatova: 'I am ready for death.' Recalling this in 1962, she wrote: 'For twenty-eight years now I have remembered that moment whenever I pass by the place' (II.179). On 13 May 1934 Mandel'shtam was arrested. Akhmatova had arrived the day before from Leningrad, bringing with her a statuette of herself by the sculptor Dan'ko which she meant to sell along with other things in order to be able to pay for her return ticket.

The order for the arrest was signed by Yagoda* himself. The search went on all night. They were looking for poems, going through manuscripts thrown out of a small trunk. We all sat in one room. It was very quiet. On the other side of the wall, at Kirsanov's, a Hawaiian guitar was playing. They found 'Wolf'† as I watched, and showed it to Osip Emil'evich. He nodded silently. When he said goodbye, he kissed me. They took him away at 7 a.m. It was completely light. Nadya went to her brother's and to the Chulkovs' on Smolensky Boulevard—we agreed to meet somewhere or other. Coming back home

---

* Genrykh Yagoda, deputy chief of the political police.
† A poem in which Mandel'shtam says he can only be destroyed by his equals and not by the wolves who surround him. It is printed in *Soch.* II.406.

together we tidied up the flat, sat down to breakfast. Again a knock on the door, again the same people, once more a search. Evgeniy Yakovlevich Khazin* said, 'If they come once more they'll take you with them.'   (II.181–2)

Pasternak, whom Akhmatova visited that day, went to see if he could contact Nikolay Bukharin, editor of *Izvestiya*, at the offices of the newspaper. Akhmatova herself went to the Kremlin to see the old Georgian Bol'shevik, Enukidze, a member of the Central Committee. To get into the Kremlin in those days was a miracle and was only made possible by the kind help of the actor Ruslanov, who knew Enukidze's secretary. Akhmatova reckoned that their efforts 'softened' the sentence.

Two weeks later Nadezhda Mandel'shtam received a telephone call early in the morning telling her to go to the Lyubyanka prison where she would be allowed to see her husband. She was asked whether she would travel with him to the town of Cherdyn', where he was to be exiled.[10] She answered that of course she would, and returned home to pack. Nina Ol'shevskaya and Akhmatova meanwhile made the rounds of the Mandel'shtams' friends and acquaintances collecting money for them. People were generous. Elena Sergeevna Bulgakova, the wife of the playwright Mikhail Bulgakov, gave them the entire contents of her purse. Then Akhmatova went with Nadezhda Mandel'shtam to the Lyubyanka to collect the necessary documents. They waited and waited for Mandel'shtam to be brought out; finally Akhmatova, with Khazin and Mandel'shtam's brother Aleksandr, left without having seen him, to catch her train for Leningrad. Later she regretted very much that she had not waited, for she learnt that as a result of her absence Mandel'shtam, whose mental balance had suffered as a result of his experiences in the Lyubyanka, became convinced that she was dead. On his way to Siberia the soldiers guarding the persecuted poet were, ironically, reading Pushkin.

Preparations were going on at this time for the first Writers' Congress. Akhmatova, sent a form to complete, found she could not do so: 'Osip's arrest made such an impression on me that I could not lift my hand to complete the questionnaire. At the Congress Bukharin declared Pasternak to be our best poet (to the horror of Dem'yan Bedny), was rude about me, and most likely did not even mention Osip' (II.184).

On 1 December 1934, Sergey Kirov, a member of the Politburo and Party boss in Leningrad, was murdered by a young Communist, L. Nikolaev, giving Stalin the opportunity for which he had been waiting. On the same day as the assassination a decree was issued depriving those accused of 'terrorist' acts of any right of defence. Thousands were

* N. Mandel'shtam's brother.

arrested, among them Akhmatova's young son Lev Gumilyov. He was released almost immediately, but the shock to his mother, following Mandel'shtam's arrest earlier that year, must have been considerable.

Faced with the intensifying reign of terror set in motion by Kirov's death, Akhmatova found that her relationship with Punin, instead of being a support, could best be described as shared loneliness:

> I drink to my ruined home,
> To my vicious life,
> To loneliness spent together
> And I drink to you—
> To the lie of lips that betrayed me
> To the deathly cold of your eyes,
> To the fact that the world is rough and cruel,
> To the fact that God did not save me.
>
> (I.240–1)

It was not a way of life that encouraged the writing of poetry, nor was it a happy marriage. Punin went out of his way to make Akhmatova aware of his flirtations with other women, emphasizing how boring he found it to spend time in her company. Yet at the same time he wanted her to stay with him. Later Akhmatova described her life with him as set in an autumnal landscape, and herself as still haunted by the house in Tsarskoe Selo where she had sensed the impending tragedy of Gumilyov's arrest and execution. Looking back over this period, she realized that it had once more been a case of losing confidence in herself, and perceived again the extreme nature of the 'testing' that was her life:

> So there it is—that autumn landscape
> Which all my life I so have feared:
> The sky like a flaming chasm,
> The noises of the town heard
> As from another world, forever strange.
> It is as if all I have struggled with
> Inside myself during my life's received
> A separate life embodied here in these
> Blind walls and this black garden . . .
> And at that moment close behind me still
> The house I used to live in followed me
> Its window unforgettable—an eye
> Squinting and malevolent.
> Fifteen years—why they'd become more like
> Fifteen centuries of granite,
> But I was also like granite myself:
> Now beg, torment yourself, call me

> A princess of the sea, it does not matter . . .
> It mattered though that I assure myself
> That everything had happened many times
> Not just to me, to others also
> And had been even worse,
> No, not worse, better.
>
> (I.310)

In 1935, however, when Lev Gumilyov and Punin were both arrested, Akhmatova described the morning when they came to take her husband away* in a poem revealing her deep attachment to him. It was to become the first poem in the cycle 'Requiem'.

> They led you away at daybreak;
> As though following a bier, I walked,
> In the dark chamber children were weeping,
> Before the Virgin the candle guttered.
> On your lips the cold touch of an icon,
> On your brow, sweat of death . . . Not to forget!—
> Like the wives of the murdered Streltsy,
> I'll wail near the Kremlin towers.
>
> (I.363)

Two weeks later both Punin and Lev Gumilyov were released.

The time of the Terror had begun a little earlier for Akhmatova than for most people. In the early part of 1934 when Mandel'shtam was first arrested, reasons for such arrests—the so-called 'crimes against the state' —were still being given; but reasons became less and less necessary as time wore on. By 1935, when her son and her husband were arrested, Akhmatova was already accustomed to that odd and usually hopeless game in which relatives and close friends of those imprisoned struggled to contact persons in high places in the hope that somehow those persons 'did not know what was really happening' or could 'do something'.

The next few years were when so-called friends in their fear for themselves and their own families turned away from one another, but also a time when friendships were formed never to be broken. In February 1936 Akhmatova went for a visit to Voronezh where Mandel'shtam had been allowed to go to live out his exile. That summer she and Pasternak managed to collect enough money to send to the Mandel'shtams that they were able to spend a short time in the country. Osip Mandel'shtam's health had been almost completely undermined by the suffering of the past two years. Akhmatova referred later to that summer of 1936, which

---

* Punin's daughter Ira recalls that morning well. She and her cousin were the children weeping.

she herself spent mainly with her friends the Shervinskys near Kolomna, as the 'last peaceful summer'.[11]

In 1936 the second of Akhmatova's Pushkin studies, on the poet and Benjamin Constant, was published,[12] and also a translation of an Armenian poem.[13] And after a period when she wrote comparatively little, at least that we know of, no less than eight poems date from that year. In one of them she considers the wasteland of her life with Punin and the general atmosphere of fear surrounding everyone:

> I have hidden my heart so well from you
> I could have tossed it into the river Neva . . .
> My wings are cut and I've been tamed—
> That's the way I live in your house.
> Only . . . at night I hear things creak.
> What's there in the alien half-light?
> Is it the Sheremetev limes . . .
> The house-elves sending messages . . .
> Like the gurgling of water
> Pressing hotly to the ear
> The black whisper of disaster
> Is approaching carefully,
> Mumbling as though its business were
> To dawdle here all night:
> 'You wanted warmth and comfort, well,
> Where do you think you'll find them now?'
> (I.234)*

4

It was an aspect of Akhmatova's fate that after she had in the poem 'To Many People' accepted her role as 'the voice of many' and in this found a justification for her existence, she should have been officially silenced, prevented from reaching her audience by means of the printed word. But when the Terror overwhelmed the country and people floundered in confusion, fear, and grief, Akhmatova was not unprepared; she found herself one of the few who could formulate clearly what had to be done: life had to be lived.

That Akhmatova was prepared for the Terror was not merely a matter of prophetic understanding. While others were literally in a state of shock she was, strange though it may seem, on familiar ground. When they struggled with feelings of horror at what was happening and with questions of love of country and loyalty to it, they did what Akhmatova

---

* Akhmatova refers in a similar way to her relationship with Punin in 'The Break', where she talks of how they 'protected' each other.

had been doing since 1917, if not since 1914. When they grieved over close relatives imprisoned and killed by an administration which twenty years earlier had promised them a beautiful future, they were living through what Akhmatova had experienced in 1921 with the death of Gumilyov. As those who had been brought up in a sincere belief in the rightness of communism saw the world crumbling around them, they turned for strength to one to whom this had already happened and who had learnt to survive.

Even when it came to a question of the loss of her child, Akhmatova was prepared. For her relationship with her son had been and remained one of progressive loss. What she was to describe in 'Requiem' was a continuation of what had begun when she had left her son as a child with her mother-in-law, in the years when she had written, 'The lot of a mother is bright torture, I was not worthy of it' (I.135) and sung to him as she rocked his cradle, 'I am a bad mother'. It was to continue years later when they parted finally, not because of outward circumstances so much as because of their characters as mother and son.*

In 1940 when Lidiya Chukovskaya was upset to hear that Akhmatova was not to get a flat she had been promised, which would have enabled her at last to move out of Punin's flat and the difficult conditions under which she was living there, Akhmatova answered: 'That is what my life, my biography, is like. Who can refuse to live his own life?' By 1934 Akhmatova had come, little by little, to accept her own 'biography'. As Mandel'shtam said to her that year, 'I am ready for death,' she might have said, 'I am ready for life.' This does not mean that her life thereafter was to be easy. On the contrary, her strength lay in her ability to face up to what was before her and to master it, the opposite to the gesture of covering her face with her hands to which Gizetti had drawn attention years before, at the beginning of the First World War. It involved an honesty and respect for the word which was fast disappearing in the literary world around her, and her fight was the more remarkable at a time when the truthful representation of fact was most often considered to be a crime against the all-powerful state, punishable by concentration camp and death. For love of a man, for a normal home, Akhmatova had tried more than once to sacrifice her 'ring', her poetry. She had also offered it up as a sacrifice to help her country. Now in her complete acceptance of her vocation she found a rock on which to build.

Early in the thirties we hear Akhmatova's voice, in a poem still not published in the Soviet Union:

---

* See p. 175. In a sense their reunion took place only after the physical death of the mother, a fact observable since then in the changed behaviour of Lev Gumilyov towards everything concerning Akhmatova.

Wild honey smells of space,
Dust—of a sunbeam,
A young girl's lips of violets
And gold—of nothing.

Mignonette smells of water
And love of apples,
But we have learnt once and for all
That only blood smells of blood.

*

Thus it was in vain that the governor from Rome
Washed his hands openly before all
While the mob yelled ominously,
In vain that the Scottish queen
Washed the crimson splashes
From her narrow palms
In the stuffy gloom of the king's house.

(II.137–8)

She was not afraid of calling evil by its name and had learnt by then that
to do this was of the utmost importance.

Prepared though she was, Akhmatova like many others found it
almost impossible to believe in the Terror. She had accepted her role
but was like Pasternak's Hamlet, watching from the edge of the stage,
praying: 'I love your stubborn purpose, I consent to play my part. But
now a different drama is being acted; for this once let me be.'[14] Like him
Akhmatova lingered, hoping that something would happen to make
things different:

The autumnal air is filled with the fifth act of the play,
Each flower bed in the park seems a fresh grave.
The pure funeral feast has been celebrated
And there is nothing left for us to do.
Why then do I linger waiting for a miracle?
It's thus a feeble hand can stay a heavy boat
For long by the pier as one says goodbye
To the person who's left standing on the shore.

(I.281–2)

If she had hoped to retreat from the disasters of her life into a happy
private life with Punin, this had failed completely. But even if, like Lot's
wife, she had had a real home, she would finally have been forced from
it into the outer world to play her part in the 'True Twentieth Century'.
In the thirties there was, in the end, no refuge. Everyone was frightened
of the moment when the knock would be not on a neighbour's door but
on his own. And with the desperation of trapped animals people sold

their honesty hoping to buy safety, only to have to pay later for the denunciations forced from them. Visiting Mandel'shtam in Voronezh in 1936, Akhmatova saw the price to be paid in this century for being a true poet and remaining one despite everything:

> And in the room of the disgraced poet
> Fear and the Muse take turns on watch.
> And the night goes on
> Which does not know of dawn.
>
> (I.236)

The year before, almost as an echo of Mandel'shtam's remark years before that his imaginary conversation with Gumilyov had never stopped and never would, Akhmatova, like the witch her first husband had described, had written a poem to him, conjuring him up to visit her.

> From behind tall gates,
> From the Okhta marshes,
> By an untrodden path,
> Through an unmown field,
> Through the night cordon,
> To the Easter bells,
> Uninvited,
> Unpromised,
> Come and dine with me.
>
> (I.232)

From the company of Dante and Pushkin Akhmatova now turned to those poets who were her own friends and contemporaries: Mandel'shtam, Gumilyov, Pasternak, Mayakovsky, Tsvetaeva. They too belong to this special company. Of Pasternak she wrote:

> For filling the world with a new ringing sound
> Of verses reverberating in new space
>
> He's endowed with a kind of eternal childhood
> With the brightness and generosity of the stars,
> And he has inherited all the earth
> And then shared it with everyone.
>
> (I.235)

Of Mayakovsky:

> Everything you touched no longer
> Seemed the same as before
> What you were destroying came to destruction
> In every word your verdict sounded.
>
> (I.241)

In October 1937 Mandel'shtam managed to get to Leningrad for a few days and saw Akhmatova. They met for the last time briefly the following spring on another of his furtive trips to the old capital. That May he was re-arrested in a convalescent home. It is believed that his death took place in a camp on 27 December 1938.* Meanwhile on 10 March of the same year Lev Gumilyov had been re-arrested, and this time it was not just a matter of days or weeks before he was released. For seventeen months he was kept in prison in Leningrad. He was sentenced to death, but then those who sentenced him were purged (they were shot) and his sentence was commuted to exile. He left Leningrad on 17 or 18 August 1939.

It is from this period of the height of the Terror, when every single day there was news of the arrest or death of someone they knew, that Akhmatova's friendship with Lidiya Chukovskaya dates. Chukovskaya first went to see Akhmatova in 1938 because her husband had been arrested. She had been told that a letter from Akhmatova to Stalin had resulted in the speedy release of her son when he had been arrested on an earlier occasion, and wanted to know what she had said. Akhmatova recited the letter to her. But nothing could save Chukovskaya's husband, whose 'crime' consisted of having the same surname as Trotsky (Bronshteyn); later she learnt that his sentence: 'Ten years without right of correspondence', had simply meant execution by a firing squad.

From this time on until shortly before the war Chukovskaya saw Akhmatova frequently. Her sensitive understanding and her deep respect for poetry and the poet's calling made her a welcome guest.† The first time Chukovskaya visited her, Akhmatova was still living with Punin. The second time, early in November 1938, the poet came out of an adjoining room and said she had moved. Later Akhmatova told Chukovskaya how she had managed finally to make the break. In front of Punin she had said to Anna Arens simply, 'Let's change rooms.' They began to move their things. Punin was quiet and then, when for a moment he and Akhmatova were left alone together, he said, 'You might just have spent one more short year with me.'‡

* This was the date Mandel'shtam's brother was given officially in June 1940. For the various reports and rumours about this, see the chapter 'The Date of Death', in N. Mandelstam, *Hope Against Hope*.

† These qualities in Lidiya Chukovskaya are reflected in the character of the narrator in her novel, *Going Under* (London, 1972). Chukovskaya recorded in detail her meetings with Akhmatova from 1938 to the end of her life, in diaries that were originally written in code. Those from 1952 to 1956 have now been published in *Pamyati A. Akhmatovoy*.

‡ Punin later married one of his students at the Academy, Marta Andreevna Golubeva. They probably met in 1935 or 1936. Golubeva (who never lived in Fontannyy Dom) died in 1963.

Next door to the poet lived a young woman named Smirnov with two little boys. During the day when the mother went out to work, Akhmatova looked after the children. Their mother boasted that she had a 'nanny of world fame'. Shortly after she had gone out in the morning the elder of the two boys would come knocking on Akhmatova's door saying, 'Val'ya is wet already.' One of the boys had perfect pitch and when Akhmatova sang to them he would cry out in protest. Chukovskaya noticed how tenderly the poet greeted these little boys. With a child in her arms Akhmatova looked to her like a statue of the Madonna, 'not so much from her expression as from the way she held herself with a sort of modest and mournful grandeur.'

In the poet's room hung her portrait by Osmyorkin, 'White Night'. Outside in the courtyard of Fontannyy Dom was the maple tree mentioned in her poems. Chukovskaya and Akhmatova spoke together about those who had died. Together they read Innokentiy Annensky and Akhmatova reiterated how much this poet had meant and continued to mean to her. She felt that in a sense all the poets of her generation, Mandel'shtam, Pasternak, herself, and even Mayakovsky, had 'come out of' Annensky. 'He contained us all,' she would say. She and Chukovskaya also read together poems by Pushkin and the Futurist poet Khlebnikov. Chukovskaya failed to appreciate the latter and Akhmatova finally gave up trying to convert her, deciding it was a hopeless task.

Akhmatova was terribly poor and living mainly on a diet of black bread and sugarless tea.* She was extremely thin and frequently ill. She would get up from bed to go and stand, sometimes in freezing weather, in the long lines of people waiting outside the prisons, hoping against hope to be able to see her son or at least pass over a parcel. When she was ill, friends would sometimes stand in the queue for her. The poems of 'Requiem', composed at this time, were learnt by heart by Lidiya Chukovskaya, Nadezhda Mandel'shtam, and several other friends who did not know who else was preserving them. Sometimes Akhmatova showed them a poem on a piece of paper which she burnt as soon as she was sure it had been committed to memory, sometimes she just recited them. Chukovskaya remembers going out late at night into the empty streets repeating a poem to herself over and over again, terrified she would forget a word or get something wrong. Once she said to Akhmatova that she visualized 'Requiem' printed with the poems numbered with roman numerals. When the cycle was finally typed out years later, in 1956, Akhmatova said to her: 'See, as you said, roman numerals.'

* Akhmatova, unable to publish her poems, had no means of earning a living. Her translation of Rubens's letters, which appeared in 1937, had earned her the first money she had had in years.

In a time when a poem on a scrap of paper could mean a death sentence, to continue to write, to commit one's work to faithful friends who were prepared to learn poems by heart and thus preserve them, was only possible if one was convinced of the absolute importance and necessity of poetry. Once a life-saving necessity for Akhmatova herself, her work now became so for those around her: at first for close friends, then for a wider and more impersonal circle, until it no longer seemed to have anything to do with her as a private individual or even as a poet in the usual sense of the word.* She was the formulator, the poet who by means of her tool, the word, could bring order out of chaos and in so doing fulfil the highest human function: 'And Adam gave names to all cattle, and to the fowl of the air, and to every beast of the field' (Genesis 2:20).

As the poet stood in the line outside the prison in Leningrad a woman who probably never read poetry 'identified' her:

A woman with blue lips standing behind me, who had of course never heard my name, suddenly woke out of the benumbed condition in which we all found ourselves at that time and whispered in my ear (in those days we all spoke in a whisper):
—Can you put this into words?
And I said:
—I can.   (I.361)

5

In 'Requiem' Akhmatova no longer needed to use a heroine as a means of linking her own life with that of other women. It was enough to formulate her own private suffering. This voice coming out of the silence was sufficient, for little by little what was happening to the country was stripping off false values, until even the blindest person was forced to realize that 'only blood smells of blood'.

But for Akhmatova to give form to this suffering she had to live through it, and because it was that of a mother it inevitably led to an understanding of the archetype Mary. The poems of 'Requiem' trace the stations of her suffering to the foot of the Cross. Lev Gumilyov's arrest for little reason other than having had herself and Gumilyov as parents could again be laid to her failure as a mother. But most awe-inspiring in 'Requiem' is Akhmatova's understanding of the

---

* A lifetime admirer of Akhmatova's work, writing to her in 1965, described what her state of 'non-existence' as a poet had meant for a student of literature during the late thirties: '1938—my first year in the faculty of literature at the Herzen Institute . . . The name of Akhmatova is forbidden and only pronounced in a whisper, but all the same it is known to a particular group of students. Even single poems, written out by hand, are passed from one to another. They are striking for the power of their content and their amazing, chased form. . . . We hear nothing about Akhmatova from the professors.'

inevitability, almost necessity, that all this had to happen: that at the Crucifixion 'A choir of angels glorified that hour' (I.368). While Mary Magdalene sobbed, 'No one dared to cast a glance to where the Mother, silent, stood alone.'

Mary the Mother is set in opposition to Mary Magdalene who has lost Christ and will only find Him again when He appears to her after His resurrection. The Mother's suffering is a reflection of that of Christ, who endures the Crucifixion to fulfil what He has been sent to do and whose suffering is not lessened but, if anything, heightened by understanding this necessity. He has no comforting illusions to place between Himself and the feeling of having been forsaken by God. And Mary, His mother, must watch Him, knowing that one cannot help anyone else, however great one's love, and that His suffering is necessary if God's purpose is to be fulfilled.

In this poem Akhmatova uses religious language to a very different purpose than years before at the time of the First World War. There is none of that feeling of suffocation that overcame her when she felt that to believe in the after life implied that it was wrong to grieve over death. Nor has this Mary, bright in her transfigured suffering, much in common with the one we met earlier. There is nothing gentle or comforting about this Mary. She is the other half of Christ: the woman who bore Him and who understands that the Crucifixion is the greatest moment in history. And as with the women of the Old Testament, Akhmatova is not observing Mary from outside. She is looking at the world through her eyes.

'Requiem' is not just a series of short poems strung together, but an organic unit documenting a precise progression through all the stages of suffering to this point and clearly set by the poet in the larger context of her life and work. The four-line poem with which it opens, written in 1961, is in a sense a triumphant vindication of a conviction Akhmatova had first formulated in 1917, that it was right and necessary for her to stay in Russia and die with her country if need be. Put at the beginning of 'Requiem' it has the quality of something coming from the other side of death:

> No, not beneath a foreign sky,
> Not sheltered by a foreign wing—
> I was where my people were,
> Where, alas, they had to be.
>
> (I.361)

It is in what she calls 'Instead of a Foreword' that Akhmatova tells of her answer 'I can' to the woman standing next to her in the queue outside the prison. In the 'Dedication' she consecrates her solitary suffering

to those other women like her who had been isolated and overwhelmed
by their grief:

> Mountains bow before this sorrow,
> The great river cannot flow,
> But strong are the gates of prisons,
> And beyond them the 'prisoners' burrows'
> And hopeless deathly longing.
> For someone the breeze blows fresh,
> For someone the sky softens at dusk—
> We are unaware, for those like us
> Harken but to the key's vile crunch
> And to the soldiers' heavy step.
> We rose as if to attend the early service,
> Walked through the hostile city streets,
> Met, more breathless than the dead themselves—
> The sun was lower, the Neva more misty,
> But far off somewhere hope still sang.
> Sentenced—and her tears stream forth,
> Cut off at once from all around,
> As though life were wrenched from her heart,
> As if they'd rudely flung her down,
> Yet she walks on . . . swaying . . . alone . . .
> Where are now those women fated to be my friends
> During those two savage frenzied years?
> What is it they see in a Siberian blizzard?
> What is it they sense in the haze of the moon?
> To them I say farewell.
>
> (I.362)

It was a time when only the dead could smile:

> Only the dead used to smile then—
> To be at peace were glad.
> Among its prisons
> Swung useless, Leningrad.
> Then, senseless from torture,
> Troops of condemned were marching,
> And the engines' whistles sang
> The brief song of parting.
> Stars of death stood above us;
> Under the wheels of a Black Maria,
> Under the heel of blood-stained boots,
> Writhed innocent Russia.
>
> (I.362–3)

The women to whom 'Requiem' was dedicated were drawn together
by the fact that in their suffering they were completely alone. In the ten

poems forming the main body of the cycle Akhmatova is no longer speaking *about* those others like herself who made up a multitude, but *for* them. She does this by speaking of that single woman, herself. Passing through that suffering she is at one with all other women forced to do the same.

In the first of the ten poems this woman is the wife who refuses to forget the moment when her husband was taken away and who will go and howl like the wives of the murdered Streltsy by the towers of the Kremlin. In the second she is much more passive.

> Quietly flows the quiet Don,
> Yellow moon slides through the door.
>
> With cap askew the yellow moon
> Sees a shadow in the room.
>
> It's a woman on her own,
> Sick woman, woman alone.
>
> Son in prison, husband dead,
> Let your prayer for me be said.
>
> (I.363)

In the third poem Akhmatova expresses the incredibility of such great suffering. It cannot be real, be hers, it must belong to someone else.

> No, not I, someone else is suffering.
> I had not strength to suffer thus,
> As for what happened, let black cloth cover,
> And take away the light. . . .
> Night.
>
> (I.364)

She stands outside, watching the suffering woman who is herself and, as once years before she had covered her face with her hands, unable to look at war, now she prays for 'black cloth' to block out the image of what has happened. The feeling of unreality continues in the next poem:

> Young mocking-bird, full of fun and mischief,
> Favourite of your friends at Tsarskoe Selo,
> Could you have foreseen what would happen to your life—
> How three-hundredth in the queue with your parcel
> You would stand beneath the prison gates
> And with your burning tears
> Cut through the New Year ice?
> There the prison poplar sways.
> No sound. How many blameless lives are ending there. . . .
>
> (I.364)

From here we move on to another stage. Now the mother no longer tries to pretend that she understands anything. Nor is pride seen in this context as having any validity. The ordinary props of exterior values have disappeared:

> Seventeen months I've cried out,
> Calling you home.
> I've flung myself at the hangman's feet,
> My terror, my son.
> All has grown confused for ever,
> I cannot now discern
> Who is man and who is beast,
> Whether I must wait for death.
> There are only dusty flowers
> And the ring of the censer,
> Only tracks from unknown places
> Leading nowhere.
> Straight into my eye is staring
> A great star;
> Its gaze is threatening
> Sudden death.
>
> (I.364–5)

In the next poem, the sixth, she has reached a state of numbness:

> Lightly the weeks fly past.
> What happened? I can't understand.
> The white nights looked in on you then,
> My child, as you sat in prison,
> The way they look in now again,
> Flame-eyed as a hawk,
> Telling of your great cross . . .
> Talking of death.
>
> (I.365)

The reference here to the suffering óf her son as a 'cross' could perhaps be taken as the first sign of a way out of this hell through which she is being asked to go. But it is only an evocation of the memory of the Crucifixion. The poet still does not claim to understand what has happened.

In the seventh poem, however, she regains her strength:

> THE SENTENCE
> And the stone word fell then
> On to my still living breast.
> Never mind—I was ready,
> Somehow I'll stand the test.

Today I am very busy;
I must see that memory's quite dead,
And that my soul has turned to granite,
Learn once more to live ahead,

But that's not it. . . . As for some celebration
Outside my window summer rustles warm.
Long ago, somehow, I foresaw all this,
The bright clear day, the empty room.

(I.365)

Akhmatova's steely 'Never mind—I was ready' shows that she has learnt the technique of how to live on. But her strength to do this may well come from another source—the feeling of the fulfillment of prophecy. In the New Testament when Christ is seized He says: 'Thinkest thou that I cannot now pray to my Father and He shall presently give me more than twelve legions of angels? But how then shall the scriptures be fulfilled that thus it must be?' (Matthew 26:53–4). But as Christ with His understanding that the scriptures must be fulfilled had still to pass through a period in which He felt Himself forsaken, so the path of the Mother to the foot of the Cross is made no easier because she once, long ago, foresaw it.

In the eighth poem, 'To Death', and the ninth, 'Already madness with its wing', she must pass through two more stages of suffering: the prayer for death—that the 'cup will pass'—which is not granted, and, finally, madness. To death she has opened her door:

You're coming anyway—so why don't you come now?
I'm waiting for you—I can't bear much more.
I have turned out the light and opened wide the door
To welcome you, miraculous yet simple.
Take whatever form you choose to visit me—
Break in, as a poisoned bullet,
Creep up with a cudgel, as a hardened bandit,
Infect me with deadly typhus.
Or make use of your little fairy tale
That has become so loathesomely familiar—
That looking past the blue policeman's cap
I see the white scared face of the caretaker.
I don't care any more. The Yenisey swirls on,
And the North Star is shining.
The blue gleam of the eyes I love
Will veil the final horror.

(I.366)

In madness she learns the final aloneness. There is no longer any question of killing memory. It must simply be left behind. Years ago, in 1914–16, Akhmatova had written of a moment of happiness which she wanted to take with her through life to ease her difficult path. Now she is not even allowed to take with her the memory of her son's suffering:

> Already madness with its wing
> Has covered half my soul,
> Gives me a fiery wine to drink
> And draws me towards the dark;
>
> I have understood that I
> Must cede the victory to him,
> Listening to my rambling voice
> As though some other person raved.
>
> He will not let me take away
> Anything at all of mine
> (However often I may ask,
> Pester him with my request)—
>
> Not the frozen suffering
> Staring out from my son's eyes,
> Nor the day that brought the storm,
> Nor the hour of prison meeting.
>
> Nor the soft cool touch of hands,
> Nor the lindens' trembling shadows,
> Nor the gentle distant murmur—
> The last words of consolation.
>   (I.367)

In 'Crucifixion', the tenth poem, we find in the three figures at the foot of the Cross not only Mary the Mother who has passed through all suffering to a point of understanding so great that we ordinary people cannot look at her, but also John and Mary Magdalene. They incarnate suffering at two points described in earlier poems in the cycle: Magdalene, the suffering of rebellion, of the Streltsy wife; John, the silent frozen suffering of one who is trying to kill memory, to continue living in blank emptiness when what gave life meaning has been taken away. In 'The Sentence' it was the soul which had to become stone; here John is as of stone:

> I
>
> A choir of angels glorified that hour,
> The heavens were melted into fire.

'O Father, why hast Thou forsaken me?'
To His Mother He said: 'Do not cry . . .'

II

Magdalene wailed and lamented,
The beloved disciple stood as though in stone,
But no one dared to cast a glance
To where the Mother, silent, stood alone.

(I.368)

In the two poems of the 'Epilogue' Akhmatova turns from the depiction of the woman alone in sorrow who becomes universal by becoming one with Mary the Mother of Christ, to describe again the many Marys to whom she has dedicated these poems. The first poem is about what fear and suffering do to people:

I learnt how faces fall apart,
How fear looks out from people's eyes,
How grief carves deep into the cheeks
Harsh characters of suffering,
How hair is silver-coloured now
That was ash-blond or black before,
How smiles fade on humble lips
And in dry laughter terror lurks.
I pray not only for myself
But for all those who stood with me
In savage cold and July heat
There, beneath that blind red wall.

(I.368–9)

This is now the other side of the coin. The understanding of the Cross produces, not a passive acceptance of horror, but rather the ability to look at it with both eyes open, full in the face. Here is no prayer for it all to be covered over with black cloth or, as long ago, with the Virgin's cloak. Nor is there any question of not understanding what has happened. The poet understands only too well. She can face up to it because she has taken suffering to its limit and so there is nothing to fear. Whereas Pushkin still prayed, 'Lord, don't let me lose my mind', Akhmatova no longer fears even madness. She has passed through it, surrendered herself to it, to learn, miraculously, that all the props to which she desperately clung for strength were not strength at all and that when they were gone and nothing more could be taken from her, she was stronger than she had ever realized was possible.

In the second poem of the 'Epilogue' her voice is stern:

The hour of remembrance draws near.
Once more I hear, I feel, I see you here:

You, whom to the window they barely led,
You, who this earth no longer tread,

And you, who shaking your beautiful head
Came here as though home, you said.

I would like to name each one in turn,
But they've taken the list; there's nowhere to learn.

From the poor words you used, which I overheard,
I have woven for you a burial shroud.

I shall remember them everywhere, always,
I shall not forget them come fresh evil days,

And if they shut my tortured mouth,
Through which a hundred million shout,

Then may you too remember me
On the eve of my remembrance day.

If they think some day in this country
To raise a monument to me,

To this solemn gesture I consent,
But with the condition that it be put

Not by the sea where I was born
(My last bond with the sea is torn)

Nor in the park by the hallowed tree
Where an inconsolable shade seeks me,

But here where three hundred hours and more
I stood and no one unlocked the door.

Because even in blessed death I'm afraid
I'll forget the noise Black Marias made

And the ugly way the door slammed shut
And the old woman's howl like a beast that was hurt.

And from my motionless bronze lids
May the thawing snow stream down like tears

And the prison dove coo from afar
And the boats go quietly down the Neva.

                                                    (I.369–70)

Here remembering is not a consolation, something to cling to when all
is lost, nor its opposite, the memory that must be killed so that one can
go on living. It is the cry of fury from the woman whose husband is taken
away at dawn: 'Not to forget!' Akhmatova consents to a monument only
if it is to be an everlasting reminder of the horror, of the old woman's
cry 'like a beast that was hurt'. And in a sense 'Requiem' is itself this
monument. It is not raised to herself, the poet, but to the women who
stood in the queues outside the prisons. If the suffering she and her
contemporaries had been forced to live through were to be forgotten or
glossed over that suffering might be repeated. Only by creating something more lasting than the short memory of man with his tendency to
forget pain quickly, can Akhmatova carry out her vow not only not to
forget but also: *not to allow to be forgotten.*

'Requiem' is a map of a journey leading through hell into the light
and it is as accurate as any chart. The poet's position as map-maker, as
formulator, is seen to be all-important, his responsibility to the word
absolute.* Only by speaking the truth can his words bring healing. Mis-
use of the word, the lie, the half-truth, the omission, are crimes against
all those whose lives have been their only formulation and who rely on
the artist with his peculiar gift of cutting across the barriers of time to
reflect this in truth, so that what has been learnt can be passed on to
later generations. Not to do this, to be silent, becomes a crime against
humanity.†

                                     6

Early in 1940 Akhmatova spent a few days in Moscow, hoping that she
might be able to do something to get her son released. While she was
there, staying with the Ardovs, Pasternak telephoned to say that Marina

---

* In this connection one can understand Akhmatova's extreme distress at the publication of Robert Lowell's 'imitations' of 'Requiem' (*Atlantic Monthly*, October 1964)
because at the time no translations of these poems had been made into English.·
  † This is the main theme of Chukovskaya's book *Going Under*, which she prefaces
with a quotation from Tolstoy, 'The integrity of a man is evident from his attitude to
the word.'

Tsvetaeva was in Moscow and would very much like to meet her. Tsvetaeva had dedicated poems to Akhmatova years before, and the two poets had corresponded, but had never met. As women poets of the same generation, they had often been compared and contrasted. Tsvetaeva had left Russia in 1922 and lived abroad as an émigré. Continually poverty-stricken, unappreciated as a poet by those in control of the émigré press in Paris, Tsvetaeva had found herself completely isolated when her husband fled back to Russia after having been exposed as a double agent. Deserted by her daughter who had already returned to the Soviet Union and under pressure from her teenage son to do the same, she arrived back in the summer of 1939 to discover that her husband had been shot. Her daughter had also been arrested and was at this time in a labour camp.

Pasternak spoke on the telephone to Nina Ol'shevskaya, who told him she would ask Akhmatova to call back and arrange a meeting. When she did, the conversation was brief. Akhmatova said she understood that Tsvetaeva wanted to see her. The latter answered that she did ('*Da, khochu*'). When Akhmatova asked if she could come to her, Tsvetaeva said it would be better the other way round. Viktor Ardov recalls letting Tsvetaeva in. He did not have to introduce his guests. They met without the usual politenesses, simply pressing each other's hands. The two poets went into the tiny room where Akhmatova usually stayed when visiting the Ardovs and remained there alone together the best part of the day. Akhmatova never spoke of what they discussed. She said only that Tsvetaeva had turned out to be a perfectly normal person, deeply concerned about her family's fate.

The following day Tsvetaeva telephoned again, 'Paris style', at 7 a.m. Akhmatova was asleep. She telephoned her later. Tsvetaeva wanted them to meet once more. Akhmatova suggested that they do so at her friend Nikolay Khardzhiev's. When Tsvetaeva asked how to get there, Akhmatova asked her how she intended to come: by taxi, metro, bus. . . . 'Only by tram.' Luckily this was possible. They sat at Khardzhiev's talking and drinking wine.

Khardzhiev well remembers the meeting. Tsvetaeva was sparkling. She was full of Paris and talked brilliantly. Akhmatova told him later that she felt herself to be dull and cow-like in contrast. But Khardzhiev, on the contrary, seeing her with the quicksilver Tsvetaeva, was struck by what he describes as Akhmatova's complete and utter genuineness.

They had planned to go that evening to the theatre. Ol'shevskaya was playing in *A Midsummer Night's Dream*. Tsvetaeva insisted that they should not change their plans. They all left Khardzhiev's house together. As they walked along the street, someone stepped out of the shadow and began to follow them. Akhmatova wondered, 'Her or me?' In 1921 in a letter to Akhmatova, Tsvetaeva had written:

> Oh, how I love you, how I rejoice in your existence, how I suffer for you, how elated I am because of you! If there were magazines, what an article I would write about you!—Magazines—an article—I must be joking! A heavenly fire! . . .
> . . . It's such a pity that all this is just words—this love—I can't bear it—I would like it to be a real bonfire on which I was burnt. . . .[15]

Akhmatova had carried everywhere with her in her handbag the manuscript of the cycle of poems dedicated to her by Tsvetaeva in 1916, until it had finally disintegrated. She herself had written a poem to Tsvetaeva a few months before they finally met, in which she imagined the two of them walking at night through the wintry streets of Moscow, and likened Marina Tsvetaeva's return to Russia to that of the historical Marina, the wife of the False Dmitri. She did not, however, manage to recite the poem at either of their meetings—perhaps because she found it less easy than Tsvetaeva to communicate her feelings openly. Akhmatova's regard for the other poet remained high, but the two were not to meet again. On 31 August 1941 Tsvetaeva hanged herself in the little town of Elabuga, in the Tatar Autonomous Soviet Socialist Republic, to which she had been evacuated shortly before.

In B. Mikhaylovsky's *Russian Literature of the Twentieth Century*, published in 1939, Akhmatova had been described as having 'fenced herself off' from the revolution and its consequences. The same old criticisms were levelled at her poetry:

> Akhmatova's lyrics are in fact limited to the poetic treatment of intimate day-to-day life, incidental and trifling experiences. Just about Akhmatova's only theme is that of rather similar amatory experiences, the same old story sung over and over again. Moreover, this theme remains within the confines of narrowly personal circumstances and moods—it does not widen out (as in Blok), does not link up with philosophical and social problems.[16]

Then, quite unexpectedly, in the grim days of 1940 the ban against the publication of Akhmatova's poems was lifted. Permission was given for a collection of poems to be printed and her work began once more to appear in magazines. *From Six Books*, a selection of poems from her previous books, with some new poems in a section called 'Willow', appeared in the early summer of 1940. Boris Pasternak wrote to her at the time:

I have long been writing this letter to you in my head, long been congratulating you over this great triumph which people have been talking about for over a month.

I have not got a copy of your book, I borrowed it from Fedin* to read and couldn't mark in exclammation marks, but I've made separate notes and I'll mark them in my copy when I get the book.

When it came out I was in hospital (with inflammation of the spinal nerve) and I missed the sensation accompanying its appearance. But stories reached me even there about queues of people trying to get it trailing over two streets and incredible stories about its circulation. A few days ago Andrey Platonov was here and was telling me that the fights over the book continue although it has already sold out and that the price for a second-hand copy has reached 150 roubles.

It is not surprising to find that you have only to appear and already you have won again. What is so striking is, that in a period of obtuse controversy about everything on earth, your victory should be so complete and irrefutable.

Your name is once more AKHMATOVA in the same way it was when that name stood for the best part of the Petersburg you described. It has its previous power to recall the time when I would not have dared believe that I would ever know you, or have the honour and good fortune to write you a letter. This summer it stands for all it stood for then and, as well, for something new and extremely great, which I have observed lately but have never before connected with the former.

The significance of your new work is so authentic and powerful in 'Willow', that it seems to be an extension or a new aspect of your earlier work. One could speak of the appearance of a new artist unexpectedly arising in you next to your former self, one is struck by the preponderance of absolute realism over the impressionistic element which is oriented towards sensibility and the complete liberation of the thought from the influence of the rhythm.

The ability of your early books to evoke the time when they first appeared has become even stronger. Once more one is convinced that except for Blok, no one has had such power of eloquence about the particular, like the early Pushkin you are altogether unique. No doubt, I, Severyanin,† and Mayakovsky are far more indebted to you than is usually thought and this debt is deeper than any admission by us because it is unconscious. How all this impressed itself upon the imagination, repeated and called forth a reaction! What examples of inventive depiction and instantaneous accuracy! . . .[17]

Pasternak went on in the letter to illustrate his points in detail, quoting page numbers, finally apologizing for getting carried away. His letter also brought greetings from friends and the news that the wife of the

---

* The novelist Konstantin Fedin.
† Igor Severyanin, the poet who founded the Ego-Futurist movement; he was extremely popular in the period just before the revolution.

writer Boris Pilnyak had been released. He asked hopefully if Akhmatova's son, Lev Nikolaevich, were home yet and thanked her deeply for her two 'undeserved gifts' to him, a poem dedicated to him and the use of an epigraph from his work at the beginning of 'Willow'. He also mentioned that the tone of an article by Pertsov about her book had 'shocked them all' and that some people (including the novelist Aleksey Tolstoy) felt that a 'real writer' should publish something about her in a journal and not in a newspaper.

The article by Pertsov in the *Literary Gazette* could, however, have been worse. Pertsov points out that Akhmatova had not ceased to write during her so-called years of silence and the new poems in *From Six Books* show that she is writing certainly as well as if not better than before. He finds that certain poems ('Slander', 'Lot's Wife', 'Dante', 'Cleopatra', etc.) show a 'desire to leave the enclosure of subjective experience for objective themes'. Leafing through her earlier poems reprinted in this book, he considers that the contemporary reader feels a 'lack of air': 'Akhmatova's heroine and us—we are too different one from the other. It is impossible not to point this out, despite her past and present high standard of poetic craftsmanship.'[18]

But Akhmatova's return to print was short-lived. A few months after the appearance of her book, its publication was declared to have been an error and it was withdrawn from sale and from libraries. According to Akhmatova, it had taken a while for it to fall into Stalin's hands and this was the result. Her distress at becoming once more the target for abuse at a time, not only of intense personal suffering, but also when the whole culture of western Europe seemed threatened by Hitler's initial success in the war, is reflected in another moving letter she received in November 1940 from Pasternak:

Dear, dear Anna Andreevna,
    Can I do anything to cheer you up even if only a tiny bit and to interest you in further existence in this darkness that has once more come over us, whose shadow I feel with a shudder every day over myself? How can I do enough to remind you that to live and to want to live (not according to someone else's rules, but in your own way) is your duty to the living,* because one's conceptions about life are easily shattered and are rarely supported by anyone else and you yourself are their chief creator.
    Dear friend and unattainable example, I would like to say everything that I

---

* The same idea can be found in one of Pasternak's poems:
                And yet you must defend
                Each inch of your position,
                To be alive, only
                Alive, only alive to the end.[19]

should have said to you on that grey August day when we saw each other last and when I was reminded again quite simply how dear you are to me. And meanwhile I was missing chances to be with you, going off for days on end to Moscow trying to meet a special train not in the timetable coming from the Crimea with Zina and her sick son,* whom it was necessary to get into hospital, when even the *day* of its arrival was not known. In parenthesis, to satisfy natural curiosity, everything was all right and the boy after a month there recovered.

I don't read newspapers as you know. And now lately when I ask what's new in the world I learn of one happy thing and one sad: the British are holding out; Akhmatova is being abused. Oh, if only between these two bits of news, both equally close to my heart, could exist some sort of reciprocity and the sweetness of the one could weaken the bitterness of the other!

I've told you, Anna Andreevna, that my father and my sisters with their families are living in Oxford and you can imagine my state of mind when I waited more than a month for an answer to a telegram. I had buried them in my mind in the way the imagination suggests that a bomber would do and then suddenly learnt that they are alive and well . . .

In the same way Nina T.† went to Tibilisi in the forlorn hope of discovering something somehow about her husband and had even suggested to me that it wasn't certain that he was alive, and she has now written to me that he is being held in Moscow and that this is certain.

Forgive me for callously listing examples from my day-to-day life like a small boy, in order to illustrate how one should never give up hope, as a true Christian you must know all this, but do you realize the value of *your hope* and the necessity of protecting it? . . .

Akhmatova was deeply concerned, as was Pasternak, about the news of the bombing of England. The 'death' of Paris had seemed to her like the death of an epoch. Her thoughts turned to those friends of her youth who had emigrated: Ol'ga Sudeykina,‡ Salomea Halpern.§ As the news of the blitz reached Russia, she wrote a poem dedicated to the people of London:

> Time's passionless hand is writing
> Shakespeare's twenty-fourth play
> And we who take part in this grisly feast
> Would be better off reading *Hamlet* or *Lear*

---

* Zinaida Nikolaevna Pasternak, the poet's wife, and one of the sons of her first marriage to the musician Genrykh Neygauz.

† The wife of the poet Titsian Tabidze. Tabidze was tortured in prison and never returned.

‡ 'In the first part of 'Poem without a Hero', which Akhmatova read to Lidiya Chukovskaya in 1940, were the lines about Sudeykina beginning, 'You came to Russia out of nowhere . . .' (II.114, line 299).

§ A poem of 1940, 'Shadow', is dedicated to Salomea Halpern.

Or *Caesar*, there by the leaden river;
Better off going with torches and singing
To take sweet Juliet to her grave,
Better off peeping in on Macbeth,
Shuddering with the hired assassin—
Only not this, not this, not this,
This we have not the strength to read.

(I.258–9)*

The autumn and winter of 1940 were probably the blackest days of Akhmatova's life. As well as being attacked again as a writer, she had received bad news about her son's situation and knew that her present unpopularity with the authorities could only make things worse for him. The culture of Europe of which she felt so much a part seemed to be disappearing for ever. Her health, always precarious, was failing badly. Earlier that year she had·been terrified she would go mad. Her close friend from childhood, Valeriya Sreznevskaya, was at that time very close to madness and Akhmatova was convinced that the same fate awaited her. In May she had recited to Chukovskaya the poem from 'Requiem' beginning, 'Already madness with its wing / Has covered half my soul' (I.367). Early in October she had a heart attack. At the end of November when Chukovskaya came one day to visit her, Akhmatova greeted her with the news, 'Valeriya has gone completely mad. I've been looking after her for three days.'

7

But if 1940, the year of the last three poems of 'Requiem', was the year of the Crucifixion, it is also the year of the resurrection. In Akhmatova a change had taken place, reflected not only in 'Requiem' but also elsewhere. Perhaps it was the final farewell to the hope of a saving miracle, the dream of childhood. In the 'Epilogue' to 'Requiem' she noted that her last connection with the sea had been broken. In another poem written that year, she mourns the willow which as a child who understood the wind better than human speech she had loved most of all. To her amazement she finds that she has outlived it.

This surprise that she should be the one to survive is echoed in a poem written in memory of her close friend Mikhail Bulgakov:

Oh who would have dared believe that I,
The half-crazed mourner of lost days,
I, who smoulder on a slow fire,

* Akhmatova read this poem on the B.B.C. when she visited London in 1965.

Having lost everything, forgotten everyone,
Should be the one now to recall
A man whom it seems but yesterday
Spoke with me full of strength and will and bright plans
Concealing the tremor of the pain that precedes death.

(II.142)

Certainly at times she must have felt as if she herself were already dead. To her friend Lozinsky she gave a book inscribed: 'from almost a shadow from the other shore of Lethe at the hour when worlds are falling in ruins . . .' (I.229). From this strange state almost beyond the grave Akhmatova was able to look at her former self and her friends from the past in a new way. And, like Mary, she knew that what seemed like loss was illusion. No longer did she feel as in 1914 that 'to cry is a sin' (I.135):

The souls of those I love are on high stars.
How good it is that there's no one to lose
And one can weep. The air of Tsarskoe
Was made to echo songs.

By the bank the silver willow
Touches bright September waters
And rising silent from the past,
My shade comes out to meet me.

So many lyres are hanging on the branches
But there is also, it seems, room for mine
And this sparse shower full of sunlight
Brings good tidings and consolation.

(I.281)*

No longer rebelling like Magdalene against the suffering which was a part of her fate, or turning herself to stone-like John, she was able on looking back to begin to see in the frightful chaos of the past an order and meaning. From the complete impersonality of Mary at the foot of the Cross, whose triumph is outside the ordinary confines of time and space, Akhmatova returned to the details of her own particular fate set firmly in this century. And, perhaps not unnaturally, to do this she chose as her heroine (if at this stage we can still use that term) someone who in fact comes from outside time and space, from the heavenly city, Kitezh,

* Falsely dated 1944. This poem was read out to a friend before the war.

and whose life on earth is seen as a journey back to that 'place' from which she has come.

'The Way of all Earth', one of Akhmatova's few long poems, she referred to as the most *avant-garde* work she had written. Much shorter than the 'Poem without a Hero' and certainly much less complex, it is however so condensed in style that it seems longer than it actually is. In 'Requiem' Akhmatova expressed the fate of the suffering mother. In 'Poem without a Hero' she was to explore that of the poet of the 'True Twentieth Century'. In this poem, set between the two, she deals with her own fate as a poet and as a person and with the reasons for her existence. The answer here is not so much the 'I can' spoken to the woman outside the prison, as that acceptance of whatever life may bring of 'Already madness with its wing'. As then she had learnt that even when she had given up everything, all was not lost, so now she knows that she has come from somewhere else to this world of misery and trouble and that one day she will return 'home'.

Kitezh, according to legend, was a city saved by prayer from the advance of the Tatars. Some say it was lifted up to the heavens and its reflection seen on a lake into which the enemy rushed to their death, others that like other legendary cities it sunk deep into the lake where its towers can be seen on days when the water is specially clear. Akhmatova's 'Kitezhanka', the woman of Kitezh, is seen hurrying home through the bullets, across the trenches, through the wars filling half the twentieth century.

In a way the poem recalls one by the sixteen-year-old Lermontov, 'Angel', in which the child's soul is carried on its way to be born into this 'world of grief and tears' by a singing angel. To the child who recalls this sound the 'boring songs of the earth' can never bring satisfaction. So here the woman of Kitezh is called home by a sound of a different quality than those of this life:

> But I do not listen to the groan
> Of the hoarse hurdy-gurdy.
> It is not that sound
> The woman of Kitezh hears.
>
> (I.243)

This poem is not, however, about escape from life, but one which expresses faith in the most profound sense of the word. Strength here stems from the recognition that the poet has come from God and will one day return to Him, and that she must make her way through time to the place where there will be none.

> Right in the path of bullets,
> Thrusting aside the years,
> Through the Januarys and Julys
> I shall make my way there. . . .
> No one will see my wound,
> No one will hear my cry,
> I, the woman of Kitezh,
> Have been called home.
>
> (I.242)

The second epigraph to the poem is from Revelations: 'And the Angel swore to the living that there will be no Time. . . .' The poet looking back from 1940 no longer sees the single instances of suffering, but her 'time': the age into which she was born, with the Boer War, the Russo-Japanese War and Tsushima, and the Great War of 1914, the revolution, the civil war, and the present war in western Europe menacing her own country. She is frightened and alone, needs to 'press someone's hand . . .' (I.243). The Muse to whom she swears an oath laughs at her, prophesying. And not only must she pass through the trenches of the many wars but through her own crucified capital where 'familiar buildings look out from death' (I.245).

Here Akhmatova is close to the concept of the 'True Twentieth Century' formulated in the 'Poem without a Hero', also begun in this year. That those who heard the *Poema* found it different from all she had written before is not surprising.* It was born in the year of 'Crucifixion' and 'The Way of all Earth'. For twenty years and more it was to be worked on and changed, its subject matter enriched through the experience of war and exile and the meetings and persecutions of 1946. But the breadth and depth of vision, the ability to look down upon her century 'as from a tower' that made the 'Poem without a Hero' possible, came from 1940. Its power is that of someone who has gone out alone to face all that is most frightening and terrible, the greatest, most profound suffering, madness, and longing for death. She has come from Kitezh and she will return, but this, as she says in a short poem also dating from 1940, is to be her last life on this earth:

> But I warn you
> That I am living for the last time.
> Not as a swallow or a maple tree,
> Nor as a reed or as a star,

---

* Chukovskaya, who heard the first part of what became 'Poem without a Hero' in Fontannyy Dom in 1940, was so struck by it, never having heard anything quite like it before, that she asked who had written it. Akhmatova replied rather crossly that of course she had.

Not as water from the spring,
Nor even as the sound of bells
Shall I come to confuse,
Or bother other people's dreams
With my insatiable groan.

(I.260)

IV

1941-1956

That is what my life, my biography, is
like. Who can refuse to live his own life?

On 22 June 1941 Hitler's armies marched into the Soviet Union. This war, however terrible, was to be for many people a welcome escape from the unbearable isolation of the years before. The Terror had split the country in pieces: individual feared individual, yet few dared to admit fear lest it seem an admission of guilt. But now the enemy was no longer within but without. People were united once again in a common aim.

For Akhmatova it was a relief to be able to be obviously and openly at one with her fellow-countrymen once more. On 25 August Pavel Luknitsky went to visit the poet. He recorded in his diary: 'She was lying down, ill. She greeted me very hospitably, her mood is good. She said with evident pleasure that she had been asked to talk on the radio. She is a patriot and the knowledge that at the same moment she and everyone else are thinking and feeling alike cheers her.'[1]

It was in September during the worst artillery attacks and bombing that Akhmatova spoke on the radio to the women of Leningrad:

My dear fellow citizens, mothers, wives, and sisters of Leningrad. It is more than a month since the enemy began trying to take our city and has been wounding it heavily. The city of Peter, the city of Lenin, the city of Pushkin, Dostoyevsky, and Blok, this great city of culture and labour, is threatened by the enemy with shame and death. My heart, like those of all the women of Leningrad, sinks at the mere thought that our city, my city, could be destroyed. My whole life has been connected with Leningrad: in Leningrad I became a poet and Leningrad inspired and coloured my poetry. I, like all of you at this moment, live only in the unshakeable belief that Leningrad will never fall to the fascists. This belief is strengthened when I see the women of Leningrad simply and courageously defending the city and keeping up their normal way of life. . . .

Our descendants will honour every mother who lived at the time of the war, but their gaze will be caught and held fast particularly by the image of the Leningrad woman standing during an air-raid on the roof of a house, with a boat-hook and fire tongs in her hands, protecting the city from fire; the Leningrad girl volunteer [*druzhnitsa*] giving aid to the wounded among the still smoking ruins of a building. . . . No, a city which has bred women like these cannot be conquered. We, the women of Leningrad, are living through difficult days, but we know that the whole of our country, all its people, are behind us. We feel their alarm for our sakes, their love and help. We thank them and we promise them that we will be ever stoic and brave.[2]

Akhmatova herself could be seen in these days standing outside the great gates of Fontannyy Dom, a gas mask over her shoulder, on duty during air-raids. Later in the month she moved temporarily to an old house on the Griboedov canal, in which two floors were being used as accommodation for writers. The Committee of the Communist Party of the City of Leningrad had ordered that she be evacuated. Ironically it was felt that she was important enough to be one of those specially preserved. Luknitsky mentions going to say good-bye to her the day before she left, finding her '. . . in her fur coat, wearing a scarf, weak, ill . . .'[3] At the end of September she left her bombed and besieged city by plane for Moscow:

> You could all have gazed on me
> As in the belly of a flying fish
> I fled the evil pursuit
> And over the wood filled with enemy
> Was carried like her who, possessed by the devil,
> Flew over the Brocken at night.
>
> (II.131–2)

Even now Akhmatova could see herself as a witch.

On 15 October Lidiya Chukovskaya, then in Chistopol', received a telegram from her father, Korney Chukovsky, saying that Pasternak, the novelist Fedin, and Akhmatova were being evacuated from Moscow.[4] Chistopol' was a miserable small town to which various writers had come because there was a boarding school in the vicinity to which their children could be evacuated. Chukovskaya had realized very quickly that if she did not move on elsewhere, she would soon starve, having no means of earning money there. Ploughing through mud, which in some places came up to the waist, she had remarked to Marina Tsvetaeva: 'Thank God at least Akhmatova isn't here. She wouldn't survive this.' Tsvetaeva had answered, 'And do you think I can?' She had come to Chistopol' from Elabuga, where she was living with her son, on a visit to the poet Nikolay Aseev. She returned 'in a state of acute mental depression and utter hopelessness.'[5] It was only a few days before her death.

Then suddenly without further warning Akhmatova appeared at Chukovskaya's door. She had travelled by train from Moscow to Kazan and by boat to Chistopol'. The young poetess Margarita Aliger had shared a cabin with her on the boat and they had talked through most of the night.* Chukovskaya asked Akhmatova about the blockade, about the Germans.

'Germans, what Germans, Lidiya Korneevna? No one is thinking about Germans. The city is starving, already they are eating dogs and cats. There will be the plague and the city will perish. No one is concerned about the Germans.'

---

* Aliger never forgot this encounter and referred to it movingly at an evening devoted to the memory of Akhmatova at Moscow University shortly after her death.

Chukovskaya decided that their best chance was to try to get to Tashkent, where her father had already gone. They went back to Kazan, where they spent the night on the floor of the Press House sardined among other people on the move like themselves. From Kazan they travelled by train to Tashkent, by a roundabout route which took them via Siberia, the journey lasting three weeks. With them travelled the poet and translator Marshak. The train passed through scenes of terrible devastation. Akhmatova spent her time looking out of the window. She told Chukovskaya she was happy to have the chance to see so much of Russia. Chukovskaya's main concern was that all of them should arrive alive; she had little energy for anything else. She was impressed, though, by Akhmatova's ability to rise above the physical trials of the journey.

Finally arriving in Tashkent, they spent the first few days in a hotel. Then Chukovskaya went to stay with her father and Akhmatova was given a small room at the top of what had been a hotel of sorts and was at the time called the 'Hostel for Moscow Writers', at no. 7, Karl Marx Street. The room had only one window under the eaves and the building had an iron roof. During the day it was stifling, at night airless. This was meant to be temporary accommodation, but in fact Akhmatova lived in this room (except for a period of convalescence at Dyurmen' outside Tashkent) from November 1941 until May 1943. Nadezhda Mandel'shtam was also staying at the same place.[6]

Chukovskaya and Akhmatova met almost every day. Their thoughts remained centred on the war-torn city they loved. From this period dates what was to become one of the most famous poems of the war, 'Courage'.*

> We know what is hanging in balance,
> Is being accomplished now.
> The hour of courage has struck
> And courage will not forsake us.
> We aren't afraid to die by a bullet,
> Or bitter when our roof falls. . . .
>   (I.262)

Aleksey Surkov recalls reading this poem to a Moscow audience: 'I remember how, during the harsh days of the winter of 1942 when I was talking in the Hall of Columns in the House of the Unions about Soviet war poetry, I read out this poem to the accompaniment of an air-raid siren. The audience that unforgettable night, of which two-thirds were

---

* Ironically, the first time Akhmatova sent it for publication it was returned with a note saying it needed to be worked on further. Needless to say, she did not consider it necessary to follow this advice, and it was published without alteration in *Pravda* on 8 May 1942.

soldiers, received it with applause which for a long time did not die
away.'⁷

Having accepted her harsh epoch, that 'one can cry' but that 'nothing
is lost' and that to live in such an age is a privilege, Akhmatova understood her role as poet in time of war and used her gift to formulate the
strength she saw in those around her. Able to publish and feeling united
to her country and its allies in western Europe, she had an opportunity
once more to reach a wider audience and also to share a little of that
strength she had won out of her loneliness and suffering:

> And she who today says good-bye to her lover,
> May she forge her pain into strength.
> We swear to our children, we swear to our graves
> That no one will make us submit!
>
> > (I.261)

The dead, she proclaimed, must not just be mourned with passive
weeping:

> And you, my friends of the last call,
> It is to mourn you that my life's been spared!
> Not in frozen remembrance, a weeping willow,
> But to shout out your names to the whole wide world
> Names, what are names!
> > I slam shut the church calendar,
> Down on your knees!
> > Crimson light shines forth.
> The people of Leningrad march out in even rows—
> The living and the dead: there are none dead to fame.
>
> > (I.264)

Turgenev had once said of his native tongue: 'In days of doubt, in
days of deep concern about the fate of my country, you alone are my
support and prop, O great, powerful, truthful and free Russian language.'⁸ Now Akhmatova expresses this same emotion in 'Courage', for
she, perhaps naturally as a poet, finds in her raw material what seems to
be the heart of what they are trying to defend.

> And we will preserve the Russian tongue,
> The mighty Russian word.
> Free and pure we will carry you on,
> Pass you on to our grandchildren,
> Save you from slavery for ever!
>
> > (I.262)

As in 1914, when she had felt war to be the wounding of the body of
Christ, Akhmatova again expresses that sensitivity to the 'aliveness' of

things. 'Don't make a noise around,' she says of Leningrad. 'He is breathing, he's still alive and can hear everything . . .' (I.262). To the statue Night from the Summer Gardens, buried for protection, she talks as if to a daughter. The land is the Holy Body, her body, her land.

Akhmatova's relationship to soldiers has changed. Long ago they were her contemporaries and she could say to them, 'Play soldiers, I am looking for my house . . .' (I.133). Now they are her grandchildren, children, brothers, sons, as they are for the women of Leningrad: 'simple boys, Van'kas, Vas'kas, Alyoshkas, Grishkas . . .' (I.343). She notes their solemn farewells to their girls and mothers as, all dressed up, they go out as if to 'play'. Her 'children' are not only those who go to war, but also those little ones starving and threatened in Leningrad. Perhaps it was only in 1939 and 1940 when, in Fontannyy Dom, the two little Smirnov boys would run in from next door, that Akhmatova, having long understood what it meant to lose a child, began to discover something of the joy of mothering small children. It was of these little boys and of Anya, Irina Punina's daughter, that Akhmatova talked lovingly as *children* in her old age. Yet because she did not recognize in a 'non-poetical' way that someone else's children were also hers, it never occurred to her to try and take the boys with her when she was evacuated. When she learnt, in Tashkent, of the death of the younger boy, Val'ya, she recalled how he used to knock on the door and come to her:

> Knock with your little fist—I'll open the door.
> I always opened it for you.
> I am living beyond the high mountain,
> Past the desert and the wind and heat,
> But I will never let you down.
>
> .   .   .   .
>
> I did not hear you groaning,
> You didn't ask me for bread.
> Bring me a sprig from a maple tree,
> Or some bits of green grass, like last spring.
> Bring me cupped in your little hand
> Some clean, cool Neva water
> And I will wash away the blood
> Staining your golden head.
>
> (I.263)

2

Akhmatova wrote of the Tashkent period: 'Until May 1944, I lived in Tashkent, hungry for news of Leningrad, of the front. Like other poets I often gave recitals in hospitals, read my poems to wounded soldiers. In

Tashkent I learnt for the first time what the shade of a tree and the sound of water can mean in the blazing heat. I also learnt the meaning of human kindness: in Tashkent I was ill both often and badly' (I.46). Chukovskaya was stricken with typhus and Akhmatova looked after her. Once, coming into Chukovskaya's room when she had a temperature of 42 degrees centigrade, Akhmatova remarked that the temperature in the room was 100 degrees: '40 degrees of yours and 60 degrees of the weather's.' Later she herself came down with typhus.

To those who had come from Leningrad, Tashkent, with its flowers blooming peacefully in the hot sun, presented a striking contrast to their besieged and starving city. At one time there was talk of sending food parcels to friends and relatives in Leningrad by special train and Akhmatova hoped she might be able to go back on it. Although while in Tashkent Akhmatova wrote mainly about Leningrad, Chukovskaya noted that while, as on the journey there, she herself was conscious of little beyond the practical difficulties of survival, Akhmatova was fascinated with being in an Asian city, despite the hardships it involved.

One hardship was being separated from her friend Vladimir Garshin. After she had left Punin in 1938, Garshin, a medical doctor, had come to occupy an increasingly important place in her life. Part of the 'Poem without a Hero' was at one time dedicated to him, though this was later changed. Tired of everlastingly living in 'other people's homes', Akhmatova had agreed to marry Garshin. The war, the blockade, and the poet's evacuation from Leningrad had disrupted their plans. In Tashkent she waited anxiously for his letters. At one point Chukovskaya wrote to him, begging him to write, saying that Akhmatova was seriously ill and so distressed at having no news of him that they feared for her life. When he did write, his letters made Akhmatova wild. His wife, from whom he had long been estranged, had died and he wrote that she, the wife, had been the most important person in his life. Akhmatova was furious and said to Chukovskaya, 'What if I wrote to him that Lourié had been the most important person in my life?' In one of his letters Garshin made Akhmatova a formal proposal of marriage conditional on her taking his name.[9]

In April 1942, Akhmatova heard that the Punin family had been evacuated from Leningrad along with others connected with the Academy of Arts. Punin, his first wife Anna Arens, his daughter Irina with her baby, Anya, and his third wife Marta Golubeva, passed through Tashkent on their way to Samarkand. Punin was extremely ill and had been since January. Conditions on the train were so terrible that the fur coat in which the tiny Anya was dressed caught fire three times during the journey. Relations between Akhmatova and Punin had been very bad at the time of their separation, and since. But all they had gone through since the beginning of the war had put things in a different perspective. When the train stopped in Tashkent Akhmatova was there to meet them. She returned to see them off when the train left again the following day.

Punin was deeply moved. In Leningrad, convinced that death was only round the corner, he had thought a great deal about many things and about Akhmatova in particular. After arriving in Samarkand, he wrote her a letter from hospital which was to remain one of her most precious possessions:

Hello, Anya.

I am infinitely grateful for your concern and touched by it—I have not deserved it. I am still in hospital—not so much because I am ill, as because it is better here than outside. . . . There is a soft bed and food, which, although it may not be marvellous, is free. And it's peaceful. I still have not fully re-covered my strength but all the same I feel alive and find such joy in the sunny days and the spring which is quietly coming on. I look and I think: I'm alive. The realization that I am still alive brings me to a rapturous state and I call this—the feeling of happiness. Moreover when I was dying, that is, knew that I would undoubtedly die—it was on Petrovsky Island at the Golubevs, where I went to live for a while, because it seemed to me the only warm room in Leningrad—I also felt that rapturous happiness. At that time particularly I thought a lot about you. This was because in the intensity of the spiritual experience I was going through there was something—as I wrote to you in my note—akin to the feeling alive in me in the twenties when I was with you. It seemed to me, that for the first time I understood you so fully and compre-hensively—and it was just because it was so completely unselfish, as I, of course, did not expect ever to see you again. It was really a meeting and fare-well with you before death. And it seemed to me then that I knew of no other person whose life was so whole and therefore so perfect as yours, from your first childish poems (the left-hand glove) to the prophetic murmur, and at the same time, roar, of the *Poema*. I thought then that this life was perfect not through will, but—and this seemed to me to be particularly precious—through its organic wholeness, that is, its inevitability, which seems some-how not to have anything to do with you. Now I cannot express all that I thought then, but a great deal of what I could not forgive in you stood before me, not only forgiven, but something right and wonderful. You know, many people judge you on account of Lyova, but then it was so clear that you did the wisest and by far the best thing you could do in the circumstances (I am talking about Bezhetsk), and Lyova would not be the person he is without his Bezhetsk childhood. I also thought a great deal about Lyova, but I'll talk of that another time—I am guilty before him. In your life there is a fortress that seems carved of stone, all at one time, by a very practised hand. All this, I remember, filled me then with joy and some quite unusual unsentimental tenderness, contemplative, as if I stood before the gates of Paradise (altogether a lot of what happened then was like the *Divina Commedia*). I was happy not so much because of you, as because of Creation, because all this made me feel than there is no personal immortality but there is that which is immortal. This feeling was particularly strong. To die was not something terrible—and I had no pretensions to continuing to live personally or to being preserved after death. I just was not interested in that at all. But that which is immortal exists and of that thing I am a part. It was solemnly splendid. Then you seemed to me, as you do now, to be the highest expression of that which is Immortal that I have met with in my life. In the hospital I happened to re-read *The Devils*. Dostoyevsky, as always, seemed heavy and not at all my kind of reading, but at the end of the novel like the golden dawn shining through terrible, incredible gloom, I found these words: 'A thought which had been with me continuously about the existence of something infinitely more just and more happy than I, fills me with immeasurable tenderness—and as for glory—whoever I might be, whatever I might have done to anyone, it is far more necessary than to be happy myself to know and believe every minute that somewhere there is perfect and peaceful happiness for everyone and everything.' These words* were just about a perfect expression of what I felt then. Particularly—'and as for glory'—'peaceful happiness'. You seemed then to be the expression of the 'peaceful happiness of glory'. Dying, I came closer to it.[10]

In Tashkent at the end of May or the beginning of June, 1942, Akhmatova met for the first time in many years a person from the 'outside world' (or, as she called it, 'the other side of the looking glass').† This was the Polish artist, Joseph Czapski, who was attached to General Anders's army. Czapski describes meeting Akhmatova at Aleksey Tolstoy's:

The evening I am referring to, Akhmatova was seated next to the lamp wearing a dress of light material cut very simply, something between a sack and the habit of a nun; her lightly greying hair was smoothed back and held by a coloured scarf. She must have been very beautiful with her even features, the classic oval of her face, her grey eyes. She drank some wine and spoke little and in a rather strange way as if she were half joking about the saddest things.[11]

When Czapski translated extempore for them poems by the Polish poets Balinski and Słonimski she listened with tears in her eyes. She wanted to translate a poem about Warsaw by Słonimski although she told Czapski she never translated poetry.‡ Akhmatova recited part of the

---

* Punin is slightly misquoting the passage.

† Akhmatova first used this expression to me in 1964, referring to Isaiah Berlin's visit to her in 1946 as being from 'someone from beyond the looking glass' (*nekto iz za zerkala*). She may have been aware of the echo of the White Queen in Lewis Carroll's *Through the Looking Glass*.

‡ Although Akhmatova had published one translation from the Armenian, in 1936, it was only in the 1950s that she became a professional translator of verse. She never enjoyed it, claiming that it used up energy better spent in writing her own poems.

'Poem without a Hero' and the poem she had written in memory of her
little neighbour in Fontannyy Dom, Val'ya Smirnov. She talked to
Czapski of her anguish over her son's fate. 'I've kissed the boots of all the
important Bol'sheviks,' she told him, 'in order to find out if he is alive
or not and I know nothing.'

   This meeting with Czapski made a deep impression on Akhmatova.
In front of him she said to Nikolay Tikhonov, the editor: 'I don't understand why, but I feel closer to Czapski than to all the other people here....'
Czapski recognized that this was due not so much to him personally, as to
the fact that he was a representative of a different world, whose manner
of speaking was less restrained and more impulsive than Akhmatova had
become used to. She herself struck Czapski with her sincerity. When they
left the Tolstoys she detached herself from those around her and Czapski
saw her home. In 1959 Akhmatova recalled how they, two Europeans
exiled by war, had walked together through the warm Asian night:

> That night we sent each other mad,
> Only the menacing darkness shone,
> The ditches were murmuring to themselves,
> And carnations smelt of Asia.
>
> And we walked through the foreign town,
> Through the smoky song and the midnight heat,
> Alone beneath the serpent,
> Not daring to look at each other.
>
> It could have been Istanbul or Baghdad,
> But, alas, not Warsaw, not Leningrad,
> And the scent of this bitter difference
> Made us feel that we had been orphaned.
>
> And the ages strode, it seemed, alongside
> And an unseen hand beat a tambourine
> And like a secret sign the sound
> Circled before us in the gloom.
>
> Together in that mysterious dark
> We walked as if in no-man's-land,
> When over our meeting-parting the moon
> Floated, a diamond felucca . . .
>
> And if this night comes back to you,
> A man whose fate I cannot grasp,
> Know that this sacred moment
> Appeared in someone's dream.

(I.321–2)

For the beloved of the moon to watch it rise with someone else was still to share a sacred moment, just as it had been in 1913.

As well as Nadezhda Mandel'shtam and Lidiya Chukovskaya, Akhmatova's friends in Tashkent included the actress Faina Ranevskaya, the musician Aleksandr Kozlovsky* and his wife Galya, Evgeniya Berkovskaya, Eduard Babaev, and Professor Vladimir Admoni. She also renewed her friendship with Aleksey Tolstoy, whom she had refused to know earlier, on his return from abroad, because of her strong feeling against those who had emigrated. Tolstoy called her Annyushka and helped her with *Selected Poems*, the volume she published in Tashkent in 1943. Together they talked of the good times they would have when they were able to return to Leningrad and Moscow.

The Tashkent volume appeared with a foreword by Kornely Zelinsky, who noted: 'The collection shows the themes in Akhmatova's poetry. Russia, nature, art, love, the human portrait—those are the most important. . . .' In a review of·the book, intended for the magazine *Literature and Art*,† Boris Pasternak wrote in the autumn of 1943: 'A collection of Akhmatova's poems has appeared. The book convinces us once again that the poet has never been silent and has responded, albeit irregularly, to the problems of our time. . . .'

Far from Leningrad and only too conscious of the contrast presented to it by Tashkent, Akhmatova all the same felt a curious sense of recognition in Asia. 'I have not been here for seven hundred years but nothing has changed . . .,' she wrote (I.272). Elsewhere we find, 'Who will dare say to me that this is a wicked foreign land' (I.270), and again, 'On this ancient dry earth I feel once more at home, the Chinese wind sings in the haze and everything is familiar . . .' (I.271). Instead of feeling a stranger she felt surrounded by 'millions of friends'. Asia revealed something of itself to her:

> It is your lynx eyes, Asia,
> That spied something in me,
> Teased out something latent
> Born of silence,
> Oppressive and difficult
> Like the midday Termez heat.
> It is as though pre-memory
> Flowed into consciousness
> Like molten lava,

* Her poem, 'The Rising of the Moon', is dedicated to Kozlovsky.

† Pasternak wrote two reviews of *Selected Poems*, neither of which was published, so far as is known. The reasons for this may have had less to do with Akhmatova's reputation, or his own, than with the fact that it was wartime.

> As though I drank tears of my own weeping
> From a stranger's cupped palms.
>
> (I.275)

Having learnt in Tashkent to value 'the sound of water and a tree's shade in the blazing heat' (I.46), Akhmatova's longing to return home and for the war to end finds expression in the recollection of the cool of the north, its forests and birches. Even when speaking of her *Poema* she talks of 'coolness' (I.269).

Two poems simply called 'Death', written at this time, reflect the experience of being near death with typhus. Akhmatova's earlier poems on this theme, by contrast, seem to be the fruit of the imagination of death, rather than the experience of coming close to it. Here is no prayer for death as a deliverance, nor is it seen as something putting an end to poetry or even affecting those close to her. If these poems resemble anything written earlier, it is the last part of 'The Way of All Earth':

> For the great winter
> I've waited long,
> Like a white vestment
> Received it.
> Quietly I'll sit
> In the light sleigh . . .*
> Before night I'll be back
> With you in Kitezh.
>
> (I.246)

But now when faced with the actuality of death the poet sees it as something both simpler and greater:

> I
>
> I was on the edge of something
> For which there is no true name . . .
> The drawing on of drowsiness,
> The slipping away from oneself . . .
>
> II
>
> But already I stand on the threshold
> Of something we all reach, though the cost differ . . .
> On this boat there is a cabin for me
> And wind in the sails—and the terrible moment
> Of parting with my native land.
>
> (I.264–5)

On a different level she expresses the confusion of delirium in what she calls a *chastushka*—a form of short humorous folk poem.

* This would refer to the custom of going for burial in a sleigh.

Somewhere there is a young night,
A starry night, a frosty night—
Oh how bad, oh how bad
Is my typhus head.
It conjures up things for itself,
On the pillow twists and turns,
Does not know at all, at all,
What it answers for and why—
That past the garden, past the stream
The hag drags a coffin along . . .
There's no need to bury me,
I am just the teller of tales.

(II.138)

As counterparts to poems like 'Already madness with its wing' and 'Death'
are others in which far from welcoming a release from memory and time,
Akhmatova is terrified of it. It is the darkness from which formulation,
poetry, saves her and in one strange poem she cries: 'Night is coming
and I have little strength left. Save me as I saved you and do not let me
disappear into the seething darkness' (II.143).*

Marina Tsvetaeva's suicide in 1941 near Chistopol' shortly before
Akhmatova's arrival there had had a profound effect on her. Faced
shortly afterwards with the 'purity' of an Asian people whose life had
followed the same simple pattern for centuries, Akhmatova again experienced that feeling of guilt that she always seemed to carry with her: guilt
at being the person she was, from whom however there was no escape.
Death to her at times like this is seen not as a release but as the horrible
drinking of emptiness:

Oh what can I do with this purity,
With this simple incorruptibility
Oh what can I do with these people!
I was not able just to be the observer,
And for some reason always pushed myself
Into nature's most restricted zones:
Curer of tender infirmity,
Other women's husbands' truest friend,
Inconsolable widow of many.
Not without cause am I crowned with grey
And already my sun-scorched cheeks
Frighten with their swarthiness.
But soon my arrogance must end
And like that other: Marina the martyr

* In Akhmatova's posthumously published notes on Pushkin[12] she quotes his lines:
'Poetry like an angel of comfort / Saved me, and my soul rose again.'

> I too must drink of emptiness
> And in a long black cloak you'll come,
> Bearing a candle green and vile
> And not reveal your face to me . . .
> But now I have not long to puzzle
> About whose hand the white glove covers
> And who sent him who comes by night.
>   (II.142–3)

It is tempting to assume the poems 'Death' were written later than this, to assign all fear of emptiness and darkness to a previous state—one that must surely have changed after the experience of death's approach so calmly and beautifully expressed. But Akhmatova records over and over again in her poems the all too human experience of knowing, forgetting, and having to relearn something; the situation where the 'answer' is continually tested and refound until only its bare elements remain. The fact that Akhmatova at one point understood Mary at the foot of the Cross in no way implies that at all times she could look upon life from that position of strength.

Yet because she had 'been there' and, perhaps most important, *recorded* it, she could no longer pretend to be weaker than she was. Thus too the experience of 'Death' would become less powerful but still remain on record. The fact that, at times of fear and weakness, she could find her way back to the strength expressed in her poems through the poetry itself, would explain her cry to her poem 'Save me!' Her poetry was witness to her ability to transcend suffering not only for others, but for herself. Perhaps too it was a protection from the solitude and loneliness of the writer's position. In 'Ballad', written in Tashkent in 1943, we find Akhmatova lingering with a finished work: 'But already in just a moment all will be over and the author once again irrevocably alone . . .' (I.256).

The Tashkent poems with their description of delirium and hot nights heavy with stars have an unreal quality. It is as if Akhmatova had suddenly been put down among the nomads of the Old Testament pictured so vividly in her Biblical poems—yet she is an observer, not one of them. Although all is 'familiar' this is but a temporary haven. It is in this unreal and yet familiar world, with its contradictions in time, where the delirium of typhus and the nearness of death confused even more the distinctions between imagination and reality, that Akhmatova wrote a large part of 'Poem without a Hero'. In some of the shorter poems written at the same time we recognize that tone of authority and that continual conversation with herself, a putting in order of the past combined with a deeper understanding of a poet's fate, that we are to find in the *Poema*. Of Pushkin and the price of fame she writes succinctly in Tashkent:

> Who knows what fame really means!
> What was the price he paid for the right,
> The opportunity, the gift
> So wisely and so archly to make fun
> Of everything; mysteriously to keep quiet;
> To speak familiarly of someone's little foot.
>
> (I.257)

Czapski described Akhmatova as speaking 'as if she were half-joking about the saddest things. . . .' It is as if her suffering and that of the people around her has now passed the point of the credible and so cannot be talked about completely seriously. It is with gentle irony now that she talks of her strength and how she can no longer be touched by super-stitious fear of the sort which first appeared in her poetry after Gumil-yov's death. It is not so much that she herself is no longer a witch as that she has passed on to something greater:

> In this chamber a witch
> Dwelt before me, alone:
> Her shadow can be seen
> On the eve of the new moon.
> Her shadow still stands
> By the high threshold.
> Evasive and strict,
> She is looking my way.
> Other people's spells
> Cannot touch me at all,
> I, in fact . . . No, I won't
> Give my secrets for free.
>
> (I.278)

In complete contrast to the poem 'Fear picks out objects in the dark', written in August 1921, is a poem written in 1944. Here although the house is 'under a spell' and frightening, undefined things appear and disappear in the Rembrandtean corners, the poet doesn't even shudder and her sleep is peaceful (I.274–5).[13]

In 1943–4 in Tashkent, Akhmatova also wrote the play 'E nu ma elish' which she later burnt.* The title of one of its parts perhaps best sums up

---

* According to Akhmatova, the title of the play was taken from the first words of an Assyrian epic poem about Creation, 'When up above . . .' It consisted of three parts: (1) 'On the stairs' (*Na lestnitse*); (2) 'Prologue, or a Dream within a Dream' (*Prolog ili son vo sne*); (3) 'Under the stairs' (*Pod lestnitsey*). At the end of her life Akhmatova talked about rewriting this play.

the quality pervading most of her poetry written in Tashkent—'A Dream within a Dream'.

3

In 1943, at no. 7 Karl Marx Street, the painter A. Tischler did a series of drawings of Akhmatova. Later that year she finally got another room, in the 'white house on Zhukovsky Street' which she mentions in a poem (I.316). After this she stayed for a while with her friends the Lugovskys. Slowly her exile drew to a close.

On 15 May 1944, Akhmatova flew from Tashkent to Moscow. Looking down from the aeroplane at the land stretching out below she had the feeling that she was looking at her own body and soul. She arrived in a Moscow 'already filled with joyful hopes and expectations of victory in the near future' (I.46). 'Home, home, is it really home! How new and how familiar it all is,' she wrote (I.267). In Moscow she stayed with her friends the Ardovs. While there she read a poem at a poetry recital in the auditorium of the Polytechnic Museum, where the reception she was given was so enthusiastic that it frightened her.

On 1 June she returned to Leningrad. There she discovered that Garshin, without telling her, had married a nurse during the siege. It was a tremendous shock. He had not even bothered to see that her room was kept for her. Chukovskaya later said that Garshin, whom she personally had liked and respected, must quite simply have lost his reason as a result of suffering and hunger during the blockade. Of him the following year Akhmatova wrote:

> . . . And the man who now to me
> Means nothing but who was my care
> And comfort in the bitterest of years
> Already roams along the outskirts,
> The alleyways and backyards of life,
> Heavy, stupefied with madness
> And with a wolfish grin . . .
> O God, O God,
> How I have sinned grievously before Thee
> Leave me pity at least . . .
>
> (I.282)

Emma Gershteyn felt that Tashkent had completely changed Akhmatova from the person she had known. To begin with she looked different: the famous fringe had gone and after typhus she had begun to put on weight. Her manner too seemed different and her circle of friends wider. Garshin's conduct towards her had inevitably resulted in a certain reassessment of her life, reflected both in her behaviour that year and in the poems she wrote. Sometime during her first month back she had burnt the manuscript of her play, 'E nu ma elish'. Various other works written in Tashkent may also have been burnt at this time, apparently for purely personal reasons.

Pavel Luknitsky went to visit the poet shortly after her return to Leningrad:

> For her patriotic poems Akhmatova has been awarded the medal 'For the Defence of Leningrad'. She looks peaceful and in good spirits. She was hospitable, recited some poems.
>
> Tomorrow is her birthday and, laughing, she asked me: 'What will they give me tomorrow, Cherbourg?' 'Probably Medvezhegorsk!' I answered. 'In Karelia our forces are attacking along the whole front.'[14]

In January 1944, while still in Tashkent, Akhmatova had 'presented' her 'silence to that great martyr Leningrad, the final and highest reward of all'.[15] Now back in this, her city, she wrote:

> I cannot brush aside
> Leningrad's misfortune
> With my hands.
> I cannot wash it away
> With my tears.
> I cannot bury it. I walk
> A mile to avoid it.
> It is not with my glance
> Or by some hint
> Or by a word or a reproach
> But with a bow deep to the earth
> In the green field
> I mark it.[16]

If during her exile she had learnt that she could never be separated from her city, St. Petersburg–Leningrad, the events of the century still seemed determined to destroy all that might recall the days of her youth. Earlier she had lamented the death of a willow she had loved in childhood. Now she mourns the 'little toy town' of her youth, Tsarskoe Selo, destroyed by the Germans.

> They've burnt my little toy town,
> And I've no loophole back to the past.
> There was a fountain there, green benches,
> And the huge park of Tsarskoe behind;
> On Shrove Tuesday—bumpy roads and pancakes,
> Finnish cabs with bells and ribbons;
> In April—the smell of earth and rotting
> And the first kiss . . .   (I.376)

Akhmatova could join with her fellow-countrymen in delight at the news of victories and the feeling that the war would soon be at an end. Her hope, however, that after the war she would be able to lead a 'normal' life with Garshin—a life like other people lead—had been sadly misplaced. Instead she found herself alone once more, walking the tightrope of poetry from which there was no escape:

> From poetry where every step's a secret
> And there is an abyss to left and right
> And fame, a withered leaf, lies underfoot—
> Apparently for me there's no reprieve.[17]

But again, as often before, it is when talking of poetry that we hear that voice of unquenchable authority:

> Our sacred craft has existed
> For thousands of years . . .
> Even where there is no light
> It has lit up the world.
> But up till now
> Not one poet has said
> That wisdom does not exist,
> Nor age, nor, maybe, death.
>   (I.257)

In 1944 Akhmatova wrote what was perhaps the clearest and most profound statement, not only of her acceptance of her fate, but also of her realization that she would not have wanted to live in any other way. Here once more, as in 'The Way of All Earth', she looks upon her whole life as from a distance. The image she uses to describe it is that of a river. Standing in contrast to her actual life is the 'normal' one she might have lived had not the 'harsh age' changed the river's course:

> As if I were a river
> The harsh age changed my course,
> Replaced one life with another,
> Flowing in a different channel
> And I do not recognize my shores.
> Oh, how many sights I must have missed.
> The curtain must have risen there without me
> And then come down. How many of my friends
> Did I not even meet once in my life.
> How many cities' different skylines
> Could have drawn tears from my eyes
> While I really know only one city
> And can find it by touch in my sleep . . .

How many poems have I not written—
Their secret chorus wanders round about me
And maybe one day will even manage
To suffocate me . . .
I know the beginnings and the ends
And life after the end and something
Unnecessary to recall just here.
And some other woman has usurped
My rightful place, carries my legal name
Leaving me a nickname out of which
I've done the best I can.
It won't, alas, be in my grave I'll lie . . .
But sometimes the playful wind of spring,
The combination of words in some chance book,
Or someone's smile suddenly draws me
Into that life that never happened—
Such and such would have taken place
That year and something else, another:
Travelling, seeing, thinking, remembering,
Entering new love like a mirror
With a dull consciousness of betrayal
And of that wrinkle that just yesterday
Had not appeared . . .
But if from there I had looked back sometime
And seen my life now as it is today
I would at last have known what envy means . . .
(I.311–12)*

To know 'the beginnings and the ends and life after the end . . .' is all
very well, but it can be a barrier separating one from one's fellow-men,
who in their weakness can only occasionally, for a few seconds if at all,
bear to face the truth one has learnt to live with. In such situations what
is in fact plain truth may be spoken in accents of irony, as Czapski
described Akhmatova's manner of speaking in Tashkent. But where
irony is really intended it must be written into a poet's work and not
depend merely on the intonation of the reader's voice. Chukovskaya
found it impossible to believe that Akhmatova was not being ironical
when she read to her the lines from the end of the sixth[18] of her 'Northern
Elegies':

> We recognize that we could not fit in
> That past within the boundaries of our life,
> And that it's almost as strange to us
> As to the person in the flat next door;

* Lines 26–36 are replaced by an ellipse in I.311–12.

That those who died we would not recognize
And those from whom God separated us
Did fine without us—and even perhaps
Everything's been for the best . . .

(I.313)

And yet this poem, written sometime between 1943 and 1954, not only
does not sound ironical now, but was read 'straight' by Akhmatova when
she recorded it towards the end of her life.

4

For a while after her return to Leningrad, Akhmatova attempted to
live with her friends the Rybakovs, but this did not work out. Finally she
succeeded in getting back two rooms in Fontannyy Dom (flat 44). When
the Punins returned in the spring of 1945 little Anya saw someone with an
enormous bouquet of flowers there to welcome them. It was Akhmatova.

In 1945, to the poet's great joy, her son Lev at last returned home. In
exile since August 1939, he had, as it turned out, been released to fight in
the war. For a time after his return, mother and son were very close.

Towards the end of 1945, the *Literary Gazette* printed an interview
with Akhmatova[19] in which she made it clear once more that for her,
lyric poetry was not something which could be written to order but was
the result of inspiration: 'Of course I will continue to write lyric poems.
But it is hardest of all to talk of these: they come of their own accord . . .'
(I.48). In the same interview she announced that a large collection of her
poems was due to be published early in 1946 by Goslitizdat in Leningrad.
She also said that she was in the process of putting her studies of Pushkin
—some 25 in all, written between 1926 and 1936—in order with a view
to making them into a book. Neither of these books ever appeared.

In the autumn of 1945 another event occurred which was to make a
very great impression on Akhmatova. It was a visit from another representative of that 'looking-glass' world with which she had felt in contact
during her meeting with Joseph Czapski. This time the conditions for a
meeting, while perhaps not perfect, were much better than they had
been with Czapski: it was possible to talk with her visitor alone for many
hours. In this case the person, who became by the very circumstances of
their meeting more than just a private individual, was Isaiah Berlin.

Berlin was at this time temporary First Secretary in the British Embassy in Moscow. In Leningrad on a visit, he went into the Writers'
Shop on Nevsky Prospect. There in the inner room where writers and
book dealers buy and sell books not for sale in the outer shop, and into
which he was able to penetrate owing to his special position as a foreigner,

Berlin met a critic whom he asked about the fate of many writers of whom nothing had been heard since before the war. Mikhail Zoshchenko, the writer, was, as it turned out, in the next room, looking yellow and frail. When he asked about Akhmatova, Berlin was told that she was living just round the corner. He was asked if he would like to meet her. They telephoned and found she was willing to receive them.

At Fontannyy Dom they found Akhmatova with friends. They had not been there long when to Berlin's stunned horror there was a call of 'Isaiah, Isaiah' from outside in the courtyard. It was Randolph Churchill. Apparently he had turned up in Leningrad as a representative of the press and needed an interpreter. Discovering from another member of the Embassy at the Hotel Astoria that Berlin, whom he had known slightly at Oxford, was also in Leningrad, Churchill had somehow managed to trace him to Fontannyy Dom and even to penetrate the courtyard garden at the back of the house.

It was a nightmarish moment. Berlin's only desire was to prevent Churchill from bursting in. He and the man who had introduced him to Akhmatova rushed downstairs and left with Churchill as quickly as possible. But the incident had destroyed any hope Berlin might have had that his visit to the poet would remain unremarked. For a Soviet citizen to meet a foreigner privately outside a place of public resort or without authority had for many years been almost synonymous with treason. The war had changed things slightly but not much. Managed quietly, with tact, a meeting might well have been 'overlooked', but to have the son of Winston Churchill shouting wildly in one's garden as one entertained another foreigner could hardly pass without notice.

Akhmatova must have been fully aware of the danger involved in allowing Berlin to return. Yet when he telephoned to apologize and asked if he could see her again she agreed and told him to come that evening at nine o'clock. At first other friends of hers were present, but as it got late they left. Akhmatova was embarrassed that she had only boiled potatoes to offer her guest. At one point her son Lev came in. He told stories of his experiences in Central Asia. Then he too went to bed. But the conversation between Akhmatova and Berlin continued. It began to grow light. It was about eleven o'clock in the morning before Berlin returned to his hotel.

Their meeting seemed to Akhmatova to have been by its very timing outside the confines of the everyday world:

> We breathed no slumbrous poppies
> And are unaware of our fault.
> Beneath what star-signs were we born
> To our mutual grief?

What was the black and terrible brew
The January darkness brought?
What invisible glow led us on,
Out of our minds until dawn?

(I.284–5)

They talked together of many things: of people they knew in common
—many of whom, such as Salomea and Aleksandr Halpern, Akhmatova
had had no word of for years—of Gumilyov, Lourié, Shileyko, Pasternak,
and Mikhail Lozinsky, to whom she was devoted. Punin, who was living
in the room next door, was hardly mentioned. Akhmatova spoke with
feeling about Boris Anrep and Marina Tsvetaeva. She could not yet
bring herself to speak of Mandel'shtam. The tragedy of his imprisonment and death was still too close. Trying to do so she dissolved into
tears.

The poet's room was very bare. There was a chest of drawers full of
poems and the Modigliani line drawing hung on the wall. When Berlin
mentioned Modigliani's fame, Akhmatova was surprised. She had not
known it was so great.

The talk turned to literature. Akhmatova expressed her dislike of
Tolstoy and Chekhov. *Anna Karenina* suffered, she said, from the
morality of Tolstoy's aunts. In Chekhov everything was a dull uniform
grey.[*] 'No swords flash.' The poet also spoke at length about her childhood in the Crimea, her 'pagan youth' as she called it, and the connection between the pagan Tatars whom she saw there and the traditional
old Jews of Central Asia whom she saw in Tashkent, who had made an
immense impression on her. Akhmatova recited her poems to Berlin,
among them 'Poem without a Hero', which he told her sounded to him
like a requiem for the whole of Europe.[†] Berlin wanted to write down
what she recited but she said it would all appear in a one-volume edition
of her poems in the spring, which she would send.

Akhmatova told Berlin that she did not approve of emigration. She
felt it was important to die *with* one's country. Compared to this dying
for one's country was easy. She said that because of this she had refused
to meet Aleksey Tolstoy and Ilya Ehrenburg when they first returned to
the Soviet Union, but had later relented towards both, and spoke of her
friendship with Tolstoy in Tashkent during the war.

When Berlin left in the morning the huge wrought-iron gates of
Fontannyy Dom through which he had entered the evening before were

[*] Pasternak disagreed with Akhmatova on this, Berlin recalls, saying Chekhov was
Russia's answer to Flaubert, the only author who does not preach to the reader.
[†] Later Berlin recalled being oddly surprised at the way Akhmatova refers in the
Poema to Byron as 'George'.

wide open—an unusual and ominous occurrence. On 5 January 1946 he came to see the poet again as he passed through Leningrad on his way out of the Soviet Union. The day after this Akhmatova realized, when pieces of plaster started falling from the ceiling, that microphones were being installed in her room.[20]

Her fateful contact with the 'other world' was to do Akhmatova no good but it was precious and important to her. For even in her times of greatest strength Akhmatova remained in need of reassurance. And to those who gave her this, Boris Anrep, Isaiah Berlin, and even Nikolay Punin when he wrote to her during the war, she remained for ever grateful. To Berlin she wrote:

> Never since long long ago
> Have I wanted someone's pity,
> But one drop of yours and I
> Feel as if the sun's inside me.
> That's why you can see the dawn
> And I do miracles as I go,
> That's why!
>
> (I.284)

And later, despite the fact that she firmly believed all her troubles in the following years were directly connected with it, she still proclaimed his visit had been something wonderful.*

5

In April 1946 Akhmatova went with a delegation of Leningrad poets† to Moscow, where they gave readings in the Hall of Columns and at Moscow University and the Writers' and Artists' Clubs.[21] In the previous three years (1944–6) her poems had been appearing regularly in journals and papers. But on 14 August all this changed. The Central Committee of the Communist Party passed a resolution which, as Gleb Struve says, 'marked the starting point of a new era in Soviet literature which has been associated with the name of Andrey Zhdanov'.[22] The resolution censured the magazines Star (Zvezda) and Leningrad for publishing the ideologically harmful and apolitical works of the writer Mikhail Zoshchenko and the poet Anna Akhmatova.

'Akhmatova is a typical representative,' said the resolution,

---

* Akhmatova described her meeting with Berlin in the cycle 'Cinque', written in 1946, as well as in the 'Poem without a Hero', where the third dedication is to him.

† The delegation included O. Berggol'ts, A. Prokofiev, N. Braun, V. Rozhdestvensky, and M. Dudin

of that empty poetry lacking in ideals that is foreign to our people. Her poems are saturated with the spirit of pessimism and degeneration and express the tastes of the old salon poetry frozen in attitudes of bourgeois-aristocratic aestheticism and decadence of 'art for art's sake' with no wish to move in step with one's people. They will be harmful in the education of our young people and cannot be tolerated in Soviet literature.

The magazine *Leningrad* had 'been behaving particularly badly', the resolution went on, 'continually opening its pages to Akhmatova's empty apolitical poems.'[23] *Star* was ordered to reform, *Leningrad* simply suppressed.

A week later Zhdanov issued reports on the situation to the Leningrad branch of the Union of Soviet Writers and the Committee of the Communist Party of the City of Leningrad, in which he made quite clear the new official policy for literature and the arts. Publishing Akhmatova in the present day, he said, is equivalent to publishing Merezhkovsky, Kuz'min, Vyacheslav Ivanov, Gippius, Sologub, and others from the same 'literary swamp'.* The Acmeists, of whom she was one, propagated, he maintained, the theory of 'art for art's sake' and 'beauty for beauty's sake' and had no desire to know anything about their people's needs and the socio-political life of the country:

Acmeists, like the Symbolists, Decadents, and other trumpeters of aristocratic-bourgeois ideology, were the propagators of decadence, pessimism, and a belief in the other world. Akhmatova's themes are completely individualistic. The range of her poetry is so limited as to seem poverty-stricken; it is the portrait of a frantic little fine lady flitting between the boudoir and the chapel. . . . The basis of her poetry is made up of amatory erotic themes, interwoven with themes of sadness, longing, death, mysticism, and doom. The feeling of doom is one we can expect to find in the social consciousness of a dying group. The gloomy tones of hopelessness before death, mystic experiences intermingled with eroticism—this is the spiritual world of Akhmatova, a left-over from the old aristocratic culture which has sunk once and for all into the oblivion of 'the good old days of Catherine'. Half nun, half harlot, or rather a harlot-nun whose sin is mixed with prayer.

Completely ignoring the fact that Akhmatova had been publishing for the past six years, Zhdanov stated:

And suddenly twenty-nine years after the socialist revolution some museum pieces out of the world of shadows appear again on the scene and begin to instruct our young people how they should live. The pages of a Leningrad journal open wide before Akhmatova and freely allow her to poison the youth with the pernicious spirit of her poetry. . . . ˙

* By equating these Symbolist poets and writers with Akhmatova, Zhdanov was, not surprisingly, ignoring the sharp distinction between Acmeist and Symbolist theory.

What is there in common between this poetry and the interests of our people, our government? Absolutely nothing. Akhmatova's work belongs to the distant past; it is alien to modern Soviet reality and cannot be tolerated on the pages of our magazines. . . . What positive contribution can Akhmatova's work make to our young people? It can do nothing but harm. It can only sow despondency, spiritual depression, pessimism, and the desire to walk away from the urgent questions of public life, to leave the wide paths of public life and activity for the narrow little world of personal experience. How can we place the education of young people in her hands![24]

The attack came as a complete surprise both to writers in the Soviet Union and to the outside world, after the more relaxed cultural atmosphere of the war years. Zhdanov's reports marked the beginning of a period of the most ferocious chauvinism and rigid control, characterized by anti-western witch-hunts which outdid anything that had passed before. Akhmatova and Zoshchenko may have been singled out to bear the brunt of the attack because of their great popularity. On 4 September 1946 Akhmatova was expelled from the Union of Soviet Writers. Her book of poems, which was already in print, was destroyed.*

This new attack affected Akhmatova's life profoundly. She claimed to have found out about it in a characteristically unorthodox way. She told Lidiya Chukovskaya that on the day after the 14 August resolution of the Communist Party was published she had for some reason to go to the Writers' Union building. As usual, she had not read the papers, and wondered what had happened when everyone she came across rushed hurriedly away; one woman was obviously in tears. She left the building and bought some salt herring to take home. On her way back she saw Zoshchenko on the other side of the street. He crossed over to meet her and said, obviously in a state of great distress: 'Anna Andreevna, what can we do?' She wondered what he was referring to but having heard that he had been having some personal troubles (although how they could concern her she could not imágine), thought these must be the cause of his distress and said soothingly: 'Bear with it, one must bear with it.' Zoshchenko later recounted with awe how unmoved by it all she had managed to seem. Unwrapping the fish on her return home, Akhmatova realized what he had been talking about. In the newspaper in which it was wrapped was printed the resolution of the Central Committee.

In the weeks that followed, she found herself more isolated than she had ever been, for those few people who would still speak to her she avoided at first for fear of doing them harm. Her friend Nina Ol'shevskaya

* One copy, at least, has survived, which was lent to Akhmatova probably by the Writers' Union, in 1964, when she was preparing *The Flight of Time* (1965). N. Mandel'shtam reckons as many as twenty copies may have survived (*Hope Abandoned*, p. 375).

came to Leningrad from Moscow to be with her. At first the poet tried
to discourage her from doing this but Ol'shevskaya was adamant. Later
Akhmatova stayed for a time with the Tomashevskys. Irina Tomashevskaya recalls how one day she came out of her flat with Akhmatova to go
and see Zoshchenko in the same building two floors down. The occupant
of the flat below hers had just come out of his door. Seeing Akhmatova
coming down the stairs he froze on the spot, moving only when they had
passed, as if nodding to her might compromise him. During this period
as never before Akhmatova realized clearly who her true friends were.
In Leningrad, other than her family, only a handful of people continued
to see her as before. Without actually refusing, others found themselves
suddenly too busy. But slowly, as more and more people began to suffer
from the Zhdanov era, she became slightly less isolated.

According to Akhmatova, many Russian writers (Ivan Bunin was said
to have been among them) had been preparing to return to Russia after
the end of the war. The 1946 resolution made them change their minds.
It also made the world aware that Stalin's Russia had not changed
basically since the days of the Terror. 14 August 1946 could thus be
considered the beginning of the Cold War. She was also sure that she
knew why she had been singled out in this way. She had received at home
not just a foreigner but a British diplomat and thus destroyed what had
previously protected her—Stalin's image of her 'nun-like' conduct. In the
third dedication to the 'Poem without a Hero', she says of Isaiah Berlin:

> He will not become a dear husband
> But together we will manage
> To confuse the Twentieth Century.
>   (II.102)

There was a direct link, she was convinced, between their meeting and
the beginning of the Cold War. Stalin by this time was subject to irra-
tional furies often sparked off by seemingly insignificant occurrences.
Akhmatova never claimed that this was the only cause of the Cold War
but, whereas the 1925 ban had been a secret affair, for the most part only
affecting her personally, now the ban was entirely public with endless
repercussions both in the Soviet Union and abroad. If, as she was convinced, this had been caused by her meeting with Berlin, then what had
seemed to be part of their personal lives was in fact part of history, a
meeting that had helped 'confuse the Twentieth Century'. Years later
Akhmatova told Berlin that Stalin at this time used to ask occasionally,
'Well, how is our nun getting on?' and that she had to appear at her
window at least twice a day so that the guard who stood in the street
outside could see that she had not escaped or committed suicide.

After 1946, Akhmatova was not only unable to publish, she found she had become the officially approved target for all forms of literary abuse. Zhdanov's reports were followed by a less crude but, in its way, more pernicious article in the erring Leningrad journal *Star* by I. Sergievsky, in which he traces Akhmatova's 'literary history', quoting Gorky, Zhdanov, and Stalin. Akhmatova, Sergievsky says, had not managed to change as some of the Symbolists had; for instance, Blok with his poem 'The Twelve'. Her heroine has no wish to live and the love theme is always confined to pain and suffering. Sergievsky admits that Akhmatova had not been one of those who 'spat on the revolution' after 1905. He claims, however, that it was proved long ago that poetry with no ideological content becomes the tool of political reaction. Akhmatova, he says, has not changed since her youth: 'She has remained deaf to everything that stayed outside the confines of her little indoor world.' Faced with her war poems, Sergievsky, ignoring among others the famous poem 'Courage', quotes one of the little poems written in memory of Val'ya Smirnov as proof that all she could see in war was pain and suffering.[25]

A general article in *Novyy mir* on the poetry of the year 1946 by V. Pertsov, who had written quite fairly about Akhmatova when *From Six Books* had come out in 1940, clearly shows the effect the Central Committee's resolution and the Zhdanov reports had had on the literary scene. 'This year,' Pertsov writes, 'is marked in our literary-political life by events which outline all our literary development for many years ahead: with new force the Party has reminded us of the task of poetry, of the "place of the poet in the work plan". As never before the poet is called upon today to solve independently the most complex problems of life, to raise up the people and draw them after him.'[26] Pertsov felt that he could add little to what Zhdanov had already said about Akhmatova. Others were less restrained. V. Sidelnikov, in an article entitled 'Against Distortion and Grovelling in Soviet Folklore Study', accused Akhmatova of treason in suggesting that Pushkin had taken the story 'The Golden Cockerel' from a non-Russian source. 'Can there be a clearer example of grovelling before all things foreign?' he asked.[27] Another critic, A. Egolin, picked out Akhmatova's little poem about the burning of the 'toy town' of Tsarskoe Selo by the Germans as proof of her sympathy for and attachment to the past.[28]

6

If the Terror and the war had found Akhmatova prepared, then the same could be said of the events of 1946. They were just another chapter of a biography with which she had schooled herself to live. She had not grown used to it in the sense that she in any way condoned what was happening around her or had become less sensitive to it. If there was anything she feared it was not pain and suffering, but that she might forget what they meant and thus betray those women who had stood with her outside the prisons in 1937 and 1938:

> Was it not I who stood at the Cross
> Was it not I who drowned in the sea,
> Have my lips forgotten your taste
> O pain.[29]

Viktor Ardov described Akhmatova as 'someone who could not bear to see another person's pain'. Of Pushkin and also probably of herself, she wrote:

> Pushkin sees and knows what is happening around him and does not want it to be like that. He does not agree with it, he protests and fights with all the means he has against this terrible untruth. He demands the one and only highest Truth. And at this point he becomes (and it is time to use this word) a moralist, reaching his goals not by straight moralizing, a thing with which as we have shown he wages a continuous battle, but by means of art.[30]

Akhmatova could bear her life because she had learnt to fight with all the means she had against 'this terrible untruth'. She had understood that it could be a privilege to be present at the Crucifixion. Not all, as she was to express in the 'Poem without a Hero', are lucky enough to be called to be poets of the 'True Twentieth Century'.

Akhmatova's longest work, the beautiful but extremely difficult and complex 'Poem without a Hero', was written over a period of twenty-two years. She began it in Leningrad before the war, continued it in Tashkent and in postwar Leningrad and Moscow, and was not finally to admit that it was finished until 1962. It is a work written on so many levels and so rich in reference and quotation both to the poet's life and times and to the literature of western Europe that interpretation is difficult—the more so because of the piecemeal way in which it was published, so that many readings have been based on faulty or incomplete texts.* Akhmatova herself categorically refused to explain the *Poema*, and in fact would ask other people's opinions about it, which she collected and read out, never commenting herself as to whether she agreed or disagreed. In 1944 she announced that the poem did not have 'any third, seventh, or twenty-ninth meaning' (II.100). But in the actual text she admits to having used 'invisible ink'; that her casket has a 'third bottom'; that she is writing a

---

* In the Appendix, p. 208, I have given a brief account of the publication of the *Poema*, and a list of corrections to the Russian text printed in *Soch*. II.

'mirror letter'. No other path, she wrote, remained open to her. 'It was a miracle that I stumbled upon this one and I will not be in a hurry to leave it' (II.126).*

Although it can of course be taken that Akhmatova was forced to use 'invisible ink' because of the pressures of censorship, it seems more likely that she used it because she was speaking to people as yet unborn as well as to those living, and also to the inner self in each reader who hears and stores away to remember later things to which at the time he is deaf. Here censorship is no longer by the state, but in the mind of the reader. We are not always ready or able to hear the voice that speaks with the authority of experience of the 'other side of Hell'.

Akhmatova with her close ties to the actuality of life in this world had reacted early in her career against the Symbolists, who seemed to her to be using a private language. But her inability to write poetry except about intensely personal experience, combined with her need to understand and thus to bear the weight of the tragic circumstances of her life, had forced her to recognize that that life itself had a symbolic value. In the 'Poem without a Hero', in order to solve the 'riddle' of her own life, she sets a whole group of people—her friends and contemporaries now mainly dead—in a larger structure, thus closing the gap between symbol and reality: her symbols are flesh-and-blood people with their own historical existence.

The poem is in three parts and begins with three dedications. The first is ostensibly to Vsevolod Knyazev but bears the date of Mandel'-shtam's death. The second is to Akhmatova's friend, the actress and dancer Ol'ga Glebova-Sudeykina. The third bears no name but is dated 'Le Jour des Rois, 1956', and is to Isaiah Berlin.† This is followed by a six-line 'Introduction':

> From the year nineteen forty
>   I look at everything as from a tower.
>   As if I were once more saying good-bye
>   To what I said good-bye to long ago,
>   And having crossed myself I were to go
>   Down beneath the dark vaults.
>   (II.103)

'1913', by far the longest part of the poem, is in four sections. It opens

---

* Akhmatova commented on this 'path' and its connection with Pushkin in her notes on the *Poema* (I.133, note 10). In her writings on Pushkin we also find: 'To *conceal* in a box with a false, no with two false bottoms'; 'There are quite a few such *coded* characteristics'; 'Pushkin's *secret* way of writing'; 'That first stratum, which *poets hide* almost from themselves' (italics mine).[31]

† The date is a reference to Twelfth Night, the day of the visit of the Three Kings—i.e. 5 January, the day of Akhmatova's last meeting with Berlin ten years before, in 1946.

with the poet waiting in Fontannyy Dom for a mysterious 'guest from
the future' on the eve of 1941. Instead, to visit her come the shades of the
past as New Year's mummers in fancy dress. In the masquerade that
follows is re-enacted the suicide in 1913 of the young poet Knyazev who
killed himself out of unrequited love for Ol'ga Sudeykina. He is 'Pierrot'
and the 'Ivanushka from an old fairy tale'; she is the 'Columbine of the
1910s', the 'goat-legged one', 'Psyche the Confuser',* 'Donna Anna'.
Knyazev's rival is also a poet and one with whose fame he cannot com-
pete, Aleksandr Blok, here cast in the demonic role of Don Juan. Most
important of all, Sudeykina, this beautiful and frivolous Petersburg
'doll', who receives her guests in bed in a room full of birds, is Akhmatova's 'double'. As this personal tragedy unfolds, however, the 'non-
calendar, True Twentieth Century' is already approaching along the
legendary banks of the Neva river.

The second part of the poem, 'Tails' (the other side of the coin), is in
a sense Akhmatova's poetic apology. It starts off with an ironical description of the editor's reaction to this poem:

> My editor was not satisfied,
> Swore he was busy and sick,
> Hid his telephone number
> And muttered 'Three themes at once!
> Reading the last sentence,
> You don't know who loves whom,
>
> Who met whom when or why,
> Who died and who remained alive,
> Who is the author and who the hero
> And why today we need these thoughts
> About the poet and some sort of
> Host of spectres.'
>
> (II.122–3)

Akhmatova goes on to explain how she wrote the poem and to trace her
path through shameful silence to the 'other side of Hell' until she
stumbled miraculously on a means of escape from an impossible situation: the 'invisible ink', the 'mirror letter' mentioned earlier. This is
linked with the revival of the *Poema* which is at once her poem and the
Romantic poem of European literature, whose existence is independent
of the poet. Just as her Muse is the same as the one who visited Dante, so
the *Poema* is known to Byron ('George') and Shelley. This frivolous

---

* Sudeykina took over the role of Putanitsa ('the confuser') in the play *Putanitsa or
the Year 1840*, by Yury Belyaev, when the actress Vadimova who had opened in the
role fell ill.[32]

lady who drops a lace handkerchief and languidly half closes her eyes is subservient to no one, least of all to the poet. When threatened with the Star Chamber and chased to the attic or told to behave, she answers:

> 'I'm not that English lady,
> And certainly not Clara Gazul,
> I have no pedigree at all
> Except from fable, from the sun.
> July brought me along itself.
>
> And as for your double-sided fame
> That's lain in the ditch for twenty years,
> I won't serve it in any way.
> We will feast together again,
> And your wicked midnight will
> Be repaid with my royal kiss.'
>
> (II.127–8)

The last part of the poem, 'Epilogue', is dedicated to the city of Leningrad under siege. It is here that Akhmatova records her recognition in exile that she and her city are inseparable. It is also here that she recognizes that in her homelessness she is one with all exiles.

Korney Chukovsky, who in 1964 published a useful article which can serve as an introduction to the *Poema*,[33] considered that the hero of Akhmatova's hero-less poem was none other than Time itself. But if Akhmatova is recreating time past, summoning up from their graves the friends of her youth, it is because she is looking for a solution to what she calls the riddle of her life. She prefaces 'Tails' with the quotation 'My future is in my past', and in '1913', as the harlequinade passes, says:

> As the future sees into the past
> So in the future the past decays,
> Fearful festival of dead leaves.
>
> (II.107)

On the literal level the theme of the poem would certainly seem to be what time or history did to a specific group of people, mainly poets, the friends of Akhmatova's 'hot youth', people who include the person she was then and to whom she refers as her 'doubles'. But even to penetrate thus far we have actively to participate with the poet in recreating time past. She describes the moon 'growing cold over the Silver Century', the winter of 1913 when

> Christmas time was warmed by bonfires,
> Carriages slipped and fell from bridges,
> The whole mournful city was swimming
> To a destination unknown to all,
> With or against the Neva's current,
> As long as it was away from its graves.
>
> (II.117)

She recalls Pavlova ('our incomprehensible swan', II.112), Meyerhold, Chaliapin. Most important, she manages to evoke the mood of the era which was to end so abruptly and completely with the beginning of the war.

> How comically soon is the denouement:
> Punch's mask peeps out from behind the screen,
> Round the bonfires the coachmen dance for warmth
> The black and yellow standard hangs over the palace.
> Everyone who has to be is in his place;
> From the Summer Gardens wafts the smell of the fifth act,
> A ghost from the hell of Tsushima passes
> And a drunken sailor is singing.
>
> (II.113)

The stage is set, both for the private drama of the young man's suicide and also for the cataclysmic events of the 'True Twentieth Century'.

At no point does Akhmatova simply offer us material for our passive reception. The beauty of the words and the extraordinary power of the poem's rhythm force us to study its 'code': find out who the people actually were to whom it is dedicated, consider the significance of its many epigraphs, follow up its oblique references. What we discover is that the activities described in the first part, '1913', stand in contrast to all that happened later. For this was the last year when the activities of individuals seemed to have meaning as such, while after, from 1914, the 'True Twentieth Century' slowly invaded the life of everyone. The blockade of Leningrad was perhaps the culmination of this invasion. If in 'Epilogue' Akhmatova can become the voice of Leningrad, it is because during the war the suffering of this particular group of people once close to her had finally merged completely with the greater collective suffering of the besieged city.

To understand the riddle of her existence Akhmatova is doing what she has always done—using the raw material of her own life: friends, places she had known, historic events in which she had taken part—but doing it on a much larger scale. In choosing to have the New Year revellers act out the tragic suicide of a young poet and to link him with another close friend, Mandel'shtam, who was to live to be a poet of the 'True

Twentieth Century' and to die tragically in one of its camps, she is examining the Poet's role and hers in particular. Knyazev in 1913 could still choose to die and this was a personal matter. The poets of the 'True Twentieth Century', caught up in the madness and suffering of their country, no longer had this choice—that is if they chose to die it could no longer be of merely personal significance. Unwittingly they had found themselves to be either their country's 'voice' or its 'silence'. Yet they would not have exchanged their harsh and bitter lives for other 'ordinary' ones despite all their suffering.

Thus Akhmatova could say of Knyazev that she pitied him. And this pity is not only because he committed suicide as a young man, but because he thus failed to play the extraordinary role awaiting those poets who lived on:

> How terrible was the poet's fate,
> Silly boy: he chose it himself—
> He could not bear the first insults,
> He did not know on what threshold
> He was standing and what path
> Was opening out before his gaze . . .
>   (II.120)

The third dedication to Isaiah Berlin underlines this widening of the poet's role after 1914 and it would seem to be him that the poet is awaiting on the eve of 1941 when the shades from the past come instead to haunt her.

In the second and third parts of the poem, however, Akhmatova describes the cost of having lived on. In 'Tails' she describes that shameful silence that was yet inevitable because it was the 'enemy' who wanted her to break it:

> Just ask my contemporaries:
> Camp women, prison women, martyrs*
> And we will tell you of numb terror,
> Of raising children for execution
> At the block, or back to the wall,
> Of raising children for the prisons.

* In Russian the line reads: 'Katorzhanok, stopyatnits, plennits.' About the word 'stopyatnitsa' N. Mandel'shtam writes: 'Permission was given to reside no closer than one hundred and five vyorsts from the capitals and all the places the railway reached in this zone were absolutely packed with people who had been in the camps and with exiles. The local people called them "one hundred vyorsters" (*stovyorstniki*) and the women, more precisely "one hundred and fivers" (*stopyatnitsy*). The second expression reminded them of the martyr, Paraskeva-Pyatnitsa, as well as of the distance. I told Anna Andreevna of the expression and it found its way into the *Poema.*' (*Vospominaniya*, New York, 1970, p. 313.)
Most of the above is left out in the translation, *Hope Against Hope.*

Pressing our blue lips together
We, who are like crazed Hecubas,
Like Cassandras from Chukhlomy,
Thunder out in silent chorus
(We, who are crowned with shame for ever)
We've crossed Hell to the other side . . .[34]

In 'Epilogue' it is Leningrad–Petersburg, the city once cursed by
Eudoxia, wife of Peter the Great, the city of Dostoyevsky, that becomes
the hero of the poem. In its crucifixion at the time of the blockade
Akhmatova found the symbol for all that she had meant by the 'True
Twentieth Century'. Just as her role as a poet had ceased to be something of solely individual significance, so individual suffering had become one with the suffering of the city which now reached its apex as
bombed from above its citizens slowly died of cold and starvation. The
horrors of the war were, however, faced collectively, not singly as during
the Terror. Only when this had happened and the ghastly drama of the
century had passed the point of the imaginable and Akhmatova herself
was exiled from her city, was she able to draw together all the threads
and become not the shameful silence but the voice of her age, of her city,
of those who stayed and of its exiles in New York, Tashkent, and
Siberia. She was part of it:

Our separation is illusion:
You and I cannot be parted,
My shadow is on your walls,
My reflection, in your canals,
The sound of my steps in the Hermitage halls
Where I wandered with my love,
And in the old Volkov Field,
Where my tears can freely flow
Over the silent communal graves.

(II.131)

Akhmatova has discovered she has little in common with the ghosts of
1913 or the person she was then. What she shares with them is the suffering that followed; the fear too terrible to be remembered in which they
lived; the imprisonments, interrogations, and deaths in Siberia; the
'bitter air of exile' that tastes of poisoned wine; the silence of the communal graves of Leningrad. And in this contrast between the world of
1913 and the 'True Twentieth Century' she finds her reward, for,
despite everything, the world she lost in 1914 was incredibly poorer than
the one she gained and the poet and person she was then little by comparison with what she has become.

Émigrés to whom the setting of '1913' was familiar, have found it difficult to judge the importance of the second and third parts of the poem, and fully to take in Akhmatova's clear rejection of the person she had been to them long ago, the author of *Rosary*:

> I don't wish to meet again
> Till the plains of Jehosaphat
> The person that I was then
> Wearing jewellery of black agate.
> (II.106)

And her contemporaries, although fascinated by her ability to recreate the atmosphere of their youth, were confused and even upset at the way she 'uses' her friends.* They found it difficult enough to see Ol'ga Sudeykina or Aleksandr Blok, for example, as symbolic images of the period as well as the individuals they had known, let alone to cope with the overlapping image of Knyazev–Mandel'shtam, or the strange role of the 'guest from the future' and the idea that Akhmatova and Isaiah Berlin had together 'confused the Twentieth Century'.

It would have been interesting to hear Sudeykina's opinion about her role in the 'Poem without a Hero', for much of it was written during her lifetime, although Akhmatova treated her as if long dead. Curiously enough, Sudeykina figures in another poem, Kuz'min's 'The Trout Breaks the Ice', which Akhmatova must have known because she borrowed a copy of it from Chukovskaya shortly before she recited the first lines of what was to become 'Poem without a Hero' to her in Fontannyy Dom before the war. The remarkable rhythm of Akhmatova's poem is close to that of a section, 'The Second Blow', of Kuz'min's poem, in which not only do we find Knyazev and Sudeykina, but the former comes to tea with other people already dead (including 'Mister Dorian'), suggesting Akhmatova's visitation on the eve of 1941 by the New Year's mummers of 1913. Perhaps it was Kuz'min's description of Ol'ga Sudeykina† sitting in a box at the theatre that made it possible for

* In 1965 Akhmatova wrote about this: 'You cannot imagine how many wild, absurd, and funny judgements this "Petersburg Tale" gave birth to. Strange though it may seem, my contemporaries were its harshest critics and their complaints were formulated by Kh. [possibly Nikolay Khardzhiev] in Tashkent when he said I was paying off some old accounts with the period (the 1910s) and with people who were already dead or could not answer back. To those who did not know certain facts about Petersburg at that time, the poem would be incomprehensible and uninteresting. Others, especially women, considered that the "Poem without a Hero" was a betrayal of some sort of former "ideal" and what's worse, the rejection of my old poems from *Rosary* which they "so loved".' (II.98)

†The connection between the *Poema* and 'The Trout Breaks the Ice' was noted after Akhmatova's death, in an article by Roman Timenchik.[35] Lidiya Chukovskaya does not agree that the beautiful woman in Kuz'min's poem is Sudeykina.

Akhmatova to realize a link between life and art that she had previously grasped only semi-consciously:

> A beauty from a Bryullov canvas.
> That kind of woman lives in novels
> And can be met with on the screen . . .
> People steal for them, commit crimes,
> Lie in wait for them in carriages
> Go and poison themselves in attics.

In 'Tails' (II.126) Akhmatova anticipated an accusation of plagiarism, and indeed the *Poema* is saturated with quotations and allusions to the work of other poets, some of whom, like Blok and Mandel'shtam, also play a part in the poem.* In the first dedication, to Knyazev and Mandel'shtam, Akhmatova writes: 'and as I did not have enough paper, I wrote on your rough draft. And here one of those words came through . . .' (II.101).

In the 'Poem without a Hero' Akhmatova seems to have gained conscious control over a world of symbol and allegory shared by all poets and in which they too play out their symbolic roles. Thus she becomes able to take their words and re-use them: sometimes it seems her poem could be taken as an answer to all those literary statements which have concerned her, while at other times, as she suggests, their voices seem to mingle with her own as her verse echoes theirs. But most important of all is the way in which she not only sees the friends of her youth as 'natural symbols'—much as Dante had seen his contemporaries in the *Divina Commedia*†—but also as playing roles in an allegorical masque, linked with characters from fiction, mythology, history, and fairy tale until what she has created is a series of psychological types connecting literature, allegory, and symbol with life. Among the revellers are Sancho Panzas and Don Quixotes, Faust, Don Juan, Thomas Glahn, and Dorian Gray. Once her contemporaries and the heroes of literature and antiquity and the folk tale have been connected, there is no longer any sharp distinction between literature and life. People become symbols and symbols become people. Their interchangeability depends not upon some imaginary link, but upon Akhmatova's insight that Mandel'shtam

---

* 'It's a strange thing,' Akhmatova said to Chukovskaya in December 1955, 'very strange. I always wrote my poems by myself. But the *Poema* was different. I wrote the whole of it as if in chorus with others prompting.' (*Pamyati A. Akhmatovoy*, p. 174.)

† It was probably due to Dante more than to anyone else that Akhmatova was able to look back in this way at the period of her youth. In the late twenties and thirties when she had been trying to understand more deeply what it meant to be a poet, she had turned to Dante as well as to Pushkin. She had read the *Divina Commedia* with Mandel'shtam; her close friend Mikhail Lozinsky had translated it into Russian; the same Muse that had dictated the 'Inferno' to Dante visited her sleepless nights.

and Knyazev were in a sense the same type, in sharp contrast with Blok; that she and Sudeykina were doubles. We have come into the world of the dream:

> But in the dream it seemed all the time
> As if I were writing a libretto for someone
> And from the music there was no retreat.
> And, after all, a dream *is* something,
> 'O soft embalmer', 'The Blue Bird',
> The parapet at Elsinore.
>
> (II.123)

Having understood on one level that she and her contemporaries were playing out their roles on a stage set for the coming destruction of their world in 1914, as she probes deeper into the reason for it all Akhmatova comes to questions of fate, of guilt, and of the understanding of what is outside the normal structure of our lives. The criss-crossing of time, the mingling of dream and reality, which at first confuse, are seen to be an important device freeing us from the bonds of ordinary time and space. From besieged Leningrad we look back to 1913 and forward to 1946 and to 1956, the tenth anniversary of a visit that not only 'confused the Twentieth Century', but for which the poet had to pay in terms of private suffering—a visit that was like the gift of myrrh brought to a queen on Epiphany:

> For you I had to pay
> Cash down
> Walked with a gun at my back
> Ten years,
> Not daring to glance
> Left or right
> And behind me came rustling
> Ill fame.
>
> (II.131)

The question of guilt varies according to the point of view. On one level Sudeykina is guilty for her indifference to the young cornet's suffering; on another it is inevitable that, she being who she is, this should be so. What has to be paid for has to be paid for. To her friend the poet says:

> 'Do not be angry with me, darling,
> That I must even touch on this:
> I'm punishing myself, not you.
> The account will be settled all the same—'
>
> (II.112)

and then later:

> I'm not marking houses with crosses,
> Just come bravely out to meet me—
> *Your horoscope was cast long ago . . .*
> (II.116)

Knyazev's words 'I am ready for death' (II.109), exactly those used by Mandel'shtam to Akhmatova in Moscow in 1934, seem to echo the finality of a predestined fate. In answer to the poet out of the darkness come the words:

> There is no death—we all know that,
> It is stale to say it again,
> But let them explain to me what is—
> (II.109)

The three heroes described to her editor: the poet disguised as a striped milestone, the sinister Don Juan connected with Blok, and the poet who only lived to be twenty, seem at once guilty and yet guiltless. 'Sins did not suit poets' (II.108), Akhmatova writes, using the past tense as if now perhaps things have changed. The question as to how it has happened that she is the only one left alive leads on to a further one. Why has this happened? To be free of sins like the poet-lawmakers of 1913 does not mean freedom from conscience. She has no sympathy for those who do not 'cry with me over the dead, or know what conscience means and why it exists' (II.124).

Constantly we return to the same point: the role of the poet in the 'True Twentieth Century' and of Akhmatova in particular is self-vindicating. The poet-lawmaker, guiltless on one level, bearing the guilt of others on another, is the creator or tool of the thing that can overcome death, the Word. It is this that makes a poet's silence something shameful, what earns Akhmatova's departing shade a bunch of lilac from the hands of an unknown man in the future. It is as a poet that she conquers space and time, understands her contemporaries, shares the world of Dante, Byron, Pushkin, Cervantes, Oscar Wilde. Formulation is the bridge that crosses time and space and provides the entry into another world in which we walk usually unaware and where we are all living symbols 'manifesting forth a greater reality'.

If a poet can be said to have a philosophy then this poem is Akhmatova's: it is the prism through which she looks forward and back. Whether we consider, as Akhmatova did, that her meeting with Isaiah Berlin had repercussions on a world scale or not; whether we consider that Sudeykina, Knyazev, and Blok were playing the roles she saw them in or not, is unimportant. The completion of a structure large enough to contain all her experience and knowledge allowed her to be at one again with those of her contemporaries from whom she had been estranged, it linked her with other poets through her use of their work in hers, and freed her from the necessity to try and formulate a further explanation of her life. In the 'Poem without a Hero' Akhmatova found that explanation, in an affirmation of the necessity both for things to be as they are and for them to change. In her mirror the 'True Twentieth Century' becomes not unendurable chaotic suffering, but a strange and beautiful, and yet cruel and horrible drama in which not to be able to play a role is seen as a tragedy.

7

In the years after the decree of 1946 the *Poema* lived with Akhmatova, constantly being reworked and changing through a time in which her ability to continue to affirm reality, to accept her fate, was being tested. When, in 1949, on 30 September, Nikolay Punin was arrested, and, on 6 November, Lev Gumilyov, there was little doubt in Akhmatova's mind and in the minds of those close to her that their arrests were due to the same cause: her 1945 meeting with Isaiah Berlin. Lev Gumilyov was to spend almost seven more years in prison camp, and Punin was to die there.

In 1950, fearing for the life of her son, Akhmatova wrote a cycle of poems, 'In Praise of Peace', praising Stalin. Misha Ardov, Nina Ol'shevskaya's young son, was detailed to take them to Aleksey Surkov for publication. Akhmatova's close friends feel that this sacrifice of her pride probably saved her son's life. It was, however, an extremely painful moment for Akhmatova. But just as to have done this earlier would have been a betrayal of herself, not to have done so now would have been vanity. In the cycle of poems she made for Lyova, her son, a sacrifice that she had not been allowed to make before, when as a young woman she had tried to give up being a poet for the sake of a more 'normal' existence as a woman. In doing this now she proved that she had come the whole way, not only as a poet but as a woman. It is a measure of a person's greatness if having sacrificed all to be true to one thing, he can give even that up if it should be necessary. Akhmatova could write praise of Stalin and it became not a sad thing—proof of a proud poet brought finally to heel—but a joke on the very times themselves when a handful of bad poems by someone who had written the poems of 'Requiem' could actually result in saving someone's life. But that it was a sacrifice there is no doubt and for Akhmatova the cycle did not exist as poetry.*

* Akhmatova expressly requested (in my presence) that the cycle be omitted from her collected works. Although it is understandable that the editors of *Soch.* II went against her wishes, it is unfortunate that the story of the cycle's publication (II.392–4) is not given with the poems, or referred to where they occur in the main body of the text (II.147–54).

Meanwhile, practical life was made difficult for Akhmatova in a number of ways. The main part of Fontannyy Dom had been taken over by the Institute for Arctic Studies, and she was no longer allowed to pass through it to her flat, which was in the north wing and only accessible this way, without showing a special pass which she had to have with her at all times. Once she and Nadezhda Mandel'shtam were photographed with a flash bulb on entering the house.* Although in 1949 she was told she would be able to continue living there, in 1952 she was told to leave. Accommodation was finally provided for her and Irina Punina, together with Anya and Punina's second husband, in a flat on Krasnaya Konnitsa (no. 3, flat 4). Here she lived until 1961.

In the early fifties, although Akhmatova's situation was far from pleasant, it had become in many ways more bearable. In 1949 she had received a commission to translate Radishchev's letters from the French and this was followed by one to translate from Victor Hugo. This meant that she had at least semi-official standing as a translator if not as a writer.† Although technically resident in Leningrad, she began to spend more and more time away from the city. Some of this was spent convalescing—her health was as shaky as ever and her heart suffered further from the strain under which she was living. Early in 1952 she was for some time in the Pine Wood Sanatorium of the Academy of Sciences near Moscow. That summer, 'the last Stalin summer', was spent mainly with her friends the Shervinskys at Starki.

In Moscow Akhmatova usually stayed with the Ardovs. Once later she said she had spent twenty years 'secretly' in Moscow. Asked why, she answered, 'Moscow loves me. Leningrad does not love me.' She certainly felt freer and happier in Moscow in the latter part of her life, for a complex of reasons, both personal and to do with the persecution she had gone through.

In Moscow, at the Ardovs' flat in June 1952, Akhmatova was visited by Lidiya Chukovskaya whom she had not seen since Tashkent. Their meetings continued after her return from Starki. Chukovskaya recalls long discussions about Gogol, Tolstoy, and Chekhov. As usual she found Akhmatova's ideas about literature extremely original.‡

Early in 1953 Nikolay Punin died in a prison camp at Abez in Vorkuta

---

*According to N. Mandel'shtam this took place shortly before the 1946 troubles. See *Hope Against Hope*, p. 18, and *Hope Abandoned*, pp. 371–2.

† Chukovskaya mentions how translation impeded Akhmatova's original work (*Pamyati A. Akhmatovoy*, pp. 65, 69, etc.). 'It is the same as eating one's own brain,' she once said.

‡Chukovskaya also recalls Akhmatova saying to her, later in the fifties, of Tolstoy's *Kreutzer Sonata*: 'In the whole of his long life it never once entered his head that the woman isn't only the victim but a partner with an equal stake.'

in Siberia. To this man, towards whom she had had such very mixed
feelings, Akhmatova wrote later:

> And already that heart will not respond
> To my voice that both exults and grieves.
> All is over . . . My song will be borne
> Into the empty night where you are no longer.
> (I.298)

On 5 March 1953, only a few weeks after Punin's death, Stalin died of
a stroke.

In May 1953 Akhmatova received the first real money she had had for
years when a considerable sum was paid to her for her translations of
Victor Hugo.[36] Thanks to this she was able to pay off a considerable debt
to Pasternak* and to fulfil the dream of Alyosha Batalov, Nina Ol'shevskaya's eldest son, in whose little room she usually stayed when she came
to Moscow. He received a Moskvich car (christened 'Bibishka') as her
'rent'. There was also money for a badly needed typewriter for Emma
Gershteyn and a fur coat, gloves, and shoes for Nina Ol'shevskaya.

A letter of 18 April 1954 from Pasternak to the poet in Leningrad
reflected her Moscow friends' impatience that she return once more:

Dear Anna Andreevna!
You are terribly needed here. Why won't you come? I thought you would
come for Easter. Nina Antonovna [Ol'shevskaya] is in despair that she can't
manage to entice you here. Perhaps the thought of Alyosha [Batalov] who is
here now is stopping you? N.A. says he is going away on the twentieth and that
you know this. If you are feeling sad, then set against my mood for two or three
days your gloom will be dispelled. Neygauz† is terribly proud that you were at
his concert and was telling how low he bowed to you from the stage. I can guess
what is keeping you in Leningrad. You probably do not want to miss the
Comédie Française and are waiting for it to arrive. In that case there is little
we can do. But how we all miss you and what a joy it would be to see you soon.[37]

Two years before, in a little poem of dedication, Pasternak had defined
his feelings about Akhmatova:

> To Anna Andreevna Akhmatova,
> To the source of precision and clarity,
> To that which has always strengthened me,
> And given me joy,
> To that which has always seemed close and familiar
> And which is higher and greater than myself.

* N. Mandel'shtam says that after the 1946 resolution, when Akhmatova was visiting
Moscow, Pasternak came to see her and left 100 roubles (1,000 old) under her pillow
(*Hope Abandoned*, p. 375).
† Neygauz, a pianist, was a teacher at the Moscow Conservatory of Music.

But while her friends waited hopefully for her in Moscow, Akhmatova had to undergo in Leningrad one of the most painful experiences connected with the 1946 attack upon her work. It was not, for once, caused by her compatriots, but by the misplaced well-wishing of a group of foreigners who had no real idea of the situation as seen 'from inside'. A delegation from Oxford had asked to meet and talk to the persecuted writers Anna Akhmatova and Mikhail Zoshchenko. Akhmatova received a telephone call from the Writers' Union telling her to attend a meeting with them. The thought of having to go back over the whole matter once more was highly distasteful. She asked hopefully if they couldn't 'send some other old woman along'.

At the meeting she and Zoshchenko sat opposite the group from Oxford. Members of the Writers' Union were present. Akhmatova was asked what she thought of the resolution of the Central Committee. The poet felt very strongly that it was not the business of those who had come from abroad to ask such questions. She answered simply that she agreed with both the resolution and Zhdanov's speech. No more questions were asked.* Zoshchenko was not able to deal with his interlocutors so simply, and began to explain what he really thought, which only made his position worse.

But this was one of the last really unpleasant incidents connected with the 1946 affair. Akhmatova's position as a translator made it possible for her to be treated as a writer even though she had been expelled from the Writers' Union. In May 1955 she was informed that she might be able to have a small *dacha* at the writers' colony in the village of Komarovo near Leningrad. Later that year her name was mentioned in a quite normal fashion, without the usual derogatory epithets, in conjunction with the publication of some of Aleksandr Blok's letters in the magazine *Novyy mir*.[38]

In March 1956, the author Aleksandr Fadeev wrote to the Chief Military Prosecutor, enclosing a letter from Akhmatova about her son. The month before, Nikita Khrushchev had made his famous speech to the Twentieth Party Congress denouncing Stalin. The way lay open for the Thaw, but Lev Gumilyov was still in a labour camp.

'I do not know L. N. Gumilyov,' wrote Fadeev,†

but consider that a speedy consideration of his case is necessary, because the justice of isolating him is considered doubtful by certain prominent members

---

* Evidence of the emotional strain of this encounter can be seen in the fact that eleven years later, in Oxford, Akhmatova suddenly stiffened at the sight of a man who had come to make some recordings for the University of her reading her poetry. She had mistaken him for one of the 1954 delegation.

† Fadeev, who had been Secretary General of the Writers' Union from 1946 to 1953, committed suicide later the same year.

of the scientific and literary intelligentsia. He himself (this is agreed by those who know him and is further confirmed by the enclosed documents by well-known Soviet academics) is a serious scholar and, what is more important, in a sphere which with our present links with the countries of Asia is particularly important—he is a historian and specialist in Eastern affairs.

His mother, A. A. Akhmatova, after the well-known decree of the Communist Party concerning the magazines *Star* and *Leningrad*, has shown herself to be a true Soviet patriot; she has decisively rebuked all attempts of the western press to make use of her name and has printed patriotic Soviet poems in our magazines. At present she has shown herself to be a translator of the highest calibre of the west or of the east. The patriotic and courageous behaviour of this fine, elderly poet after such a stern decree has called forth deep respect in writers' circles and Anna Akhmatova was a delegate to the Second All-Union Conference of Soviet Writers.

In considering the case of L. N. Gumilyov, it must be taken into consideration that, despite the fact that he was only nine years old when his father died, he, Lev Gumilyov, as the son of N. Gumilyov and A. Akhmatova, may have been 'used' by careerists and inimical elements in making what accusations they chose against him. I think that it is perfectly possible for this matter to be considered objectively.[39]

On 14 May Akhmatova arrived at the Ardovs' flat in Moscow for a visit. On the 15th Lev Gumilyov walked in. He had just been released and had not known she was there.

The ordeal was over. But for Akhmatova the price had been very high. In a poem written in the 1930s, 'In Imitation of the Armenian', she comes in a dream as a sheep to those who have just eaten, asking them if they had enjoyed the meal they had made of her son. In another poem written later she says:

> Everyone has gone and no one has returned.
> Only, true to the promise of love,
> You, my last one, only you glanced back
> To see the sky now full of blood.
> The house was cursed, the deed was also,
> The sound of the song more tender in vain
> And I did not even dare lift my eyes
> Before the full horror of my fate.
> They sullied the word most pure,
> The sacred word was trampled on
> That I should wash the blood-stained floor
> With the sick-nurses of thirty-seven.
> They took away my only son,
> Tortured my friends locked in casemates,
> Built round me an invisible fence
> Of their close-netted shadowing.

My award was to be made dumb
As they cursed me so all the world could hear
And gave me slander for my drink
And gave me poison for my food.
They took me out to the very brink
And for some reason left me there—
I will roam the silent squares,
As if I were the town's mad fool.[40]

V

1956–1966

. . . all the same it would be strange to
write a normal review about Akhmatova.
L. NIKULIN, 1961

Opposite: A. Tischler's drawing of
Akhmatova in Tashkent, 1943.
Overleaf: Akhmatova in 1966. *Facing page:* Iosif Brodsky and Anatoly
Nayman at Komarovo; the woods
at Komarovo; Akhmatova's work
table; profile of Akhmatova, 1963.

The last ten years of Akhmatova's life were in many ways a sharp contrast to those that had gone before. With her son at last returned from prison, and herself able again to publish and awarded distinctions abroad, the poet had still to fight illness and the exhaustion of old age as she tried to accomplish all that she felt it was necessary for her to do before death.

Her gift for poetry did not diminish during the last decade of her life, but continued unimpaired to her death. Continually plagued by demands upon her to do more translation, she continued all the while to write. From this final period date some of her most perfect poems— some looking back over the events of her life and to the people she had known, others contemplating life and death. For several years she went on completing and retouching 'Poem without a Hero'. And to the end of her life she wrote poems about love.

At sixty-seven, impressive and stately, Akhmatova was yet someone upon whom her fate seemed to rest lightly and who was grateful at last to have reached the stage where she was loved, by some at least, as a person, not only as a poet. And yet the inspiration for most of her late poetry comes from those special relationships she had always been able to form and which had sustained her throughout the difficult times of her life—relationships which she described as outside ordinary time and which depended upon the depth of meetings rather than on their frequency or the length of time she had known the person.

In the summer of 1956, while she was staying with the Ardovs in Moscow after Lev Gumilyov's release, Isaiah Berlin who was on a visit to Russia telephoned to ask her if they could meet. Akhmatova refused, terrified that it might result in the re-arrest of her son. Their conversation and the present impossibility of meeting brought back vividly to Akhmatova their meeting in 1946. This time, however, their only contact must be a 'non-meeting'. In the beautiful cycle 'The Wild Rose Comes into Bloom', dedicated to Berlin, this meeting which never took place, 'crying round the corner', is seen to have given Akhmatova strength to face whatever life has left in store for her:

> I walked as though beneath the sea . . .
> The fragrance of the wild rose
> Was so sweet it turned into words
> And I was ready then to meet
> The final, highest, wave of fate.
>
> (I.291–2)

'The Wild Rose Comes into Bloom' contains thirteen poems written in 1946, 1957, and 1963, and a final four-line poem written in Rome in 1964, in which the poet compares her turbulent age with that of the Roman Emperor Vespasian:

> And people will think of this time
> As they do of Vespasian's age,
> And it was in fact just a wound
> And a little cloud of torture over it.
>
> (I.295)

This last touch emphasizes once more how strongly Akhmatova felt that her meeting with Berlin had brought them both out of the personal into the world of history. The paradoxical fact that this meeting had caused most of her subsequent troubles, yet at the same time had given her strength to survive them, seemed to her to reflect the peculiarities of her fate and her ability to triumph over them.

Although some of the poems in the cycle date from after 1946, Akhmatova subtitles it 'From a Burnt Notebook'.* As her meetings are outside the bonds of the ordinary, so even her poems in the notebook seem to have a life which is more than just physical and she talks to them as to a friend:

> How you implored me, wanted to go on living,
> How frightened of the caustic flame you were!
> Then suddenly your body gave a quiver
> And, as it flew away, your voice cursed me.
> And all at once the pines began to whisper,
> Reflecting in the depths of moon-filled water.
> While round the fire, spring's most sacred spirits
> Already had begun their dance of mourning.
>
> (I.289)

In this cycle more clearly than anywhere else is described the kind of spiritual relationship which was the sustaining factor in Akhmatova's life. For these are more than just poems concerning a particular person, they are about the very immortal quality of those meetings which paradoxically makes it unnecessary for them to recur. It is as if Akhmatova has distilled some elixir out of ordinary life without which it would have been unbearable. The people who assisted in this process may or may not have been aware of what she was to make of their brief meetings. The poems here form part of the larger group which includes the poems to Anrep in *White Flock*, the poem to Czapski written in memory of

---

* It is possible that the subtitle refers to a notebook also containing poems dedicated in 1944 to Garshin, which Akhmatova said she had burnt.

their meeting in Tashkent, and the love poems Akhmatova wrote at the very end of her life, particularly the cycle 'Midnight Poems', when she knew that soon she would die. They belong to that world described in the 'Poem without a Hero' in which she and her city Leningrad remain inseparable despite exile and death and which stands in contrast to the world of everyday occurrence.

In a poem telling of a 'non-meeting' Akhmatova tries to formulate its quality, forcing language to describe the indescribable often by stating what it is not, recalling Mandel'shtam's battles to tell of the non-formulated world:

> Of a non-meeting full of secrets
> The desolate splendours,
> The unspoken sentences,
> The words silent.
> Glances that never crossed
> Don't know where to lie,
> Only tears are happy
> That they can flow long.
> A wild rose near Moscow
> Alas! Why here . . .
> And all this is what they'll call
> Immortal love.
>
> (I.290)

It is the very fact that this meeting is a 'non-meeting' and that this does not matter, which proves to her that she has won over her fate.

In this world set in contrast to that of everyday, the dream once more plays an important role. For here meetings denied in waking time can take place:

> Black and lasting separation
> I share equally with you.
> Why weep? Instead give me your hand,
> Promise you'll come in a dream again.
> Like two mountains which stand apart
> On earth we have no meeting place.
> Only if you would just send me a word
> At midnight sometime through the stars.
>
> (I.289)

Dream is also the vehicle of prophecy. In 1916, awaiting her 'true lover', Akhmatova had written how everything had promised him to her: 'the sky's edge of dim vermilion, the sweet dream just before Christmas, the many sounds of the Easter wind . . .' (I.157). Now she writes:

That dream was prophetic or maybe it was not . . .
Mars glowed among the heavenly constellations;
It became scarlet, sparkling and ominous,
And it was that night that I dreamt you'd come.

It could be sensed in everything. . . . In a Bach Chaconne
And in the roses blooming for no reason
And in the sound of the village church bell
Over the blackness of ploughed-up earth.

(I.291)

Even reality has taken on the quality of a dream:

It's as though I live in a stranger's house
I've dreamt about, where I may have died,
Where, in the languor of evening, the mirrors
Keep something peculiar to themselves.

(I.293)

The meeting in 1946 which was to be the 'precursor to all the troubles' had taken place despite everything that should have made it impossible. For this kind of relationship exists despite, not because of, ordinary life, and later, despite death. It can only take place through an ability to rise above so-called reality and realize the impossible among people who are 'souls at the edge of the world' (I.290). The ordinary stands in sharp contrast:

We met in an unbelievable year,
When the world's strength had already been drained,
Everything was in mourning, drooping from misfortune,
And the only thing that was fresh were graves.
The Neva embankment without lights was dark as pitch
And the night stood thick around like a wall . . .
That was when my voice called you!
I didn't know what I was doing myself.

(I.292)

And yet Akhmatova remains, as always, honest. She knows that there is nothing even this visitor can do to help her cope with ordinary life. Only she can live that out. 'Away with time and away with space . . . But even you cannot help me' (I.289), she writes. Nor does she admit to being the person her visitor imagines: 'You dreamt me up', she says. 'There is no person like that in the world. There couldn't be' (I.294). The emphasis on the sacred quality of this kind of meeting is also found in the poem written to Czapski in 1959. There the meeting seems to have an eternal existence of its own and can return in a dream. It too takes place in the dark and, similar to the 'non-meeting', is a 'meeting-parting'. As the two of them walk through Tashkent at night they seem to be walking in another dimension.

2

Akhmatova watched with a certain amount of ironic detachment her rehabilitation by Soviet critics, as slowly but surely she was reinstated as a poet considered suitable for the Soviet reader. Although Stalin died in 1953 it was only after Khrushchev's speech in 1956 to the Twentieth Party Congress that things really began to change. Akhmatova's name appeared in print a few times that year not as a target of abuse, if not of praise either, and her book of translations of Korean poetry,[1] published in 1956, was reviewed favourably even though one notice, according to the poet, did not mention her name as translator.

Poems by Akhmatova were printed that year in the two 'Thaw' anthologies, *Literary Moscow* and *Poetry Day*,[2] and the debate began as to the value of her poetry. Akhmatova's poem, 'Memory has three epochs', published in *Poetry Day*, left the reviewer V. Ognyov completely unmoved: 'How much is there here of that weak-souled, cold, devastating lack of faith in life, in its creative force,' he says.[3]

In a review of *Literary Moscow* E. Serebrovskaya contrasts Tsvetaeva, who emigrated, with Akhmatova who did not. The latter, she writes,

was aware of the strong link between her own fate and that of her country. That is why in 1942 during our country's most difficult minutes she was able to write '. . . But we will preserve the Russian tongue, the mighty Russian word . . .' 'My land', wrote Akhmatova and in this lies her power. And it was not anyone else's prompting but her own civic pride that taught her how to answer those unceremonious bourgeois guests who came to Leningrad in search of newspaper sensation shortly after the decree of the Central Committee about *Star* and *Leningrad*.* What in fact is patriotism? For some it is only a word of foreign origin, for others it is the basis of their whole life, their main emotion on which all others depend in some way or other.[4]

It was in fact because of her patriotism and loyalty to her country that Akhmatova had won the respect of many writers who did not like her poetry, or at least felt it to be alien in spirit to the literature they hoped to see created.

In May 1957 Akhmatova's name was again linked with that of Tsvetaeva in the reports on the Third Plenum of the Governing Body of the Union of Writers. A. Dymshits expressed his concern lest certain poets

* Serebrovskaya is, of course, referring to the visit of the group from Oxford mentioned above.

be overpopularized in an attempt to restore them to their historic places in Russian literature. Tsvetaeva, he felt, was being made too much of. 'What are we to do then with Akhmatova?' he asks. 'Why if you compare her with Tsvetaeva, she's far above her.'[5]

In 1958 the first post-Stalin collection of Akhmatova's poems appeared. *Poems*,[6] a slim volume also containing a number of translations, was published in an edition of 25,000. In a short review of this collection in the *Literary Gazette*, L. Ozerov seems to be discussing more of Akhmatova's work than appears in the volume, although he is careful to draw his examples from poems in it with which even the sternest and most dogmatic Soviet critic would be hard put to find fault. He draws attention to the fact that in her poetry of the last fifteen years, especially in her love poetry, Akhmatova had been holding what he calls 'a conversation with a contemporary'. Her poems are, he says, 'lyrics of the conquest of loneliness, confessions of a daughter of the century who understood that solitude and isolation forces the artist into an impossibly difficult role.' Akhmatova has, he insists, never departed from her own poetics and intonation, but like all true creators, continually moved on along her own way. 'It is possible to speak of the complexity and difficulties of her long creative path', writes Ozerov, 'but not to point out that it is a path is impossible. The poetess made every effort to find a way to her new reader. This path leads in the direction of the present day and not away from it.'[7]

Akhmatova's poems were again printed in newspapers and journals— 4 in 1956, 21 in 1957, 18 in 1960, 8 in 1962, 12 in 1963, 24 in 1964, 7 in 1965—even though there was a certain amount of confusion behind the scenes as to what her official position really was.* The 1958 collection was followed three years later by *Poems 1909–1960*, a much fuller collection edited and with an afterword by A. Surkov, published in the Poets' Library series in an edition of 50,000.[8]

In contrast to Ozerov, who had trod delicately, suggesting that a deeper interpretation of Akhmatova's work was perfectly in tune with the present climate of opinion, Surkov created what could be called a recipe for rehabilitation, superimposing upon the poet's life and work a pattern which he considered would make it possible for her to be fully

---

* I witnessed an example of this in 1964. Akhmatova was due to have some poems published in *Novyy mir*. The editor dealing with the matter had to be away unexpectedly and returned to discover that the proofs had been put aside, as someone else on the staff of the journal had panicked. The censor had not even seen them. I was present when the editor came to apologize to Akhmatova, saying that she had taken the proofs to the censor immediately on her return, who said their being put aside was complete nonsense. *Novyy mir* then arranged to publish a larger selection of poems in the following issue to make up for this embarrassing incident.

accepted as a Soviet poet, much as the monks of the early Church created the official lives of the saints. Surkov emphasizes Akhmatova's difficulties in coming to terms with the revolution, which he says was hardly reflected in her work. She was, he says, saved from the fate of emigration by her strong feelings of patriotism (he quotes 'I heard a voice'*). Suddenly, however, he continues, her poems began to sound in unison with the post-revolutionary world. Following years of extreme difficulty and tragedy, during the war she began to look at the world around her with new eyes (he quotes 'Courage'). Her love for her country which had saved her from emigration now brought her into the rank of Soviet poets. Akhmatova's war poems, he says, though sometimes expressing a mother's grief, also express anger and a conviction of the inevitability of victory, not hopelessness and despair.

Over the 1946 incident Surkov passes uncomfortably quickly: 'In the first year after the war,' he writes, 'a note of weariness and despondency appeared in the poetry of certain Soviet poets. This also affected Akhmatova. In many of her poems a note sounded which was thought to have been dispensed with for ever. In 1946 this tendency received a strong social reprimand.' But this situation, Surkov goes on to say, did not last long and soon the poet was back publishing poems similar to those she had published in the war years (he quotes 'Song of Peace'). The critic's final statement has a ring of irony for those who know the circumstances under which 'Song of Peace'† was written: 'With her poems written in the last few years Anna Akhmatova has taken her own special place in Soviet poetry, a place not bought at the cost of any moral or creative compromises.'‡

Although not all Akhmatova's poetry was considered suitable for immediate publication, in the last few years of her life her path to her readers was no longer officially blocked. Her work was not necessarily appreciated by the die-hard Stalinist critics, but a body of opinion in the literary world supported her and endeavoured to remove whatever obstacles might stand in the way of publication of more and more of her poetry written over many years and hitherto known only from manuscript. Her silence, her refusal to compromise except to save another person, her dignity when abused, her loyalty to her country despite all

* This is the ninth line of the poem 'When in suicidal anguish' (I.378) quoted at p. 47. First the sixth, seventh, and eighth lines were left out (I.185); then it appeared in 1940 in *From Six Books*, and in subsequent collections, with the first eight lines omitted.

† Part of the cycle 'In Praise of Peace'.

‡ N. Mandel'shtam registers in Surkov's favour the fact that he slipped money into her husband's pocket unnoticed once when they were completely penniless (*Hope Against Hope*, p. 302). Akhmatova discovered when he was editing the 1961 collection that he knew all her early poems by heart.

that had happened to her, above all the fact that her poetry had survived
and continued to delight new generations, had made it impossible to
ignore her. 'Criticism has buried her alive more than once,' wrote N.
Rylenkov of Akhmatova in *Poetry Day 1966*, 'as something long ago
part of the past, when she suddenly appeared to a new generation as
their contemporary.'[9] And A. Pavlovsky, re-examining the polemics of
the twenties in a monograph on the poet published in 1966, wrote:
'Akhmatova's love elegy, played on muted strings, should according to
all the laws of logic have been forgotten, have disappeared without
trace. . . . This did not happen.'[10]

'I am easy in my mind now,' said Akhmatova to Nadezhda Mandel'-
shtam in the sixties. 'We have seen how durable poetry is.'[11]

3

In the winter of 1958, while convalescing from one of her heart attacks
at the sanatorium of the Academy of Sciences at Bol'shevo, Akhmatova
began to write her short poetic memoir of Modigliani. She was also busy
trying to help get her son's book on the people of Central Asia published.

At first, Akhmatova had felt only happiness and relief at having her
son back from prison. Before long, however, her joy at his return was
tempered by the difficulties of living in the same place as he. By now a
man in his forties, Lev Gumilyov had spent fourteen years of his life in
camps and prisons because of having had Nikolay Gumilyov and Anna
Akhmatova as parents. He and his mother were in many ways too much
alike to live together in peace. Finally free, he intended to live as he
chose. His mother was deeply hurt at his lack of consideration and as
stubborn as he in her desire to have her own way. Quarrels were frequent
and very bitter. Once after a quarrel Akhmatova had a heart attack.
Finally Lev Gumilyov got accommodation elsewhere. They ceased to
meet. Akhmatova was, however, extremely proud of her son and would
praise him highly as a scholar.

The loss of her son was in some degree made up for by her relationships with young people. Akhmatova was particularly interested in the
generation growing up around her. She noticed that young people with
qualities which in their parents' generation had been very rare, now
seemed to be appearing everywhere. In Moscow, in the noisy Ardov
flat, she enjoyed having 'parties' with the younger generation: Aleksey
Batalov, Misha and Borya Ardov and their friends. Vodka, she said, was
good for people with bad hearts—it enlarged the arteries. When in
Leningrad Akhmatova continued to live in the same flat as the Punins,
and in 1961 they all moved to Lenin Street. Akhmatova was extremely

fond of her step-grandchild, Anya Kaminskaya, who was now following her grandfather and mother by studying to become an art historian; and later of Anya's young husband, Lev Zykov, and his brother Vladimir. She kept Anya's picture pinned up over her bed.

In Leningrad she became particularly close to three young poets: Anatoly Nayman, Iosif Brodsky, and Dmitri Boboshev. Now in these easier times other young poets made pilgrimages to recite their works to her and she recited hers to them. Others came for advice or to ask questions about those who had been alive in the early part of the century or who had died in the purges or the war, people with whom Akhmatova was a living link.* And from all over the Soviet Union came a stream of letters from people thanking her for her poems, thanking her for existing, telling her what she meant to them. For many Akhmatova stood, with Pasternak, as proof that even in the 'True Twentieth Century' it had been possible to keep one's integrity.

At last during these years Akhmatova had a home of her own, at least during the summer months. In the writers' colony at Komarovo in a pine wood a small *dacha* had been built for her, to which she moved each summer as soon as it was warm enough. At her 'cabin', as she called it, she was looked after by Lev Arens and his wife. Arens, the brother of Nikolay Punin's first wife, a delightful old gentleman with a long white beard, would go on his bicycle every day from early summer to swim in the cold Finnish lake nearby.

It was in Komarovo that she usually received foreign visitors, and there, at the *dacha* of Professor Alekseev, in the summer of 1962 she met the American poet, Robert Frost. F. D. Reeve† has described the meeting of the two aged poets:

Akhmatova arrived. She came in a dark dress, a pale lilac shawl over her shoulders, august and dignified with her white hair and deep eyes. She and Frost greeted each other with polite deference. At table Alekseev toasted Frost and then toasted both Akhmatova and Frost, referring to their meeting as one of the great literary events of our time. . . . We sat around the table in the sun-filled dining room, the lunch a seven-course dinner, the conversation turning both to American and English writers and to the Greek and Latin classics, topics on which Akhmatova, Frost, and Alekseev were all extremely well read. Akhmatova, Frost, and Alekseev, some twenty years younger than the other two, were people intellectually of the same generation. Akhmatova

---

* Akhmatova's constant stream of visitors could be exhausting for others. When in the spring of 1962 her friend Lyubov' Bol'shintsova spent a while with the poet at the Writers' Hostel in Komarovo she found the visitors almost more than she could cope with.

† Akhmatova used to refer to Reeve as '*samyy krasivyy amerikanets*'—the handsomest American.

and Frost had both begun to be recognized poets just before the First World War. They both had had long and exceptional careers, bringing them in their different ways, to the same point: each was the leading poet of his country, of a whole national literary culture and tradition. . . .

Akhmatova recited the short poem 'I cry no longer over my affairs' in which she talks of how it hurts her to see other people's lack of success. 'Then,' continues Reeve,

she said in her soft but emotionally strong and expressive voice, a poem which refers to 'four powerful, passionate women from the world's history who directed their passion to serve the integrity of the nation in which they had transcendent faith . . .'* Hearing Akhmatova recite the poem moved us all. The whole group was so caught up in the immediacy of the poem and by the life and understanding which it represented that for a few seconds we were silent, still. The incommunicability of the poem's substance had fallen like a shadow over the room. Frost remembered this, and he remembered Akhmatova's expression, for he commented later how grand she was but how sad she seemed.[12]

Contact with the west was much easier now, and Akhmatova received most of the things published about her abroad through various friends and members of the Writers' Union. Late in life she began to be extremely irritated at some of these publications. Because she had been more or less continually in official disfavour since 1925, her later work had not been considered in detail by serious critics in Russia. Nor had much biographical information been published about her or Gumilyov. But several acquaintances living abroad, taking advantage both of the lack of published material in the Soviet Union about both poets and the émigré conviction that Akhmatova was really 'one of them', had decided to write their memoirs. Although Akhmatova had not believed it would be possible for anyone to take seriously the first of these volumes, Georgy Ivanov's highly fictitious account *Petersburg Winters*,[13] she saw now that unless works of this nature were contradicted, both her poems and those of her first husband were likely to be interpreted in the light of such distorted 'facts'. She was particularly incensed by Georgy Ivanov's description of a poetry reading where Vyacheslav Ivanov was credited with discovering her. In her notebook she recorded what had, according to her, really happened:

In actual fact it was like this. N.S. [Gumilyov], after our return from Paris (summer 1910) took me to V. Ivanov's. He did ask me if I wrote poetry (the three of us were alone in the room), and I read to him 'And when we cursed each other' (1909 Kiev notebook) and something else (probably 'They came

* 'The Last Rose'.

and told me'*) and V. Ivanov said with indifference and irony: 'What pure Romanticism.'

Akhmatova was irritated by the false picture given in these memoirs of her relationship with Gumilyov. She found herself being described as someone who had been madly in love with a husband who thought she should not write poetry and who, after hurting her cruelly, had divorced her. 'Proof' of Gumilyov's attitude towards her as a poet was often drawn from a poem she had written in 1914 where her heroine is told by a friend she meets on the embankment that 'it is absurd for a woman to be a poet' (I.115). Akhmatova pointed out that she was able to talk to her husband over breakfast and did not have to go on to the embankment to do so. The usual assumption, she found, was that all her early poems up to 1918 had been dedicated to Gumilyov. Nothing was known of the fact that for nearly ten years a large proportion of Gumilyov's poems had been dedicated to her.[14] In fact Gumilyov had played a far less significant role in Akhmatova's early poetry than she had done in his, mainly because what for her was the most important part of their relationship took place before their marriage, while the bulk of her mature poetry was written after it.

The memoirs of Sergey Makovsky,[15] the former editor of the magazine *Apollon* in which she had published much of her early verse, were among those which made Akhmatova furious. These had been written in Paris shortly before Makovsky's death and in them he claimed erroneously to have been a close friend. She wrote to Georges Nivat, in whose French translation she first read these memoirs, expressing her displeasure at their content.[16] Nivat answered on 20 July 1963: 'I am very sorry that you were so displeased with Makovsky's article. I certainly understand your reaction if there are so many mistakes. . . .' Akhmatova promised him a letter about the mistakes and Nivat offered to publish it but she never wrote to him again.

Almost equally unpopular with the poet was Gleb Struve's introduction to Volume I of the collected works of Gumilyov published in the United States.[17] Akhmatova considered it commendable that Gumilyov's poems had been republished, but she felt it was farcical to attempt to write about his life on the basis of émigré memoirs, when ample documentation existed in the Soviet Union, no longer cut off, as in previous years, from western scholars. For one thing, an untrue impression was being created, that Gumilyov's poetry had been popular during his lifetime; this gave a false bias, she felt, to the consideration of his work both as a poet and as a critic.

---

* An unpublished poem dedicated to N. Gumilyov, written in 1909.

Thus at the very end of her life Akhmatova, who felt to a degree that knowledge of a poet's private life was not essential to an appreciation of his work, was herself drawn into the stream of memoirists in her recollections of Modigliani and more particularly Mandel'shtam. But while performing what she considered to be her duty to poets dead and now in danger of being misunderstood, such as Gumilyov and Mandel'shtam, and to poets living, such as Nayman and Brodsky and all the others to whom she drew readers' attention in interviews, she also continued to write about the process of writing poetry and the Poet. Sometimes she does so with a touch of ironical humour:

> Do not repeat—your soul is rich—
> The thing that someone said before,
> But who knows, perhaps poetry itself
> Is just one splendid quotation.[18]

Akhmatova's ability not to take her calling too seriously was that of a true professional. It did not mean that she was not aware of its value but rather that she understood it deeply. In a poem in which Alexander the Great demands the destruction of Thebes, she had him add: 'But be sure the Poet's house is not destroyed' (I.325).

In 'The Four of Us', written in 1961, she again emphasized, through epigraphs from Mandel'shtam, Tsvetaeva, and Pasternak, her links with these poets of the 'True Twentieth Century'. At Pasternak's death the year before she had written:

> Yesterday the inimitable voice fell silent
> And he who spoke the language of the groves
> Abandoned us.
> He has turned into a life-giving ear of grain
> Or into the most gentle rain
> Of which he sang.
> And all the flowers growing in this world
> Came into bloom to meet
> This death
> And suddenly it has grown quiet here
> Upon this planet modestly named
> Earth.
>
> (I.322)

The deaths of those few friends who had survived all the rest seemed now almost unreal. In memory of Valeriya Sreznevskaya, with whom as a small child she had played in the garden of their house in Tsarskoe Selo and with whom she had shared some of the worst moments of the darkest years, Akhmatova now wrote:

It barely can be true, for you've been always there;
In the blessed lime trees' shadow; during the blockade;
In hospital, in prison cell and also in that place
Where there are evil birds, lush grass and terrible water.
How everything has changed, but you've been always there
And now it seems as if I have lost half my soul,
The half you were and where somehow I knew the reason
For something most important. Suddenly it's gone . . .
But your ringing voice is calling me from yonder,
Asking me not to grieve, saying to wait for death
As for a miracle. What can I do! I'll try.

(I.329)

During these years Akhmatova seldom looks back, in her shorter poems, or when she does it seems to be more to the days of her early youth in Tsarskoe than to the terrible times that followed. In a poem written in 1958 she talks of being the 'inheritor' of Tsarskoe; elsewhere she recreates the period of the nineties. One poem, a beautiful meditation on death, 'Seaside Sonnet', written in Komarovo, links her end with this beginning:

Here everything will outlive me,
Everything, even the old starling houses
And the air, this air of spring,
Which has completed its sea crossing.

The voice of eternity is calling
With unearthly, irresistible power
And the light moon spills its radiance
Over the cherry tree in blossom.

And it looks so easy to step on
That road, white in the emerald chalice,
Leading I will not say whither . . .

Brighter there among the tree trunks
Looking exactly like the *allée*
By the pond at Tsarskoe.

(I.317–18)

It is mainly in the 'Poem without a Hero' that we find Akhmatova dealing with her relationship with the past. But in one short poem written in 1960, 'Echo', there is a description of that forgetting and yet not forgetting that is part of this, and from the following year date the four lines at the beginning of 'Requiem' in which the poet writes about how she had chosen not to leave her country for 'foreign skies' but to remain

with her people. Time has vindicated her decision to stay. In 'Native
Soil', also written that year, Akhmatova recalls in the epigraph her own
words about her countrymen in 1922: 'But there is no people more tear-
less, prouder or simpler than we' (I.327). This poem is perhaps an answer
to the cycle 'In Praise of Peace', for here she defines her people's feeling
for their native soil as something quite apart from the bombastic slogans
of conventional patriotism:

> We don't wear it in amulets over our hearts,
> We don't sob forth verses about it,
> It does not trouble our bitter sleep
> Or seem like the Land of Promise.
> We don't make of it in our soul
> Something to buy and sell,
> Sick and poor and silent on it
> We don't even call it to mind.
>> Yes, for us it's the dirt on our galoshes,
>> Yes, for us it's the grit on our teeth.
>> And we grind and crumble and crush this dust
>> That's not guilty of anything.
> But we will lie down in it one day
> And become it ourselves so we freely can say
> It is ours.
>
> (I.327)

4

In 1963, 'Requiem' was published in Munich 'without the author's
knowledge or consent'.[19] At the end of that year Akhmatova came to
Moscow to prepare another fuller collection of poems, *The Flight of
Time*. She was also busy translating from Rabindranath Tagore. As
usual she stayed with various friends, moving from one to the other.

On 18 January 1964 in Leningrad her young friend and protégé Iosif
Brodsky stood trial for the crime of not taking regular work and thus
being a 'parasite on the state'. Asked why he had not tried to learn how
to be a poet in some institution of higher learning, Brodsky answered:
'I did not think it was something that could be learnt. . . . I think, it's . . .
from God. . . .'[20] In a farcical second trial on 13 March at which, along
with others, Akhmatova's friend from the years in Tashkent, Professor
Admoni, spoke out courageously on behalf of the young poet, Brodsky
was sentenced to five years' exile with compulsory labour. He was sent
to a village near Arkhangel'sk and for a while was in a bad mental
state.

Akhmatova was deeply distressed at all that had happened to Brodsky.

She persuaded various friends to go and visit him and with other people collected money for things to help make his life more bearable. At the same time she was concerned lest something similar should happen to Anatoly Nayman, who, although officially 'all right' until the summer, as far as working went (he was on a film scenario course in Moscow), would, after that, be in a position as vulnerable as Brodsky's, not being a member of the Writers' Union. In April, partly as a result of the strain he had been under since his friend's arrest, Nayman had a heart attack. Akhmatova had been asked to translate a selection of works by Leopardi. Despite her increasing dislike of doing translations, she agreed on the condition that Nayman, for whose poetry she had the greatest respect, could be her co-translator.

Akhmatova had been awarded an Italian literary prize and was to go to Taormina in Sicily at the end of 1964 to receive it. She finished her memoir of Modigliani and gave it to the Italians to publish in conjunction with her forthcoming visit. There was also talk at the time of her being given the Nobel Prize. In June she left Moscow to celebrate her seventy-fifth birthday in Komarovo. Many of her Moscow friends joined her. It was a beautiful summer, and she took walks in the woods with Nina Ol'shevskaya, an impressive finder of mushrooms, and had bonfires lit during the day, something the poet particularly loved. The occasion was only marred by the absence of Iosif Brodsky and the death, later in the summer, of Valeriya Sreznevskaya. In the autumn Ol'shevskaya, who by comparison with Akhmatova was still quite a young woman, had a stroke. The poet had been hoping that she would travel with her to Italy. Instead when Akhmatova left for Taormina in December she was accompanied by Irina Punina.

It was the first time Akhmatova had been abroad since 1912. In Oxford the following year she described Rome to Isaiah Berlin as a place where the struggle for supremacy between the pagan and Christian worlds was still going on. In Taormina, true to the spirit of western Europe, the award was presented to her by the Italian Minister of Tourism. Akhmatova arrived back in Russia worn out and went to the Writers' Hostel in Komarovo to recuperate. In February she returned again to Moscow—this time as a delegate from Leningrad to the Writers' Congress.

At this time an incident occurred, ironical in the context of Akhmatova's life. A young poet who had copied down one of her poems years before into his notebook, on rediscovering it thought it to be his own. After a few 'improving' alterations he sent it to the magazine *October* which published it. It was immediately picked up and Vasily Zhuravlyov was accused of plagiarism. Poor Zhuravlyov apologized in a letter to

Izvestiya. He was particularly ashamed of having dared to correct the poem.[21]

In a long interview printed in April 1965 in the journal *Literary Questions*,[22] Akhmatova took the occasion to put in a good word for many of her fellow-poets, both of the younger and middle generations, whom she did not feel had had the recognition they deserved.* She made sure Nayman's name was mentioned as co-translator with her of Leopardi. For many years she had been the one isolated and un-recognized; now that she was in a position to help others she never missed a chance.

It was at this time that Akhmatova told Anatoly Nayman one day: 'When I was young I loved architecture and water, now I love music and earth.' In her poetry music is both the comforter and that which leads towards another world:

> And music shared peace with me,
> Most compliant of all companions.
> Often she would lead me out
> To the very edge of my existence.[23]

Now it is death that will cause separation and so even more clearly does the poet define what is not affected by this—the relationship that may not even require a meeting.

'Midnight Poems', a cycle written near the end of Akhmatova's life, stands by itself as a group of love poems. The love sung here is menaced not by some new demand by fate in the form of history or war or revolution, but because it stands in the shadow of death. Ordinary separations foreshadow this inevitable final parting, and so it is the lovers' ability to surmount these that conquers death itself. Separation may in fact be easier to bear than a meeting. And what cannot take place on earth may in music or in the sharing of a dream.

'In 'Midnight Poems' the poet's previous 'true lovers', whose love existed outside time and space, fuse together in the love between her and this, her final lover. It is as if she has found the last piece of the image of her tsarevich shattered so many years before. He is made up of many people who are yet one person—as Mandel'shtam and Knyazev in the 'Poem without a Hero' are two shadows merging together. In the four lines originally prefacing the cycle Akhmatova describes this:

---

* These included Mariya Petrovykh, Tarkovsky, Shefner, Lipkin, Kornilov, Gito-vich, Korzhavin, Samoylov, and Shengeli. Akhmatova also expressed her feeling that the present practice of young poets reading their poems aloud, frequently to large audiences, might easily result in a confusion between good poetry and success on the stage.

> If the pieces of glass
> Which once shattered with a ring
> Had come together again—then this
> Is what would be there.[24]

As before this love has about it nothing earthly. 'What in fact has it to do with us that all will turn to dust', the poet asks (I.304). In a poem called 'Through the Looking Glass' this other world stands in strange and frightening contrast to the ordinary one of the relationship between her lover and his wife:

> The pretty girl is very young
> But she's not of our century,
> We cannot be alone together
> For she will never leave us.
> You move the armchair up for her,
> I generously share my flowers . . .
> What we are doing, we don't know,
> But every second makes it worse.
> Like people who have been in jail
> We each know something terrible
> About the other. We are in
> Hell's circle, or maybe it isn't
> Even us at all.
>
> (I.305)

In this other world the word retains its ultimate importance:

> And then at last you spoke the word out loud,
> And not like some do . . . down upon one knee—
> But like someone who's broken out of jail
> And sees the sacred canopy of the birch
> Through the rainbow of involuntary tears.
>
> (I.305)

In the three poems of Akhmatova's 'Moscow Trefoil', written between 1961 and 1965, we find the poet similarly preoccupied. Once more it is the triumph over parting that is important:

> You will hear thunder and remember me
> And think: she wanted storms . . .
> The streak of sky will be harshly crimson
> And your heart, as then, will be on fire.
>
> And it will happen thus on that Moscow day
> When for ever I leave the city
> And hasten to those heights I have longed for
> Leaving my shadow still among you.
>
> (I.298)

Akhmatova had lived out her life nearly to the end. Although it had not been easy, she had tried when she could to keep true to the harsh laws imposed upon her by the role she had been asked to play during her time 'as a guest on earth' (I.191). Now, tired, she asked just to be able to enjoy the gift of life itself in all its wonder and beauty:

> Bowing to the ground with Morozova,
> Dancing with Herod's step-daugher,
> Flying up with the smoke from Dido's pyre
> To burn again with Joan at the stake—
>
> Lord, can't You see I'm weary
> Of this rising and dying and living!
> Take it all, just let me once more
> Sense the freshness of this scarlet rose.
>
> (I.328–9)

Her way back to the enjoyment of the scarlet rose for its own sake, to Paradise, had been through bearing the consequences of the Fall. She had been to the 'other side' of Hell and returned with this boon: the key to the Garden of Eden.

With the 'Poem without a Hero' Akhmatova had in a sense completed her poetic pilgrimage. Working from the position of the Acmeist through life and experience into a deeper understanding of the language of the living symbol, she could not only set her early life in the larger context of her country's fate, but also in that of world literature. She quoted with pride the critic Viktor Zhirmunsky's statement that the 'Poem without a Hero' was the fulfillment of the Symbolists' dream— what they had preached in theory, but had never been able to realize in their creative work. In her search for her beginning in her end, Akhmatova began to rediscover Gumilyov's poems written for her and about her as a young girl and woman and realized that he, the Symbolist creator of the theories of Acmeism, had not only been concerned with the very same problem, but had also reflected in his poetry an image of her as that very living symbol which it had taken her nearly her whole life to accept and to formulate for herself.

Looking back, Akhmatova could see how Gumilyov long ago had 'recognized' her when she herself had little more than a confused presentiment of what her life would bring. Others had too, but she had found their recognition and praise like some nightmare of happiness:

> And the more they sang my praises,
> The more delight they took in me,
> The more terrible it was to live in the world,
> The more strongly I longed to awake.[25]

In turning to re-examine the poems that Gumilyov had dedicated to her in her youth, Akhmatova realized that his violent love for her had been for that tsaritsa, that person from the 'other world' which she had tried to deny in favour of 'real life'. It was this that had forced her young lover to attempt suicide when she had refused to marry him and yet caused him to flee physical bondage as soon as she had become his wife. In Gumilyov's description of her as a young woman, Akhmatova found her final heroine, the expression of all that she had been and become and of all a woman could be and could become. From Mary, from the women of the Old Testament, Akhmatova reached back to the earliest expression of woman at the roots of Judaeo–Christian culture, to Eve.

In his poem of 1908, 'The Dream of Adam', Gumilyov had pictured his Eve as both wanton and saint,

> Sometimes a moon-girl sometimes an earth-girl
> For ever a stranger, eternally strange.[26]

Perhaps this strangeness which had been at the root of the failure of the marriage of these two poets* could also now be seen as having been the actual cause of Gumilyov's passion. In 1921, probably with him in mind, Akhmatova had written:

> He told me that I had no rivals,
> I was for him no earthly woman
> But the soothing light of winter sunshine,
> The wild song of his native land.
>
> (I.212)

With these poems in mind we may turn to 'From the Tragedy *Prologue, or a Dream within a Dream*', published in 1964, which seems to contain the poet's final word.† It takes the form of a dialogue between 'he' and 'she', followed by two sections: 'Heard from Afar' and 'Blind Man's Song'.[27] In Gumilyov's poem quoted above, the life of the Fall is seen as a dream from which Adam awakens at the end in Paradise. Akhmatova too had spoken of her longing to awake from the dream of her life, in 'And I had no rosy childhood'; but in 'Poem without a Hero' and elsewhere the dream was the vehicle of meetings from that other world of spiritual love. Perhaps this is the dream within the other dream

---

* Akhmatova paused in the middle of a conversation with me in 1964 to recite this poem; commenting on the relationship between her and Gumilyov, she pointed to the word 'strange' (*chuzhaya*) and said: 'That was the whole tragedy.'

† The poem takes its title from a part of the play 'E nu ma elish', written in Tashkent and later destroyed. According to V. V. Ivanov,[28] the 1964 poem is not at all like the play. N. Mandel'shtam describes the latter in *Hope Abandoned* (pp. 350–7); she did not like the former (ibid., pp. 362–3).

of life, as at night sometimes we know within one dream that we are dreaming.

In the first part of 'From the Tragedy *Prologue* . . .', 'She speaks', the poet talks of her homelessness. 'No one in the world', she says, 'lacks shelter more, is more homeless than I.' She is, she continues, the cruel voice coming through the ghostly dawn beyond the grave. He to whom she is talking has penetrated her last dream. She asks him to curse once more the ordinary beauty of everyday life that she has defended:

> Curse once more the creak of the bucket at the well,
> The whisper of the pines, the black croaking of the crows,
> The earth upon which my feet have walked,
> The yellow star that shone in at my window,
> What I was then and what I have become
> And the hour when I said to you
> That I thought you had appeared in my dream.
>
> (I.300)

Yet within this cursing she recognizes something else, 'words tauter and more intoxicating than an embrace, more tender than the first grass of spring.' Perhaps what lies behind the denial of the beauty of ordinary life once more concerns that other love—the love by which Gumilyov had been obsessed for the tsaritsa, the witch, the fallen Eve, not for the flesh-and-blood woman he had made his wife. When 'he' speaks we recognize the voice of fallen Adam speaking to fallen Eve:

> Though you be three times more charming than the angels,
> Though you be the sister of the willows by the river,
> All the same with my song I will kill you,
> I will kill you without spilling your blood upon the earth.
> I will not touch you with my hand,
> Without one look I will cease to love you,
> But with your unbelievable groan
> I will finally quench my thirst.
>
> (I.301)

This battle is not of the physical world but of that other world of the dream, of poetry, of the spirit. Here Adam is bound for eternity to Eve and can only return to Paradise through her redemption, for it was through her that he left it. It is this that makes it impossible for him to live with her or without her. She remains a stranger, yet only by knowing her and becoming one with her once more, can he be freed. He must kill her and yet it is she in her non-fallen state who can save him from herself. He continues:

Because it was with you that I divided
The primeval darkness of Creation,
It does not matter whom you may have married,
For—I now no longer seek to hide it—
Our criminal marriage has continued.
Each of us has hidden it from the other,
From other people, from God, from the end.
I recall the place in Dante's circle
Like the laurel of a victory wreath.
I've seen you, the new bride in the temple,
Seen you burnt alive upon a bonfire,
Stoned to death; a toy in a demon's game.
From everywhere your eyes have looked out at me;
From everywhere you have called out to me
You've given your soul to me and your body
You've given back to God in sacrifice.
You and only you have been my fate,
For you I was ready to do all.
Oh God, the things we've done together
There, in the final layer of dreams.
Apparently I was your murderer,
Or were you mine? I remember nothing . . .
As a Roman, Scythian, man of Byzantium
I have been a witness to your shame.

(I.301–2)

Adam's fidelity has been the enchanted drink that has supported Eve. Whatever the horrors of the world, a Paradise in which there is no consciousness is something nauseating. Eve is led by a beloved hand through the dream of life, the stormy centuries, carrying Cain the murderer in her womb. We are reminded of the poet's words about herself: 'You will hear thunder and remember me / And think: she wanted storms . . .'

'Heard from Afar' tells us again of her who has known the 'horror and the honour of life beyond the grave' (I.303). To pronounce her name is 'like death' and Akhmatova's final advice to whoever sets off on this journey comes from the mouth of a blind man:

Don't take yourself by the hand . . .
Don't lead yourself over the river . . .
Don't poke a finger at yourself . . .
Don't tell stories about yourself . . .
You go on, go on and will stumble.

(I.303)

Life is to be lived but to be human is also to be blind. Ivanushka of the old fairy tale never reached his goal through intelligence or cunning, but through simple faith and goodness. The return to Paradise is through the rediscovery of faith. It is this that makes it possible to accept this blindness willingly as part of the human condition. But Paradise unsinned in and therefore without value is sickening. Only those who have completed the journey through the stormy centuries and have seen and known all can return to it. Then the memory that all is not without purpose is the sustaining factor. Faith does not ask one to take oneself in hand or to criticize oneself. It supports one as one walks blind, knowing one will stumble. . . .

5

In the spring of 1965, preparations were made for Akhmatova to go to England to receive the honorary D.Litt. to be conferred upon her by the University of Oxford. In May she was once again in Moscow. Told by her doctors (as she had been before her trip to Italy) that it would be risky for her to travel by plane, she decided to brave the journey by train and boat. With her she planned to take Anya Kaminskaya. At the Writers' Union, owing to a bureaucratic error, they were given one ticket via Ostend and one via the Hook of Holland. Kaminskaya arrived with the correct tickets only minutes before the train was due to leave. The next train would have made them too late for the Oxford ceremony.

Akhmatova later described how they travelled across 'a Europe in flower'. She joked that it was just a trip to Komarovo from Moscow via Oxford. Travelling was not easy for her. The rocking of the train made her feel sick and owing to her weight all movement was an effort. She was extremely nervous at the prospect of it all, frightened that her health would not be up to it. But there was never any question of not going. Despite the fact that she had an entry visa, the immigration officer at Dover quibbled as to why she had not brought with her a letter of invitation as well. By the time she reached Victoria she was utterly exhausted, but walked with the dignity of a queen up the platform as cameras flashed around her.

In London, nearly twenty years after their fateful meeting in 1946, Akhmatova again met Isaiah Berlin. Once when they were alone together she said: 'Before I was well known in Russia, but not abroad. All this— Italy, Oxford . . . Are you responsible?' Berlin, somewhat surprised at Akhmatova's idea of his powers, answered that he was not.

At Oxford in the Sheldonian Theatre, Akhmatova, wearing the scarlet gown of a Doctor of Literature, heard the Public Orator in his address in Latin compare her to Sappho. With her in the Sheldonian stood another poet, Siegfried Sassoon. Afterwards, sitting in her room in the Randolph Hotel surrounded by flowers, the poet received her visitors one or two at a time, as was her custom in Moscow and Komarovo—an occupation known as 'Akhmatovka' by her close friends. The entire lounge of the hotel was filled with Russian-speaking visitors. From all over the world they had come to see her honoured and if possible to see her personally: friends who had left Russia in the twenties or earlier; students of her poetry or of poets who had been her contemporaries; Russians for whom she was both a living connection with their youth and with a country to which they had never returned.

While in Oxford, Akhmatova was handed a telegram from Switzerland. It was addressed to 'Anna Akhmatova c/o Cambridge University, Oxford, England' and read:

Sir if Russian poetessa Anna Akhmatova guest of another University please forward text. Congratulations for today's award. I am the son of your brother Andrew and Maria Smuntzyla [Zmunchilla]. Mother spoke often about you. I would very much like to meet you. Cable time and place or come to me if possible . . . Love and expectation.   ANDREW GORENKO

Akhmatova sent a telegram back asking this nephew whom she had never seen to come to London. There they met, incredibly alike in looks, yet speaking together in French, as Gorenko spoke no Russian.

In London Akhmatova also saw her old friend Salomea Halpern, now living in a little house in Chelsea. Never able to cook herself, the poet was amazed at her friend's prowess. 'Salomea, when did you learn to cook?' she asked in amazement. Her friend answered that she had devoted her energies to cooking when she felt she had been a Muse for long enough. Akhmatova had described Salomea in her youth (then Princess Andronikova) in a poem she dedicated to her in 1940:

> Always more elegant than all the rest,
> Taller, with higher colour in your cheeks,
> Why do you float up from days gone by
> And does my grasping memory wave before my eyes
> Your transparent profile against the carriage glass?
> How we quarrelled whether you were an angel or a bird!
> A poet called you Solominka—a straw.
> Through the black lashes of your Georgian eyes
> A gentle light looked evenly on all.
> O Shade, forgive me, but the bright day,
> Flaubert, sleeplessness, the late lilac's bloom
> Reminded me of you, a beauty of 1913,
> And of your cloudless and indifferent day . . .
> And yet such memories don't suit me, Shade.

                                        (I.259)

Still beautiful so many years later, Salomea insisted that there had never been any reason to quarrel over whether she was angel or bird. She was both.

Not wanting to go through the tiring business of changing from train to boat and back again in order to cross the Channel, Akhmatova decided to take the wagon-lit to Paris and travel to Moscow from there. She stayed in Paris for a few days. London she had found an unexpected surprise; Paris she now found in many ways disappointing. No longer was it the capital more elegant than all others where she had sat with Modigliani on a park bench in the rain reciting Verlaine. People in the streets might have been in London, Rome, or even Moscow. Where she saw elegance she found it rather pretentious. Paris was also changing colour—it was being cleaned.

But if in England she had met again Salomea Halpern, Yury Annenkov (who came over from Paris), and friends of a later vintage such as Isaiah Berlin, in Paris she was to meet again many people whom she had known during her early married life and whom she had last seen when they were all young and beautiful. Now they came to see her one after the other, old, frail, deaf, incredibly changed: Ol'ga Obolenskaya,* Dmitri Bouchène, S. R. Ernst, bringing back memories of summers spent at Slepnyovo; Georgy Adamovich and Boris Anrep. Anrep hesitated about coming to see the poet, feeling that he had changed beyond recognition. But he was one of the people Akhmatova was most concerned to see. She too, after all, had changed greatly from the skinny tall girl of long ago with her striking looks and dark fringe. Anrep said on going into the room he felt as if he were being ushered into the presence of Catherine the Great. Akhmatova on the one hand appreciated the comedy of the situation. On the other she seemed to be acting out a part of high symbolic significance, felt by all those around her, but which they would have been hard put to explain in words. In Paris as well as friends from her youth Akhmatova also met again Joseph Czapski, whom she had not seen since Tashkent.

Back in Russia later that summer, in an interview with Misha Ardov which was printed in various papers, Akhmatova spoke about this trip to western Europe, comparing it to journeys she had made abroad early in the century. She was asked her impressions of Britain. 'It seemed to me that the English are far nicer and more hospitable at home than abroad,' she answered. 'All their Victorian primness seems to have gone—a fact which is, after all, not surprising; sixty years have passed.' Akhmatova took the chance in the interview to speak out on behalf of people whom she felt deserved more attention in the literary world, this time in the

* Formerly Kuz'mina-Karavaeva.

field of translation. She also repeated something which those close to her had heard her say many times: 'I have been witness to the literary life of half a century. I have never seen anything like the young people of today—kind, clever, brave. . . .'*

That summer as usual was spent at Komarovo. The weather was bad and the poet felt tired, unable to force herself to go out for walks. Nayman, with whom she had been working on the Leopardi translations, went off on holiday to Estonia. But as usual she was visited by a stream of people, young and old. Often Viktor Zhirmunsky, the critic and academician, now also living in Komarovo, would drop in. And almost every day would bring more letters from her devotees all over the country. There was again talk of her being awarded the Nobel Prize. People brought Akhmatova cuttings from papers abroad in which her candidacy was discussed. There was also talk of her making another trip to Paris that autumn, but this would have been as part of a delegation of Soviet poets. Akhmatova refused. It was not the way she wanted to go and anyway her trips abroad had tired her.

In the early autumn Akhmatova left Komarovo and went to Moscow. Shortly after her arrival she had another heart attack. At first she was extremely ill, but not for long. However, they kept her in hospital for some time. There she had good news: Iosif Brodsky had been released. But into the Party hospital where she lay people also brought bad news, in whispers, of the trial of two authors accused of the crime of sending their works to be published abroad under pseudonyms: Andrey Sinyavsky and Yuly Daniel. At one time she had a message that her son was coming to see her. When it turned out that he had changed his mind, his mother with typical generosity of spirit decided that he had not come because he had known that the excitement of meeting him again after so long would be bad for her.

At the end of February 1966 she left the hospital for the Ardov flat. From there she and Nina Ol'shevskaya, who was still recovering from the stroke she had had the year before, were to go together to stay at a convalescent home not far from Moscow. They went there by car. Akhmatova had been reading the scenario of the film *Last Year in Marienbad*,† and the convalescent home as soon as she saw it was dubbed Marienbad.

On the morning of Saturday, 5 March, only the second or third day

---

* According to Akhmatova, her young friend Ardov did not know quite what to ask her, so she provided both the questions and the answers. She gave me a cutting from *Smena*, a Leningrad evening paper, but I have not traced the date.

† I had sent this to her because it reminded me of certain things in 'Poem without a Hero' and 'From the Tragedy *Prologue* . . .'.

after they had arrived, Ol'shevskaya left the room for a few minutes. It was breakfast time. Akhmatova complained that the tea was cold. Ol'shevskaya on returning was warned not to go into the room. A few minutes later, after a short battle for life, Akhmatova died. Ironically it was the anniversary of the death of Stalin, a day that she always liked to celebrate.

The body of the poet was taken to the morgue in Moscow before being flown back to Leningrad. The morgue, oddly enough, was in the hospital in the old Sheremetev Palace, and like Fontannyy Dom the building bore a coat of arms with the motto used in 'Poem without a Hero': *Deus conservat omnia*. Preparations for Akhmatova's funeral were confused and delayed because of the week-end and the fact that the Tuesday following, 8 March, was a national holiday, International Women's Day. When Iosif Brodsky and Vladimir Zykov went to the graveyard at Komarovo to choose a place for the poet's burial, the gravediggers were drunk.

Akhmatova had asked that her funeral take place in the Nikol'sky Sobor in Leningrad. Here she lay in state in the side part of the church, while hundreds of people came to see her—some for the last time, but for many of the young, for both the first and the last. The official part of her funeral at the Writers' Union, in another Sheremetev palace bearing the motto *Deus conservat omnia*, was reported in the press.* It was however the sight of the crowds of people pressing into the church and overflowing into the streets that remained in the minds of those present. On the way to Komarovo a stop was made for a few minutes' silence outside Fontannyy Dom. Then those who were close to the poet made their way to the village by train or car to see her body finally laid to rest in the cemetery surrounded by pine forest on the way to the lake.

6

From a life seemingly nonsensical, cruel, and purposeless Akhmatova had made sense, seen purpose, rediscovered faith. In the west it took the explosion of the atomic bomb at the end of the Second World War at least partly to shake people into the realization that the values which resulted in the bomb's use were liable to lead to the destruction of the species; in the Soviet Union the self-destroying mad paranoia of the years of the Terror had already torn away from many the final scraps of comforting illusion, leaving them face to face with their own naked

* The Leningrad studio of Documentary Films filmed the entire funeral. Shortly afterwards the film was confiscated and the people who had made it demoted.

fear and inability to cope with a world that had gone mad. In 1939 Akhmatova had written:

> All has grown confused for ever,
> I cannot now discern
> Who is man and who is beast . . .
>
> (I.364)

Values previously taken for granted were tested and many cast aside as inadequate or simply irrelevant. The individual, forced in on himself, discovered that he could trust only the very thing his culture had taught him to fear as unsound—the dictates of his private conscience, his own feelings of right and wrong. Officially proclaimed values had too often been proven lies, the word, misused in propaganda and slogan, the vehicle for public falsehood—something which became more and more obvious as the façade crumbled showing what was beneath. Pompous bureaucratic jargon revealed its empty uselessness when compared with what it described—the real loss experienced in the heart. Yet set against the lying, inaccurate, shoddy printed words, covering up what was really happening as millions of people were shot, went mad, or were deported to rot for years in Siberian camps, there stood these few slender poems, written by a woman who recognized the importance of using the word to define accurately; to record; to communicate the truth of one individual's experience to another. In them she traced the path of her own suffering without melodrama and without self-pity. In doing so she also recorded what had happened to her—her rediscovery of the meaning of life at the very foot of the Cross.

From childhood Akhmatova had had a strange intuition of her future which had made her refer to happiness as torture. But her premonitions had given her no easy free passage through life. Instead she walked blind, and little by little learnt to recognize that if she was led it was by her Muse. Yet in her attempts at understanding herself in her early love poetry, we see how torn she was between her loyalty to that Muse and her desire to be a woman to a man. Slowly she had to learn that only by being faithful to her Muse would she find the strength to live. At the same time she began to realize the ultimate importance of the kind of relationship between individuals that survives parting and death and to understand that it was this love for which she searched:

> I do not have to stand waiting
> By the hateful window,
> Suffer wearisome meetings,
> For love's thirst is slaked.
>
> (I.112)

In many encounters during her life, Akhmatova tested again this spiritual love for the drowned tsarevich of her youth. Because of this, ordinary marriage became for her a lie and any home but a caricature of the word. Her true home was Paradise; her father's garden; Kitezh—the world outside time which she had left to embark upon this journey through space and time: life, and to which she could only return when she had accomplished what she had set out to do. Her link with this other world was in poetry, music: man's formulations in art, or further, man's incarnation of the word by acting out his part in the symbolic drama of life.

The poet was herself only the instrument of a higher power: the 'lines that are simply dictated / Appear in the snow-white notebook' (I.251). But as for the Lady of Shalott weaving her web as she watches reflections in her mirror, this very homelessness on earth was the curse the poet had to bear, preventing her from living a 'real' life here on earth as others do. When she turned away to look straight at life, the mirror broke and although she did not die like the Lady of Shalott, her curse passed to 'confuse the century'. Art was the mirror that made sense out of an otherwise senseless existence, the link between worlds that could reveal the greater purpose underlying apparent chaos, making it possible to bear life's suffering. It was also a means by which the drama of life could be completed, Paradise returned to earth. The poetic word lived longer than other things and could cross barriers of time and space. Because through the Muse the poet was granted vision, by its formulation she became a lawmaker. Not to fulfil this sacred function, to be silent, was something shameful.

But not only was Akhmatova forced to live a looking-glass life because of her function as a poet, she was also fated to sing of loss, of tragedy, of partings. That she was able to triumph over a life characterized by the recurrent loss of all that seemingly made it worth living, was because she had discovered the illusory nature of separation. It was this understanding that there is a place outside history where meetings can take place, which made it possible for her finally to accept the details of her own biography without bitterness, and even to express her honour, if not her thanks, at having been assigned a role of such magnitude.

Akhmatova recognized that for those who are able to fathom its significance, the Crucifixion is the most splendid moment of the drama of life. This was no approbation of man's cruelty and blindness, but rather an understanding that the Cross is at the turning-point of man's journey and marks the beginning of his return to Paradise. Although she knew that her origin lay in Kitezh, in some point outside time, and that she would one day return there, this did not mean the rejection of life on earth. On the contrary, she knew that it is *this* drama that *is* life, and if at times it seems purposeless, this is because of the limitation of our vision. To live 'real' life we must accept blindness as a necessary condition. To live is to stumble and if we are to be seers it can only be at the cost of this 'reality'. But like sleeping Eve we can have faith that we are being led through the stormy centuries by the hand of the beloved.

True Paradise is not, however, that nauseating Eden of innocence constantly threatened by knowledge. It is to be reached by passing the way of the Cross and to which one returns willingly having been to the other side of Hell and seen all there is to see and known all there is to know. To understand what man is and should be, it is necessary to know what he is not. The poetic word was therefore not only to be used to reveal the underlying purpose in the world, but also to reflect man's own inhumanity to himself, presenting him with his true image in degradation. No one must be allowed to forget the queues of women made numb by fear and grief outside the prisons in Leningrad, or the sound of the old woman's cry that was like that of a wounded beast.

And because Akhmatova had the courage to face and formulate man's inhumanity, she was able by that very act to restore his humanity to him. By accepting Eve's fall as a necessary part of God's purpose, and seeing that Magdalene the prostitute fulfilled as important a role as her opposite, the Virgin Mother, she restored value to this life on earth—something which the Christian message had too often lost through teaching us to distrust our deepest desires and to despise the flesh. The nineteenth-century image of woman had become a split caricature, with the fainting, delicate angel-wife contrasted with the lusty whore. By reuniting this split within herself, Akhmatova made woman once more into a whole being, finding again the sacramental value of desire and placing it firmly within God's purpose.

The function of the poet and lawmaker, of the one who has had to journey to the other side of Hell, closely resembles that of the folk-tale hero who 'performs the three-fold task of liberating those in bondage, transmitting treasures from the other world after his discovery of the elixir of life, and of perfecting himself.'[29] And it is only after the journey to the Other World has been completed, that the hero's 'real' life in this world begins: the 'happily ever after' of the end of the tale.

Akhmatova made no call to others to follow the example of her life. On the contrary:

> Could the words of Beatrice have created Dante
> Or Laura have extolled the flame of love?
> I taught women how to use their voice . . .
> But Lord, how do I make them stop!
>
> (I.254)

Her life had not been an ordinary life. This was both its splendour and its tragedy. It had had a singular purpose and this when carried out had no need to be repeated.

> But I warn you
> That I am living for the last time.
>   (I.260)

———

Forty days after the funeral, according to Orthodox custom, a service usually takes place at the grave of the deceased. In Akhmatova's case this was not possible because it was the week after Easter. Instead some close friends and members of her family went to Komarovo to lay flowers on the grave. It was a freak late winter and fresh snow lay thick on the road to the graveyard. In it were footsteps showing that someone had gone ahead of them. When they arrived at the grave, the person standing by it turned and went away. No one knew her. She was one of those anonymous Russian women in a grey scarf and quilted jacket.

SELECT BIBLIOGRAPHY

The following list includes the principal sources cited or quoted in this book (referred to hereafter in shortened form), together with certain other works which have provided background material but are not quoted directly. All other works on which I have drawn are cited in full in the Reference Notes at p. 202. For a complete bibliographical guide to works by Akhmatova and to the literature concerning her life and work, see Part II of my thesis, *Anna Akhmatova: Life and Work. An Interpretation in the Light of Biographical Material* (University of London, 1971).   A.H.

I   WORKS BY ANNA AKHMATOVA

Vecher (Evening) (St. Petersburg, 1912)
    later included in:
Chyotki (Rosary) (St. Petersburg, 1914); 9th enlarged ed. (Petersburg–Berlin, 1923)
Belaya staya (White Flock) (Petrograd, 1917); 2nd ed. (1918), 3rd ed. (1922), and 4th ed. (Petersburg–Berlin, 1923) contain changes and additions
Podorozhnik (Plantain) (Petrograd, 1921)
    later included in:
Anno Domini MCMXXI (Petersburg, 1921) (on frontispiece, 1922); 2nd enlarged ed. (Petersburg–Berlin, 1923)

Selections and collections subject to severe censorship:
Iz shesti knig (From Six Books) (Leningrad, 1940)
Izbrannoe (Selected Poems) (Tashkent, 1943)
Izbrannye stikhi (Selected Poems) (Moscow, 1946)
Stikhotvoreniya 1909–1945 (Poems 1909–1945) (Moscow–Leningrad, 1946); almost completely destroyed
Stikhotvoreniya (Poems) (Moscow, 1958)
Stikhotvoreniya 1909–1960 (Poems 1909–1960) (Moscow, 1961)

Subject to less severe censorship:
Beg vremeni (The Flight of Time) (Moscow–Leningrad, 1965)

Books first published abroad:
Requiem (Munich, 1963)

Posthumous collections:
Sochineniya (Works), 2 vols., ed. G. P. Struve and B. A. Filippov (Munich–Washington, D.C.: vol. I, 2nd ed., corrected, 1967; vol. II, 1968)
Tale without a Hero and Twenty-two Poems by Anna Akhmatova, ed. J. van der Eng-Liedmeier and K. Verheul (The Hague, 1973)

Uncollected poems and prose in periodicals published before 1971:
'Vse ushli, i nikto ne vernulsya' (poem), *Vestnik russkogo studentcheskogo khristyanskogo dvizheniya* (Paris-New York),·no. 93 (Mar. 1969), 65
'Stikhi raznykh let', *Novyy mir*, v, 1969, 53–8

'Pushkin i nevskoe vzmor'e', *Literaturnaya gazeta*, 4 June 1969, 7
'Stikhi', *Yunost'*, VI, 1969, 66–7
'Esli by bryzgi stekla' (introductory lines to 'Polnochnye stikhi'), *Novyy mir*, VI, 1969, 243
'D'yavol ne vydal, mne vsyo udalos'–' and 'Zabudut:—vot chem udivili' (poems), *Prostor* (Alma Ata), VIII, 1969, 91
'Iz neizdannogo Anny Akhmatovoy', *Zvezda*, VIII (Aug. 1969), 164
'Neizdannye zametki Anny Akhmatovoy o Pushkine', *Voprosy literatury*, I, 1970, 158–206
'Stikhi', *Prostor*, II, 1971, 101

II OTHER WORKS

G. Baran, 'Pis'ma A. A. Akhmatovoy k N. I. Khardzhievu', *Russian Literature* (The Hague–Paris), 7/8, 1974, 5
K. Chukovsky, 'Akhmatova i Mayakovsky', *Dom iskusstv*, I, 1921, 23–42.
—— "Anna Akhmatova', *Sovremenniki* (Moscow, 1967), 298–320
L. Chukovskaya, *Going Under* (London, 1972)
J. Czapski, *Terre inhumaine* (Paris, 1949)
E. Dobin, *Poeziya Anny Akhmatovoy* (Leningrad, 1968)
S. Driver, *Anna Akhmatova* (New York, 1972)
B. Eykhenbaum, *Anna Akhmatova* (Petrograd, 1923)
——'Ob A. A. Akhmatovoy', *Den' poezii* (Leningrad, 1967), 169–71 (written 1946)
——'Roman lirika', *Vestnik literatury*, VI–VII, 1921, 8–9
A. Gizetti, 'Tri dushi', *Ezhemesyachnyy zhurnal*, XII, 1915, 154–60
S. Karlinsky, *Marina Cvetaeva—Her Life and Art* (Berkeley and Los Angeles, Calif., 1966)
N. Mandelstam, *Hope Against Hope* (London and New York, 1971)—The Russian edition, *Vospominaniya* (New York, 1970), contains some passages not translated in the English version.
——*Hope Abandoned* (London and New York, 1974)
O. Mandel'shtam, 'Utro Akmeizma', *Sirena* (Voronezh), no. 4–5 (30 Jan. 1919), 69–74; reprinted in his *Sobranie sochineniy*, vol. III (New York, 1969), 31–5
N. Nedobrovo, 'Anna Akhmatova', *Russkaya mysl'*, VII, 1915, Part II, 50–68
L. Nikulin, 'Put' poeta', *Literaturnaya gazeta*, no. 153 (28 Dec. 1961), 3
L. Ozerov, 'Melodika. Plastika. Mysl' ', *Literaturnaya Rossiya*, no. 34 (86) (21 Aug. 1964), 14–15
—— 'Stikhotvoreniya Anny Akhmatovoy', *Literaturnaya gazeta*, no. 78 (4044) (23 June 1959), 3
Pamyati A. Akhmatovoy (Paris, 1974)—Contains 'Stikhotvoreniya' and 'Moya biografiya i dva pis'ma' by Akhmatova (pp. 9–28, 33–5), and L. Chukovskaya, 'Iz knigi "Zapiski ob Anne Akhmatovoy"' (pp. 45–198).
A. Pavlovsky, *Anna Akhmatova* (Leningrad, 1966)
—— 'Anna Akhmatova', *Poety-sovremenniki* (Moscow–Leningrad, 1966), 103–40
—— 'Vysokiy vecher', *Den' poezii* (Moscow, 1964), 23–6
J. Rude, 'Poème sans héros', in A. Akhmatova, *Poème sans Héros* (Paris, 1970), 9–41
——*Anna Akhmatova* (Paris, 1968)

N. Struve, 'Neizdannaya stranitsa iz vospominaniy A. A. Akhmatovoy ob O. E. Mandel'shtam', *Vestnik russkogo studentcheskogo khristyanskogo dvizheniya* (Paris–New York), no. 93 (Mar. 1969), 66–7

G. Superfin and R. Timenchik, 'Pis'ma A. A. Akhmatovoy k V. Ya. Bryusovu', *Zapiski otdela rukopisey Vsesoyuznoy biblioteki im. V. I. Lenina*, 33, 1972; reprinted with an introduction by G. Nivat in *Cahiers du Monde russe et soviétique*, XV (1–2) (janv.–juin 1974), 183–200

A. Surkov, 'Anna Akhmatova' in A. Akhmatova, *Stikhotvoreniya 1909–1960* (Moscow, 1961), 294–305

R. Timenchik, 'Akhmatova i Pushkin. Zametki k teme', *Uchonye zapiski Latviyskogo gosudarstvennogo universiteta imeni Petra Stuchki* (Riga), tom 215, Pushkinskiy sbornik, Vypusk 2, 1974, 32–55

——'Zametki ob akmeizme', *Russian Literature* (The Hague–Paris), 7/8, 1974, 23–46

T. Tsiv'yan, 'Antichnye geroini—zerkala Akhmatovoy', ibid,. 103–19

J. van der Eng-Liedmeier, 'Poema bez geroya', in *Tale without a Hero and Twenty-two Poems by Anna Akhmatova*, ed. van der Eng-Liedmeier and K. Verheul (The Hague, 1973), 63–113

K. Verheul, 'Public Themes in the Poetry of Anna Akhmatova', *Russian Literature* (The Hague), I, 1971, 73, reprinted in *Tale without a Hero and Twenty-two Poems by Anna Akhmatova*, op. cit., 9–48

——*The Theme of Time in the Poetry of Anna Akhmatova* (The Hague–Paris, 1971)

V. Vinogradov, *O poezii Anny Akhmatovoy* (Leningrad, 1925)

——'O simvolike A. A. Akhmatovoy', *Literaturnaya mysl'*, I, 1922; reprinted with the above in V. Vinogradov, *Anna Akhmatova* (Munich, 1970)

V. Zhirmunsky, 'Anna Akhmatova i Aleksandr Blok', *Russkaya literatura*, III, 1970, 57–82

——'Dva napravleniya sovremennoy liriki', *Zhizn' iskusstva*, nos. 339–40 (Jan. 1920), 1–2; reprinted in V. Zhirmunsky, *Voprosy teorii literatury* (Leningrad, 1928), 182–9 (now available in a photo-print, The Hague, 1962)

——'O tvorchestve Anny Akhmatovoy', *Novyy mir*, VI, 1969, 240–51

——'Preodolevshie simvolizm', *Russkaya mysl'*, XII, 1916, part II, 32–41; reprinted in *Voprosy teorii literatury*, op. cit., 278–321 (special section on Akhmatova, pp. 289–302)

REFERENCE NOTES

I: 1889–1914

[1] 'I nikakogo rozovogo detstva', *Novyy mir*, V, 1969, 54.
[2] N. Gumilyov, *Sobranie sochineniy*, 2 vols. (Washington, D.C.: vol. I, 1962; vol. II, 1964), I.38; I.29; I.150.
[3] *Dafnis i Khloe*, V. Sreznevskaya's memoir of Akhmatova and Gumilyov which the poet asked her to write to counteract fanciful accounts of their relationship then (1964) being published in the west, remained unpublished at Sreznevskaya's death in that same year. The present whereabouts of the blue exercise book containing the memoir are unknown to me.
[4] A. Gizetti, 'Tri dushi', *Ezhemesyachnyy zhurnal*, XII, 1915, 154–60.
[5] 'I nikakogo rozovogo detstva', op. cit.
[6] N. Gumilyov, op. cit., I.135–6.
[7] Ibid., I.56–7.
[8] Ibid., II.30.
[9] Ibid., I.166–7.
[10] Ibid., II.127.
[11] Ibid., I.179–80.
[12] See O. Mandel'shtam, 'Shutochnoe', *Vozdushnye puti* (New York), III, 1963, 24–5, and N. Gumilyov, 'Al'bomnye i shutochnye stikhotvoreniya', *Sobranie sochineniy*, II.200–3.
[13] A. Blok, *Sobranie sochineniy*, vol. VII (Moscow, 1963), 75–6.
[14] N. Gumilyov, 'Nasledie simvolizma i akmeizm'; S. Gorodetsky, 'Nekotorye techeniya v sovremennoy russkoy poezii', in *Apollon*, I, 1913, 42–50.
[15] V. Pyast, *Vstrechi* (Moscow, 1929), 155.
[16] N. Mandelstam, *Hope Against Hope*, 263.
[17] V. Vinogradov, *O poezii Anny Akhmatovoy*, 56.
[18] 'Neizdannye zametki Anny Akhmatovoy o Pushkine', *Voprosy literatury*, I, 1970, 160, 182.
[19] For the Russian version of this letter see A. Haight, 'Letters from Nikolay Gumilyov to Anna Akhmatova 1912–1915', *Slavonic and East European Review* (London), L, no. 118 (Jan. 1972), 100–6. Copies of the six letters published here were given to me by Akhmatova in 1965. She told me that the original letters had been stolen from her, and that she knew who had them but did not want to make a fuss for fear they might be destroyed.
[20] *Dafnis i Khloe*. See n. 3 above.
[21] N. Gumilyov, op. cit., I.150.
[22] Ibid., I.165–6.
[23] Ibid., I.160–1.
[24] Ibid., I.163.
[25] 'Letters from Nikolay Gumilyov to Anna Akhmatova', op. cit., 102.
[26] Ibid., 103.
[27] N. Gumilyov, op. cit., I.223.

²⁸ B. Livshits, *Polutoraglazyy strelets* (Leningrad, 1923), 261–3.
²⁹ V. Pyast, op. cit., 155.
³⁰ Y. Annenkov, 'Anna Akhmatova', *Vozrozhdenie* (Paris), no. 129 (Sept. 1962), 43.
³¹ Extracts from letters of Nedobrovo to the late Boris Anrep were given to me by Akhmatova. Anrep had given the original letters to Gleb Struve, who made copies of these extracts for Akhmatova in London in 1965.
³² O. Mandel'shtam, 'Kak chornyy angel na snegu', *Vozdushnye puti*, III, 1963, 14.
³³ Cf. A. Akhmatova, *Sochineniya*, II.381.
³⁴ M. Tsvetaeva, *Vyorsty I* (Moscow, 1922), 75–86.
³⁵ 'Snova so mnoy ty. O mal'chik igrushka', *Yunost'*, VI, 1969, 66.

II: 1914–1924

¹ 'I nikakogo rozovogo detstva', op. cit.
² 'Letters from Nikolay Gumilyov to Anna Akhmatova 1912–1915', op. cit., 103.
³ R. Ivanov-Razumnik, 'Zhemanitsy', *Zavety*, V, 1914, part III, 47–51.
⁴ D. Usov, 'Anna Akhmatova. *Chyotki*', *Zhatva*, VI–VII, 1915, 468–71; A. Gizetti, 'Tri dushi', op. cit.; N. Nedobrovo, 'Anna Akhmatova', *Russkaya mysl'*, VII, 1915, part II, 50–68.
⁵ N. Gumilyov, '*Chyotki*. Anna Akhmatova', *Apollon*, V, 1914, 36–8.
⁶ K. Chukovsky, 'Aleksandr Blok kak chelovek i poet', in A. Blok, *Stikhi* (Petrograd, 1925), 34–5.
⁷ V. Zhirmunsky, 'Preodolevshie simvolizm', *Russkaya mysl'*, XII, 1916, part II, 32–41.
⁸ V. Zhirmunsky, *Voprosy teorii literatury*, 322–6.
⁹ D. Vygodsky, 'O novykh stikhakh', *Novaya zhizn'*, no. 210 (204) (24 Dec. 1917), 5–6.
¹⁰ Letter of 21 Jan. 1962 to Salomea Halpern (the former Princess Andronikova), with whom, late in life, Lourié began a correspondence as a result of some message from or about Akhmatova.
¹¹ See K. Verheul, 'Public Themes in the Poetry of Anna Akhmatova', *Russian Literature* (The Hague), I, 1971, 73, reprinted in *Tale without a Hero and Twenty-two Poems by Anna Akhmatova*, 9–48. Verheul is wrong, however, in suggesting that the poem 'Ne byvat' tebe v zhivykh' (You are no longer among the living) (I.208) also refers to this incident; Akhmatova told A. Nayman that it referred to Gumilyov.
¹² A. Blok, 'Bez bozhestva, bez vdokhnoveniya', *Sobranie sochineniy*, vol. VI (Moscow, 1963), 174–84.
¹³ N. Mandelstam, *Hope Against Hope*, 154.
¹⁴ K. Chukovsky, 'Akhmatova i Mayakovsky', *Dom iskusstv*, I, 1921, 23–42.
¹⁵ E. Zamyatin, 'Ya boyus' ', ibid., 43.
¹⁶ A. Lunacharsky, 'Dom iskusstv', *Pechat' i revolyutsiya*, II, 1921, 225–7.
¹⁷ V. Mayakovsky, 'Vystuplenie na pervom vechere *Chistka sovremennoy poezii*, yanvarya 1922', *Polnoe sobranie sochineniy*, II (Moscow, 1959), 460–1.
¹⁸ L. Brik, 'Mayakovsky i chuzhie stikhi', *Znamya*, III, 1940, 166–7, and V. Shklovsky, *O Mayakovskom* (Moscow, 1940), 28–9, 69, 93.
¹⁹ L. Ozerov, 'Melodika. Plastika. Mysl' ', *Literaturnaya Rossiya*, no. 34 (86) (21 Aug. 1964), 14–15.

[20] G. Gorbachev, 'Pis'ma iz Peterburga', *Gorn*, II, 1922, 130–3.
[21] B. Eykhenbaum, *Anna Akhmatova*, 114.
[22] N. Osinsky, 'Pobegi travy', *Pravda*, no. 148, 1922.
[23] A. Kollontay, 'O drakone i beloy ptitse', *Molodaya gvardiya*, II, 1923, 162–74.
[24] V. Arvatov, 'Grazhdanka Akhmatova i tovarishch Kollontay', ibid., IV–V, 1923, 147–51.
[25] P. Vinogradskaya, 'Voprosy morali, pola, byta i t.Kollontay', *Krasnaya nov'*, VI, 1923, 204–14.
[26] L. Trotsky, *Literatura i revolyutsiya* (Moscow, 1923), 30.
[27] G. Lelevich, 'Anna Akhmatova', *Na postu*, II–III, 1923, 178–202.
[28] See *Soch.* I. 398.

III: 1924-1941

[1] L. Grossman, 'Anna Akhmatova', *Svitok*, IV, 1926, 295–305. Reprinted in Grossman's books *Bor'ba za stil'* (Moscow, 1927), 227–39, and *Mastera slova* (Moscow, 1928), 301–11.
[2] *Russkaya poeziya XX veka*, ed. I. Ezhov and E. Shamurin (Moscow, 1925), with a foreword by Shamurin.
[3] See also N. Mandelstam, *Hope Abandoned*, 222–3.
[4] K. Stanislavsky, 'Pis'mo K. K. Alekseevnoy i K. F. Fal'k, 17 iyuniya 1927', *Sobranie sochineniy*, VIII (Moscow, 1961), 158.
[5] M. and S., 'Anna Akhmatova', *Literaturnaya entsiklopediya*, I (Moscow, 1929), 280–3.
[6] R. Ivanov-Razumnik, *Pisatel'skie sud'by* (New York, 1952), 28–9.
[7] 'Poslednyaya skazka Pushkina', *Zvezda*, I, 1933, 161–76.
[8] See also the posthumously published notes and articles, most of them written in the fifties: 'Neizdannye zametki Anny Akhmatovoy o Pushkine', op. cit., 163, 190–2, etc., and 'Pushkin i nevskoe vzmor'e', *Literaturnaya gazeta*, no. 23 (4 June 1969), 7.
[9] *Tale without a Hero and Twenty-two Poems by Anna Akhmatova*, 50.
[10] N. Mandelstam, *Hope Against Hope*, 29–33.
[11] For some idea of the difference in atmosphere and in the behaviour of those in authority between 1934 and 1938 see N. Mandelstam, ibid., 8–9.
[12] '*Adol'f* Benzhamena Konstana v tvorchestve Pushkina', *Pushkin. Vremennik Pushkinskoy Komissii Akademii Nauk SSSR*, I, 1936, 91–114.
[13] See *Zvezda*, VII, 1936, 3–4.
[14] B. Pasternak, *Doctor Zhivago* (London and New York, 1959), 467.
[15] A. Haight, 'Anna Akhmatova and Marina Tsvetaeva', *Slavonic and East European Review*, Oct. 1972, 590–1.
[16] B. Mikhaylovsky, 'Akmeizm', *Russkaya literatura XX veka* (Moscow, 1939), 333–48.
[17] This and the following letter from Pasternak to Akhmatova were copied by me from a typescript in Akhmatova's possession, in Moscow in 1964. She told me the originals were in the Pasternak archive.
[18] V. Pertsov, 'Chitaya Akhmatovu', *Literaturnaya gazeta*, no. 38 (889) (3 July 1940), 3.
[19] B. Pasternak, *Kogda razgulyaetsya—Poems 1955–1959* (London, 1965), 14.

IV: 1941-1956

[1] P. Luknitsky, *Skvoz' vsyu blokadu* (Leningrad, 1964), 42.
[2] Quoted in O. Berggol'ts, *Govorit Leningrad* (Leningrad, 1964), 15-16.
[3] P. Luknitsky, op. cit., 99.
[4] All information on Akhmatova's evacuation from Moscow is from three conversations with Lidiya Chukovskaya, in Moscow in 1964 and in Moscow and Peredelkino in 1966.
[5] S. Karlinsky, *Marina Cvetaeva—Her Life and Art*, 105.
[6] N. Mandelstam, *Hope Abandoned*, 351-5, 376, 445, 610.
[7] A. Surkov, 'Anna Akhmatova', in A. Akhmatova, *Stikhotvoreniya 1909-1960*, 301.
[8] I. Turgenev, *Sochineniya* (Moscow–Leningrad, 1930-4), vol. X, 333.
[9] N. Mandelstam, *Hope Abandoned*, 449.
[10] For the Russian text of this letter see A. Haight, 'A Letter from N. N. Punin to A. A. Akhmatova', *Russian Literature Triquarterly* (Ann Arbor, Mich.), no. 2 (Winter), 1972, 456-7. Akhmatova first showed me a copy of the letter in 1964; she later asked me to make copies of it to send to Boris Anrep and Isaiah Berlin. A part of the letter was read on the B.B.C. in an obituary broadcast to Russia following Akhmatova's death.
[11] J. Czapski, *Terre inhumaine*, 180-4.
[12] 'Neizdannye zametki Anny Akhmatovoy o Pushkine', op. cit., 158. See also N. Nedobrovo, 'Anna Akhmatova', op. cit., 57: 'The person for whom poetry is a life-saver . . .'
[13] See *Beg vremeni*, 354. For some reason the editors of *Sochineniya* I have printed an earlier version.
[14] P. Luknitsky, op. cit., 586.
[15] *Yunost'*, VI, 1969, 67.
[16] *Novyy mir*, V, 1969, 55.
[17] *Yunost'*, VI, 1969, 67.
[18] The order of 'Severnye elegii' is: I, 'Rossiya Dostoevskogo. Luna'; II, 'I nikakogo rozovogo detstva'; III, 'V.tom dome bylo ochen' strashno zhit''; IV, 'Tak vot on—tot osenniy peyzazh'; V, 'Menya kak reku'; VI, 'Est' tri epokhi u vospominaniy'; VII, 'Moya sed'maya' (mentioned in 'Reshka', *Soch.* II.124). I have not seen III or VII.
[19] In the section 'Budushchie knigi', *Literaturnaya gazeta*, 24 Nov. 1945.
[20] See also N. Mandelstam, *Hope Abandoned*, 359, 363-4, for more about these meetings and their consequences.
[21] See A. Werth, 'Akhmatova: Tragic Queen Anna', *London Magazine*, Dec. 1966, 87-93.
[22] G. Struve, *Soviet Russian Literature* (Norman, Okla., 1951), 329.
[23] KPSS, 'O zhurnalakh *Zvezda* i *Leningrad*: iz postanovleniya TsVKP(B) ot 14-ogo avgusta 1946g', *Zvezda*, VII–VIII, 1946, 3–6, and elsewhere. The resolution can also be found in the book *KPSS v rezolyutsiyakh i resheniyakh 1925–1953* (Moscow, 1953), 1019–1927.
[24] A. Zhdanov, 'Doklad t. Zhdanova o zhurnalakh *Zvezda* i *Leningrad*', *Znamya*, X, 1946, 7–22, and elsewhere. This combined and condensed stenographic version of Zhdanov's reports is reprinted in *Sovetskaya pechat' v dokumentakh* (Moscow, 1964).

²⁵ I. Sergievsky, 'Ob antinarodnoy poezii A. Akhmatovoy', *Protiv bezideynosti v literature—sbornik statey zhurnala Zvezda* (Leningrad, 1947), 81–8.
²⁶ V. Pertsov, 'Russkaya poeziya v 1946 godu', *Novyy mir*, III, 1947, 172–88.
²⁷ V. Sidel'nikov, 'Protiv izvrashcheniya i nizkopoklonstva v sovetskoy fol'kloristike', *Literaturnaya gazeta*, no. 26 (2431) (29 June 1947), 3.
²⁸ A. Egolin, 'Za vysokuyu ideynost' sovetskoy literatury', *Protiv bezideynosti v literature*, op. cit., 17.
²⁹ *Novyy mir*, V, 1969, 55.
³⁰ 'Neizdannye zametki Anny Akhmatovoy o Pushkine', op. cit., 164.
³¹ Ibid., 163, 190–2.
³² See E. Moch-Bickert, *Olga Glebova-Sudeikina—Amie et inspiratrice des Poètes* (Thesis Reproduction Service, Lille University, 1972), 102–4.
³³ K. Chukovsky, 'Chitaya Akhmatovu', *Moskva*, V, 1964, 200–3.
³⁴ Lines represented by ellipses, 'Reshka', verses XI and XII. See Appendix.
³⁵ R. Timenchik, 'K analizu "Poemy bez geroya" Anny Akhmatovoy', *T.G.U. XII nauchnaya konferentsiya studentov* (Tartu, 30 Mar.–2 Apr. 1967). Kuz'min's poem is in *Forel' razbivaet lyod—stikhi 1925–1928* (Leningrad, 1929).
³⁶ For details of Akhmatova's translations from the works of Victor Hugo, see *Soch.* II.456.
³⁷ This letter and the following poem copied from a typescript in Akhmatova's possession, Moscow, 1964. See chap. III, n. 17.
³⁸ *Novyy mir*, II, 1955, 160.
³⁹ A. Fadeev, 'Pis'mo v glavnuyu voennuyu prokuraturu', *Novyy mir*, XII, 1961; reprinted in *Soch.* II. 388–9.
⁴⁰ *Vestnik russkogo studentcheskogo khristyanskogo dvizheniya* (Paris–New York), no. 93 (Mar. 1969), 65.

V:1965-1966

¹ *Koreyskaya klassicheskaya poeziya* (Moscow, 1956).
² *Literaturnaya Moskva* (Moscow, 1956), 537–9, and *Den' poezii* (Moscow, 1956), 9.
³ V. Ognyov, 'Den' nashey poezii', *Oktyabr'*, II, 1957, 209–10.
⁴ A. Serebrovskaya, 'Protiv nigilizma i vseyadnosti', *Zvezda*, VI, 1957, 201.
⁵ A. Dymshits, 'Samyy zhiznennyy vopros', *Literaturnaya gazeta*, no. 61 (3717) (22 May 1957), 1. He goes on to blame P. Antokol'sky for praising Pasternak and to enlarge on the harm done to youth by Dudintsev's *Not by Bread Alone*.
⁶ *Stikhotvoreniya* (Moscow, 1958).
⁷ L. Ozerov, 'Stikhotvoreniya Anny Akhmatovoy', *Literaturnaya gazeta*, no. 78 (4044) (23 June 1959), 3.
⁸ *Stikhotvoreniya 1909–1960*, 294–305.
⁹ N. Rylenkov, 'Vtoraya zhizn' poeta', *Den' poezii* (Moscow, 1966), 305.
¹⁰ A. Pavlovsky, *Anna Akhmatova*, 30.
¹¹ N. Mandelstam, *Hope Against Hope*, 222.
¹² F. D. Reeve, *Robert Frost in Russia* (Boston, 1963), 80–5.
¹³ G. Ivanov, *Peterburgskie zimy* (Paris, 1928; reprinted, New York, 1952).
¹⁴ See for example a 1963 thesis, M. Maline, *Nicolas Gumilev* (Brussels University): 'Mais cette jeune femme Anna Akhmatova n'eut pas le privilège

d'inspirer les premières poésies amoureuses de Gumilev . . .' and later, 'La vie de Gumilev n'a été éclairée ni par un grand amour, ni par une fidèle et exclusive amitié . . .' (14, 27).

[15] S. Makovsky, 'Nikolay Gumilyov po lichnym vospominaniyam', *Novyy zhurnal* (New York), IX, 1964, 157-89.

[16] Akhmatova's letter to Nivat is reproduced in his introduction to the reprint of G. Superfin and R. Timenchik, 'Pis'ma A. A. Akhmatovoy k V. Ya. Bryusovu' *Cahiers du monde russe et soviétique*, XV (1-2), janv.–juin 1974, 193 (first published in *Zapiski otdela rukopisey Vsesoyuznoy biblioteki im. V. I. Lenina*, no. 33, 1972).

[17] G. Struve, 'N. S. Gumilyov, zhizn' i lichnost' ', in N. Gumilyov, *Sobranie sochineniy*, I.vii–xliv. When I was interested in writing something about the poems Gumilyov had dedicated to her, Akhmatova went with me through Struve's foreword and Makovsky's article, and got me the typescript of P. Luknitsky's *Trudy i dni N. S. Gumilyova* (unpublished) to read.

[18] *Yunost'*, VI, 1969, 67.

[19] *Requiem* (Munich, 1963).

[20] 'Stenograficheskiy otchot protsessa Iosifa Brodskogo', *Vozdushnye puti*, IV, 1965, 294-5.

[21] V. Zhuravlyov's poem was published in *Oktyabr'*, IV, 1965, 81; the accusation of plagiarism was 'Ch'i zhe stikhi', *Izvestiya*, no. 91 (20 Apr. 1965), and Zhuravlyov's reply, 'Pis'mo v redaktsiyu', *Izvestiya*, no. 99 (28 Apr. 1965), 4.

[22] 'Gryadushchee, sozrevshee v proshedshem', *Voprosy literatury*, IV, 1965, 183-9.

[23] 'Otryvok', *Novyy mir*, V, 1969, 57.

[24] Ibid., 243.

[25] Ibid., 54.

[26] N. Gumilyov, op. cit., I.150-1.

[27] The section 'Tretiy golos' printed in *Soch.* II is a separate poem dedicated to A. Nayman, inserted as a means of getting it into print; it should be removed from the sequence.

[28] In a talk given at the University of Moscow in April, 1966.

[29] M. Wosien, *The Russian Folk Tale, Some Structural and Thematic Aspects*, Slavistische Beitrage, Band 71 (Munich, 1969), 104-5.

APPENDIX

THE TEXT OF 'POEM WITHOUT A HERO'

'Poema bez geroya', Akhmatova's longest work, was written and rewritten over a period of twenty-two years. Extracts and variants of the poem-in-progress were published in the Soviet Union and elsewhere. Because of this considerable confusion has arisen over what is the final version and whether in fact such a thing exists.

What is probably the first completed version of the poem can be found in J. van der Eng-Liedmeier and K. Verheul, *Tale Without a Hero and Twenty-Two Poems by Anna Akhmatova* (1973), pp. 116–30. Sections of variants of Part I were published in the USSR in *Leningradskiy al'manakh* (1945); *Literaturnaya Moskva*, no. I, 1956; *Antologiya russkoy sovetskoy poezii 1917–57*, I (1957); A. Akhmatova, *Stikhotvoreniya* (1958); *Moskva*, VII, 1959; A. Akhmatova, *Stikhotvoreniya 1909–1960* (1961); *Den' poezii* (Moscow–Leningrad, 1962 and Moscow, 1963). A. Akhmatova, *Beg vremeni* (1965) contains Part I complete except for three lines in the third dedication and two lines in section I. Outside the Soviet Union incomplete versions of Part I were published twice in *Vozdushnye puti* (New York), in 1960 and 1961. A section of Part II was published in *Den' poezii* in 1962. Part II was also published, but incomplete, in *Vozdushnye puti* in 1960 and 1961. An extract of an early version of Part III was published in A. Akhmatova, *Stikhotvoreniya 1909–1960*. The two versions of Part III in *Vozdushnye puti*, 1960 and 1961, are incomplete.

In January 1964 I corrected the 1961 *Vozdushnye puti* text in Moscow, using Akhmatova's manuscript (dated 1962). My typescript was approved by the poet in London in June 1965 and she confirmed that this was the final version. Akhmatova did not, however, claim to be a good proofreader and advised me at all times to consult Lidiya Chukovskaya about any textual queries I might have relating to her work. I therefore asked the latter to look at my text of the poem published in the *Slavonic and East European Review* (London), no. 105, 1967. Chukovskaya corrected my text and a photo-copy of the corrections in her hand can be seen in my thesis.

In the same place can be seen the lines replaced by the poet with ellipses. I do not think she wanted the lines replaced by ellipses to be printed instead of the ellipses, but rather that they should exist separately and yet be known to come from that place—an idea perhaps not as peculiar as it first sounds when considered in the context of Akhmatova's life and the way she talked and wrote.

In 1967, C. Ricci published a text and translation into Italian in *Poema senza Eroe e altre Poesie* (Turin, 1966). Ricci's text contains a number of minor variants from my text. It does not include verse XXII of 'Reshka' or italics in 'Epilog'. It also includes various lines removed by the poet later.

In June 1968 I sent Chukovskaya's corrections to the editors for inclusion in *Soch.* II. Unfortunately they were unwilling to accept all of them, including one

I had seen in the poet's hand. Corrections which should be made to the text in *Soch.* II are:

p. 95   The quote from *Don Giovanni* should be deleted—it applies only to Part I, not the whole poem.

pp. 97–8 Removed from poem 13 May 1962.

p. 99   *Deus conservat omnia* etc. should be on a page by itself. It refers to the whole of the poem.

p. 100 Piece dated 'Leningrad 1944' should be removed.

p. 105 Lines 33–4 deleted.

p. 108 A variant exists in line 136 'No bespechna, pryana . . .'

p. 110 The three introductory lines to *Cherez ploshchadku* (Gdeto vokrug . . .) should be deleted.

p. 111 A variant exists in line 203: 'smirennitsa' for 'zateynitsa'.

p. 112 Line 236 should read 'Nad Marinskoyu . . .'

p. 122 The subtitle *Intermezzo* should be deleted. In the introductory prose the words in the line before the last: 'Sleduyushchie strofy' should be deleted and replaced with: 'ochen' gluboko i ochen' umelo spryatannye obryvki Rekviema'.

p. 124 A variant exists to the last line of verse x: 'V etom uzhase ne mogu'.

p. 125 Verse xi here is a discarded variant out of place and should be deleted. It is not the verse for which the ellipse stands.
        Verse xv, line 2 should read 'moglo' not 'mozhet'.

p. 128 There should be a semi-colon after the word 'dom' and the word 'i' following it should be deleted.

In 1970, J. Rude published in *Poème sans Héros* a text which contains numerous small mistakes and variants to my text and to that of Ricci. It includes lines discarded from the final version and some of the lines represented by ellipses in the wrong order. It retains Akhmatova's ironical note about imitating Pushkin with 'propushchennye strofy' (p. 112) which refers to lines in fact now printed here, with the exception of those at the beginning of (her) verse XIII (my text, verse X), left out for no apparent reason, except perhaps that she did not have them. Verse XII here represents non-existent text. If Akhmatova's ironic comment is to be preserved, the lines represented by ellipses in the main text must be given in the footnote.

INDEX OF NAMES

AA = Anna Akhmatova. Bold-face references indicate extended treatment.